Writing Fiction

Approaches to Writing

Series Editor: Graeme Harper

Published

Amanda Boulter, *Writing Fiction*

Forthcoming

Chad Davidson and Greg Fraser, *Writing Poetry*
Bruce Dobler, *Writing Creative Nonfiction*

Approaches to Writing
Series Standing Order
ISBN 1–4039–9999–6
(*outside North America only*)

You can receive future titles in this series as they are published by placing a standing order. Please contact your bookseller or, in case of difficulty, write to us at the address below with your name and address, the title of the series and the ISBN quoted above.

Customer Services Department, Palgrave Macmillan Ltd, Houndmills, Basingstoke, Hampshire RG21 6XS, England

Writing
Fiction

Creative and Critical Approaches

Amanda Boulter

palgrave
macmillan

First published 2007 by
PALGRAVE MACMILLAN
Houndmills, Basingstoke, Hampshire RG21 6XS and
175 Fifth Avenue, New York, N.Y. 10010
Companies and representatives throughout the world

PALGRAVE MACMILLAN is the global academic imprint of the Palgrave Macmillan division of St. Martin's Press, LLC and of Palgrave Macmillan Ltd. Macmillan® is a registered trademark in the United States, United Kingdom and other countries. Palgrave is a registered trademark in the European Union and other countries.

ISBN-13: 978–1–4039–8810–2 hardback
ISBN-10: 1–4039–8810–2   hardback
ISBN-13: 978–1–4039–8811–9 paperback
ISBN-10: 1–4039–8811–0   paperback

This book is printed on paper suitable for recycling and made from fully managed and sustained forest sources.

A catalogue record for this book is available from the British Library.

A catalog record for this book is available from the Library of Congress.

10   9   8   7   6   5   4   3   2   1
16   15   14   13   12   11   10   09   08   07

Printed and bound in China

For Ruth, Isaac and Sam
– with love

Contents

Acknowledgements

I would like to thank the University of Winchester and the Arts and Humanities Research Council for funding my research and thus enabling me to write this book. Thanks also to the tutors and students at Winchester, especially those who have studied for the MA in Creative and Critical Writing. The National Association of Writers in Education and Great Writing conferences have generated lively discussions about creativity and criticality and I would like to thank all those involved.

I am very grateful to Professor Graeme Harper, and my editors Kate Wallis, Sonya Barker, and Brian Morrison for their enthusiasm about this project and their support throughout the stages of its evolution.

Finally I would like to thank Ruth Gilbert for being my first and most perfect reader.

The author and publishers wish to thank the following for permission to use copyright material: Alfred A Knopf, a division of Random House, Inc. and Georges Borchardt, Inc on behalf of the Estate of the author for figure, 'Building climaxes' from John Gardner, *The Art of Fiction: Notes on Craft for Young Writers*. Copyright © 1984 by the Estate of John Gardner; A P Watt Ltd on behalf of Michael B Yeats and Scribner, an imprint of Simon & Schuster Adult Publishing Group, for an excerpt from W B Yeats, 'The Circus Animals' Desertion' from *The Collected Works of W B Yeats, Volume 1: The Poems*, ed. Richard J Finneran. Copyright © 1940 by Georgie Yeats, renewed © 1968 by Bertha Georgie Yeats, Michael Butler Yeats and Annie Yeats.

Every effort has been made to trace the copyright holders but if any have been inadvertently overlooked the publishers will be pleased to make the necessary arrangement at the first opportunity.

Research for this book was funded by

 Arts & Humanities
Research Council

The AHRC funds postgraduate training and research in the arts and humanities, from archaeology and English literature to design and dance. The quality and range of research supported not only provides social and cultural benefits but also contributes to the economic success of the UK. For further information on the AHRC, please see our website www.ahrc.uk.

Acknowledgements

Introduction: A Critical-Creative Approach to Fiction

> *Art lives upon discussion, upon experiment, upon curiosity, upon variety of attempt, upon the exchange of views and the comparison of standpoints; and there is a presumption that those times when no one has anything particular to say about it, and has no reason to give for practice or preference, though they may be times of genius, are not times of development, are times possibly even, a little, of dullness. The successful application of any art is a delightful spectacle, but the theory, too, is interesting.*
>
> Henry James, 'The Art of Fiction', *Longman's Magazine*

As fiction writers we tell stories. We plunge our readers into imaginary worlds, enthral them with invented lives, tantalise them with made-up events. This is the power and pleasure of fiction. In this book, I want to explore this creative process to see how we can enhance our writing through, in James' words, 'discussion', 'experiment', and 'curiosity': curiosity about ideas, experiment with creative possibilities, and discussion of writing and life. I want to think about how we as writers can improve our fiction by developing a critically creative imagination.

The approach I take in this book attempts to unpick the oppositional logic that has developed around creative writing, a logic that sets 'creativity' against 'criticism' as if they are utterly distinct elements of writing. Peter Elbow, for instance, argued that: 'creativity is strong only when critical thinking is weak, or vice versa'.[1] To help his students write, he separated the writing process into two distinct stages of unhampered creative flow and uninterrupted critical revision, suggesting that if these separate stages got muddled up it would confuse and weaken the writing produced. I understand the benefit of Elbow's technique, but the problem with this oppositional approach is that, over the years, it has become something of an orthodoxy within writing classes, and now threatens to limit, rather than enhance, creative possibilities for student writers.

I want to go beyond Elbow's opposition to explore how writers can be critically creative and creatively critical. For me, writing cannot be divided into a creative process that is purely generative (of ideas and words) and a critical process that is purely fault-finding: the process of writing balances both creative and critical skills. But if we are to re-assess the role played by the critical in creative writing, we need to move away from the term 'criticism' (with all its negative connotations). In this book I use the term 'criticality' as the complement to 'creativity', and I want to show that creativity and criticality work hand-in-hand in the conception, evolution and production of creative writing.

As I write, the importance of the critical is gradually being recognised within university writing programmes. Writers who choose to take degrees in Creative Writing are looking for something from the universities. Sometimes at (post)graduate level students are already published writers, but they turn to higher education to learn more about their own creative practice. The universities offer a creative environment, the space and time to write, and advice about the art and craft of writing. But they are also sites of cultural and critical knowledge and student writers who access this cultural-critical resource can use it to inspire their writing.

In developing a critical-creative approach to writing, I want to tap into some of the key ideas that circulate in Literature and Creative Writing departments (from philosophies of storytelling to analyses of narratives, from theories of identity to explorations of language) to see how these ideas can enrich creative work. This book attempts to give useful advice about the practical issues of writing, such as structuring, characterisation, dialogue and so on, but it also attempts to go beyond a 'handy hints' format to engage with some of the deeper and more complex questions that lie at the heart of creative fiction.

A critical-creative approach to writing

Probably, indeed, the larger part of the labour of an author in composing his work is critical labour; the labour of sifting, combining, constructing, expunging, correcting, testing; this frightful toil is as much critical as creative ... we do not assume that because works have been composed without apparent critical labour, no critical labour has been done.
        T. S. Eliot, 'The Function of Criticism' in *Selected Essays* (Faber & Faber)

For many years authors have reflected on their creative process, the agonies and the ecstasies, the successes and the failures, and while some have clung to an idea of inspiration with an almost superstitious defensiveness, others, like Eliot, have actively sought to analyse the journey from idea to text. I want to consider a couple of these writers now to outline the ways in which a critical-creative voice has been explored or resisted over the years.

The Lawrence approach

D. H. Lawrence once said: 'One sheds one's sicknesses in books, repeats and presents again one's emotions to be master of them.'[2] This constructs literature as a pseudo-psychiatric couch, a talking cure for writers, and although we will look at theories in this book that do indeed see stories as the expression of deep unconscious needs, I want to argue with the way Lawrence used this idea to theorise his writing. Talking specifically about his poetry, he made a distinction between what he called his 'real' poems which came from somewhere deep inside and created their own form, as he said, 'willy-nilly', and his 'composed' poems which were 'worked on' and therefore could be changed.[3] For Lawrence the genuine article was that which by-passed the critical altogether and was produced by creative alchemy deep within the psyche. This perception of the artist as an (almost) unconscious producer of genius is a powerful myth, but it's one that other writers have argued vehemently against. The French writer Raymond Queneau, for example, railed against the notion, developed during the early twentieth century, that a writer should submit to his or her unconscious, accepting 'willy-nilly' anything and everything dredged up from below. He said:

> Another very wrong idea that is also going the rounds at the moment is the equivalence that has been established between inspiration, exploration of the subconscious, and liberation, between chance, automatism, and freedom. Now this sort of inspiration, which consists in blindly obeying every impulse, is in fact slavery. The classical author who wrote his tragedy observing a certain number of known rules is freer than the poet who writes down whatever comes into his head and is a slave to other rules of which he knows nothing.[4]

The sense of these 'other rules' is what makes a critical-creative approach so important, because it is not only the 'rules' of the unconscious, as Sigmund Freud or Jacques Lacan might describe them, that are at issue. There are other 'rules', personal and social 'rules', that we accept without being fully aware of how they affect us: common-sense ideologies, casual prejudices, cultural myths, taken-for-granted assumptions and so on. A critical-creative approach to writing attempts to throw light upon our culture's, and our own, knee-jerk responses; to look beyond the half-forgotten habits and the half-hidden mundane that also exists in the personal and social unconscious of our time.

In everyday life, everyone who speaks or writes does so in the language and style of their cultural moment. Words take on or lose meanings, they become associated with certain ways of looking at life, certain judgements, certain affectations. If you use language 'willy-nilly', just as it comes, it might well be that you have struck linguistic riches, or it might be that you are repeating the language you are most familiar with, without asking whether it is the language that conveys the particularity of your vision. As John Gardner warns: 'language carries values with it, and unexamined language carries values one might, if one knew they were there, be ashamed of accidentally promoting.'[5] Revision, in other words, does not mean that in some way your work is no longer truly yours, it means that it is more fully yours – emotionally, sensually and intellectually – than any first or 'automatic' draft can ever be.

The Weldon approach

Another way to think about the split between the creative and the critical can be seen in Fay Weldon's essay 'Harnessed to the Harpy' in which she presents the writer as a kind of split personality. On the one hand there is the creative side, described by such adjectives as 'impetuous, wilful, emotional, sloppy' and on the other there is the critical side, 'argumentative, cautious, rational, effective, perfectionist, ambitious'.[6] Weldon suggests that these two sides of the writing personality emerge at different points in the writing process. First the writer 'creates', and this creation comes, again, from the unconscious, from what Freud termed the 'id' (in English the 'it'), the repressed unreasonable part of the psyche, the screaming child within. And then the writer revises, using the conscious/unconscious critic within that Freud called the 'super-ego', the conscience, the internalised parent figure who follows behind ready to clear up all the mess.

This is an inspiring model, perhaps just as much of a myth as Lawrence's indefinable inspiration, but one that gives many writers a sense of freedom. They can create without worrying about their own critical (which here stands for self-critical and undermining) voices, because the mop and bucket of critical revision is there when play-time has finished. It's the model that Peter Elbow recommended, one that has a strict division of labour between the critical and creative elements of writing. But in keeping the creative and the critical so far apart, these models fail to recognise the ways in which criticality can play a productive role in the entire process of creative writing. Instead of saying that critical awareness is okay as long as it knows its place, I want to show that criticality can enhance creativity.

The American poet Gary LaFemina has argued that, 'as a practicing poet, it's my critical work – whether I publish it or not – that clarifies and propels my creative endeavors (the scope of my vision as it were) and what I learn from crossing fences allows me to move forward as a writer.'[7] The critical-creative approach to writing fiction presented in this book encourages writers to cross fences, and it begins by re-thinking the relationship between creative writing and critical theory.

Creative writing and critical theory

Writers are often told to read fiction, to explore the world of words. But too often they are insulated from other writing, especially writing about fiction, literary criticism or literary theory. This, especially the latter, is seen as some sort of bloodless, life-draining pursuit: a parasite practice that writers must avoid lest they too be sucked dry of the true life-force of writing. I think this is a mistake. Whatever we might think about literary theory, it has for over two millennia been addressing what writing does and why and how it works, and as Ernest Hemingway said, 'I think you should learn about writing from everybody who has ever written that has anything to teach you.'[8]

There are hundreds of incisive, inspirational ideas in what has been termed 'theory' or even worse 'criticism', and these ideas can enrich the process of fiction writing. Even if, as writers, we reject them utterly, we can still find inspiration from our disagreement. In other words, critical and cultural theory represents a huge creative resource just waiting to be tapped. And once we start asking questions of theory we might find not a pleasure-starved intellectualism, but a resource for greater freedom and creative experiment. Within philosophy there are debates about the roles stories play in making us human, the role of narrative in understanding time, and the relation of fiction to life.

In psychoanalysis there are debates about the nature of creativity, the connections between cultural myths and personal dreams, and the universal humanity we all share. In cultural studies there are debates about identity, community, interpretation and meaning. And in literary studies, perhaps most significant of all for writers, there is a body of work that has studied the nature of narratives, plots, characters, technique, voice, style, reading and readers for many years. I, for one, do not want to turn my back on all that.

So this book attempts to address the issues that affect writers, cutting through the confusion of '-isms' to focus on those theories that expand creative possibilities. I try to be open to a range of different ideas, without being ensnared by any particular model, highlighting those ideas that I, as a writer and university teacher, have found to be the most stimulating for creating fiction.

The structure of this book

This book is divided into two parts: Foundations and Speculations. Foundations explores a range of theories to stimulate ideas and generate new ways to develop creative practice. Speculations builds upon these ideas, and integrates theory and practice to offer more direct advice about fiction writing. Each part concludes with a number of exercises that draw from the ideas in the chapters and explore their implications for fiction writing.

Part I: Foundations

Chapter 1: Establishing Practice focuses on 'prewriting', a time when we can be intensely involved in creative discovery without necessarily writing a single word. The prewriting stage is a time of 'deep drifting', a loose openness to ideas that contrasts with the 'shape-shifting' process of writing and rewriting, and this first chapter explores four different aspects of the prewriting phase: musing, reading, researching and planning.

In *Chapter 2: Form and Structure* I consider philosophical and theoretical ideas about fictional structure: from Aristotle's *Poetics* to scriptwriting guru Robert McKee's *Story*. I then consider some of the various models and diagrams that have been used to describe plot structure in order to help writers identify the best form for their own fictions.

Chapter 3: Subject develops these ideas, considering key theories about fairytale and myth to explore the subject matter of fiction. This is not just a question of what we should write about, whether that be sex or war, or fashion or football, as Virginia Woolf argued in *A Room of One's Own*.[9] Instead, my exploration of subject goes back to the question: why do we tell stories? Is there one universal subject beneath all stories? And if theorists suggest there is, should we embrace this as a creative foundation or reject it as a potential formula?

In *Chapter 4: Voice* I tackle the anxiety created by the pressure to 'find your voice' by exploring what we mean by 'voice' in the first place. All writing (and speaking) only has meaning when someone reads it (or listens to it) and I want to think about voice in this way, as a dialogue between writer and reader. If we think about the reader as our creative accomplice it can free us from the solitary search for our voice and allow us to recognise that the language we speak is never wholly our own.

In *Chapter 5: Style* I argue that our style as writers is not only found in the manipulation of words on paper but in the balance between our vision of the world and the way we express that vision. I explore key moments in the development of fiction, from Realism to Modernism to Postmoderism, to show that the vast stylistic differences between these movements can be understood simply as different answers to the same question: 'How do we perceive and represent reality?'. I also consider whether beneath all the literary debates there are some theories of style that remain unchanged.

In the final chapter in Part I, *Chapter 6: The Foundation of Fiction*, I take some of the most obvious advice about how to write ('write what you know' and 'write what you read') and consider it against Paul Ricoeur's philosophical model of writing as a 'circle of triple mimesis'. Although perhaps an unconventional pairing, the philosophy reveals interesting ways to think about the 'how to' advice and brings us closer to the simple principles at the foundation of fiction: pleasure and understanding.

Part II: Speculations

The chapters in Part II build upon the discussion in Part I, developing ideas to emphasise the ways in which prewriting, writing, and rewriting interact. *Chapter 7: Exploring Possibilities* focuses on the transition between prewriting and writing, exploring ways to 'write with power', to use Peter Elbow's phrase. I then consider how to rewrite effectively, drawing from the writer and editor Sol Stein's model of triage.

Chapter 8: Forms and Structures explores how writers have worked with the structure of 'beginning, middle and end' and offers advice about using surprise and suspense to draw the reader into the fictional world. *Chapter 9: Subjects* considers the subjects of fiction, the characters who people the fictional world. In this chapter I ask how we should think about our characters: are they people who happen not to exist, are they experimental selves, or are they empty ciphers?

Following this, *Chapter 10: Voices* focuses on dialogue and develops Mikhail Bakhtin's notion of the author as ventriloquist. I draw out the connection between voice and point of view in fiction, and argue that as writers we cannot separate the question 'who speaks?' from the question 'who sees?'. In *Chapter 11: Styles*, I then use the work of the critic Gérard Genette to consider the different modes within fiction and analyse the deep rhythms of narrative which are often overlooked in discussions of a writer's style.

The final chapter, *Chapter 12: Speculations in Fiction*, suggests how as writers we might speculate upon our own work, thinking and writing about the processes of composition in a new form of literary criticism. I also address that other form of speculation – speculating on the market – and advise how best to present work for publication.

Mainstream publication might be your ultimate goal; alternatively, you might feel that the tough commercialism of the publishing business stifles creativity, and decide to write for your own satisfaction, sharing your work with friends, perhaps self-publishing to reach a selected audience. This book is for all writers: those who strive for mainstream success as well as those whose work will only be seen by a handful of chosen readers. It focuses upon the processes of writing rather than the packaging of the ultimate product, and aims to stimulate your ideas rather than adopt a 'one-size-fits-all', 'that's-the-way-to-do-it' approach to fiction writing. I hope the book will help you to find new inspiration as you develop both critically and creatively as a writer.

Part I

Foundations

Part I

Foundations

1   Establishing   Practice

Try to be one of the people on whom nothing is lost.
         Henry James, 'The Art of Fiction', *Longman's Magazine*

Turn yourself into a stranger in your own streets.
         Dorothea Brande, *Becoming a Writer* (Palgrave Macmillan)

When we write fiction, the ideas, actions and characters don't just spring from our minds fully formed. Writing fiction is a process that takes time, perhaps even years. Sometimes, if we're lucky, inspiration conforms to cliché and strikes us like a thunderbolt (this, of course, being a cliché writers do welcome), but normally inspiration glimmers and flashes in more haphazard ways. Fiction begins, as both Dorothea Brande and Henry James have suggested, in our creative and critical responses to the world around us. Being a 'stranger' on our streets means that we try to rub away the grime of habit and see the physical, social and emotional realities of place in new ways. Being someone 'on whom nothing is lost' means that we absorb the nuances of character and conversation, whether that be on the bus or in Henry James' own fiction. The imaginary world grows slowly in our mind's eye as we explore the people, setting, and possible events of our story. We muse, we read, we research and we plan, building upon the fragments in our head until we begin to shape those glimmers and flashes into fiction.

All this and we might not yet have put pen to paper. But we *are* writing. Because writing is not simply an action, it's a practice. And the practice of fiction writing does not only involve typing on a keyboard or scribbling with a biro, it involves the creation of an imaginary world. We begin to write our fiction long before we set down the first draft, and even when the draft is finished, the practice of writing continues as we review and revise. In this way we might see writing as having three faces: three faces that Frank Smith, following D. Gordan Rohman, has labelled Prewriting, Writing, and Rewriting.[1]

Prewriting, Writing, Rewriting

Put simply, *Prewriting* is the time of incubation, when ideas are frothing in the deep recesses of our minds. This stage can involve charts, plans, copious notes or simply endless musings in the bath. It is the 'muttering before the uttering',[2] what I like to think of as 'deep drifting' when, lost in the depths of imagination, we allow our minds to drift over ideas and experiences. The *Writing* stage produces the first draft, and the *Rewriting* stage transforms it in a process of literary 'shape shifting'. Scenes and sentences are cut, changed and re-created until the true shape of the story begins to emerge.

This three-faced model of writing is useful because it provides a way for us to talk about writing as a practice, and acknowledges that we are not writers only when we sit down at our desks. But it also has its problems: not least in the implication that by dividing writing into prewriting, writing and rewriting, we set up three separate and discrete stages to be worked through one after another. Smith himself recognises the difficulty and acknowledges that rather than being separate, 'prewriting, writing, and rewriting frequently seem to be going on simultaneously.'[3]

This is certainly my experience of writing. The three faces of writing might offer different perspectives upon the process, but as a writer I can inhabit each face as I please, slipping from prewriting to writing to prewriting to rewriting in a continuous loop. For as Smith points out: ' "rewriting" of the draft just completed becomes "prewriting" of the draft to come.'[4] However, in this chapter I want to hold prewriting apart from the others stages so that I can think about how it works to establish the practice of fiction writing. Prewriting can continue throughout writing and rewriting, but here I'm thinking about it primarily as the time before the actual drafting begins, a time of freedom and possibility when we can engage in that familiar feeling of distracted potential that I call 'deep drifting'. There are many activities that we might think of as constituting this prewriting phase, but I want to focus on just four of them: musing, reading, researching and planning.

Musing

> *I must lie down where all the ladders start,*
> *In the foul rag-and-bone shop of the heart*

> W. B. Yeats, 'The Circus Animals' Desertion'
> (Palgrave Macmillan)

The organized and intelligent dream that will eventually fill the reader's mind begins as a largely mysterious dream in the writer's mind.

John Gardner, *The Art of Fiction* (Vintage)

Fiction begins with a spark in the writer's mind, a vivid fragment of an idea, a character or an event that will eventually flare into a story. This is what John Gardner calls the 'mysterious dream' at the root of all fiction, a dream that needs to be shaped and focused by the writing process. But in this early stage, all we have is the patchy sense of possibility. The musing phase of prewriting is a time of distraction, when as writers we find ourselves absorbed into the imagined spaces of the story world. It's a time when we must listen to ourselves to 'hear and reflect upon the ideas that come to us'.[5] In previous centuries these ideas might have been seen as coming from the Muses, the Greek deities who presided over the arts and sciences and inspired mortal men. For thousands of years the Muses were invoked as a way of suggesting that the writer's work was the result of divine inspiration, beyond his own self (it was normally men writing), and this has reinforced the sense that creativity has nothing to do with the critical mind of the writer.

In the twenty-first century, we use more scientific language to sustain the same separation between creative and critical, revering the mysteries of the unconscious just as the poets once revered their Muse. But I want to argue that the invocation of the Muses has always contained an invocation of a critically creative inspiration, a plea for, in contemporary terms, the conscious and unconscious mind to work together.

The Muses

Originally only three Muses were worshipped. They were the daughters of Zeus and Mnemosyne (whose name means memory) and were called Melete (meditation), Mneme (memory), and Aoede (song). When the poets invoked their help, they were invoking 'memory', asking for reminders – these were after all the days of oral tales, when poets needed to remember hundreds of lines from their own or others' work. The Muses helped poets to *remember* their songs, to re-create them. So, it is not the English word 'muse' that we get from the Greek Muses (that comes from a different source), but the word 'mind', which used to mean memory, a meaning we can still hear in 'remind' and 'reminder'. In other words, the Muses weren't invoked to bring inspiration from the outside. They were invoked to stimulate the critical-creative work of oral composition, remembering and embellishing the traditional lines and phrases of the great tales. In the twenty-first century, we can call on the same muses to enhance our prewriting, asking for 'meditation' (to listen to ourselves and reflect on our ideas), 'memory' (to recall experiences, emotions, and expressions) and 'song' (to develop the art and craft of storytelling).

Meditation, memory and song fuse the creative and critical elements of writing, and take us from the conscious to the unconscious mind. We might begin by musing, or meditating, on a particular idea, and find that we are no longer directing our thoughts and emotions; our thoughts and emotions are revealing new directions to us. The muses do not separate the critical from the creative. Instead they show how each aspect of storytelling involves both critical and creative activity.

The rag-and-bone shop of the heart

To think about how this process of meditation and memory might work, we can turn to Yeats' image of the 'foul rag-and-bone shop of the heart'. For Yeats, all writing begins in the filthy detritus of living, in the emotions and feelings that have been discarded and repressed. But it is the mind, not the heart, that produces 'masterful images'. Yeats uses the simple image of a ladder, a ladder of imagination, to connect the 'foul heart' of experience to the 'pure mind' of art. This ladder, which I see as the link between the unconscious and the conscious, between the creative and critical imagination, is what we must build, rung by rung, with memory, meditation and craft as our tools.

> Those masterful images because complete
> Grew in pure mind, but out of what began?
> A mound of refuse or the sweepings of a street,
> Old kettles, old bottles, and a broken can,
> Old iron, old bones, old rags, that raving slut
> Who keeps the till. Now that my ladder's gone,
> I must lie down where all the ladders start,
> In the foul rag-and-bone shop of the heart.[6]

It takes time to make new things out of old rags, and the sense of slow transformation in Yeats' poem, as sordid experience is transformed into high art, is also found in other metaphors of the creative process, such as Natalie Goldberg's concept of 'composting'. In *Writing Down the Bones* she argues that experience must be sifted through the body and mind:

> [F]rom the decomposition of the thrown-out egg shells, spinach leaves, coffee grinds and old steak bones of our minds come nitrogen, heat and very fertile soil. Out of this fertile soil bloom our poems and stories. But this does not come all at once.[7]

For Goldberg, we can enrich this compost by writing every day without fear or judgement. The act of writing itself is enough, no matter what we produce. And many people recommend this as an exercise for writers, ensuring that we spend some time each day writing anything that comes into our minds. This is a very useful exercise, but if I'm honest, it's not one that I've ever managed to do for more than a few days. Instead, I prefer to see my prewriting as 'disposable writing', to use Frank Smith's term, a kind of back-of-the-envelope thinking that clarifies my musings. Once I've grasped the idea or character that is born out of this writing, then my actual scribblings can be thrown away, because the work is still taking place in my head, in the 'mysterious dream', rather than on paper.

The blooming buzzing confusion of life

Disposable writing can involve writing letters to yourself from your characters (as a way of getting to know them), or charting the fragments of story so far, or following idea bubbles to see where they take you. It's writing that is loosely focused on the fiction you want to create, but writing that allows long notes to yourself about how you are feeling or why a certain character or idea will never work. It begins to focus the mess and mulch incubating within our unconscious and responds not only to what we see and hear, but what we have read, what we have learned, and what we have experienced in our life. It is a way of drawing from what William James called the 'great blooming, buzzing confusion' of life and bringing it into our fiction.[8]

To do this, writers need to muse not only upon the work they're doing, but upon the world they're living in. Walt Whitman called this loafing: 'Have been loafing here deep among the trees, shafts of tall pines, oak, hickory, with a thick undergrowth of laurels and grapevines . . . no two places, hardly any two hours, anywhere, exactly alike. How different the odor of noon from midnight, or winter from summer, or a windy spell from a still one.'[9] This is more than just observing the world around you, which every writer must do, it's being part of that world, experiencing it as a writer, experiencing it with the sensitivity of a poet.

There are other ways in which this idling time of prewriting have been described. The French poet Baudelaire saw the writer as a *flâneur* who wandered through the city, part of the crowd and yet distant from it, able to give it a new voice. This kind of prewriting, which we might call, after Clifford Geertz, 'deep hanging out', is a way for the writer to absorb the places and people of a story, to really *see* the world around them.[10] For, as John Gardner says: 'Getting down what the writer really cares about – setting down what the writer himself notices, as opposed to what any fool might notice – is all that is meant by the *originality* of the writer's eye.'[11] What any fool might notice is what our eye is first drawn to, those features or incidents, gestures or expressions that we see every night on TV as a shorthand to emotion (ones I've used myself but now know better!): the shuffling with cigarettes, the hands twisting through hair to show anxiety, the feet on the desk to show cockiness.

When we are loafing like Whitman, we train ourselves to look beyond the obvious and smell the difference between midnight and noon. We train ourselves to climb down to the foul rag-and-bone shop of our hearts and recast old iron into new art. Dorothea Brande puts it most simply: 'It is well to understand as early as possible in one's writing life that there is just one contribution which every one of us can make: we can give into the common pool of experience some comprehension of the world as it looks to each of us.'[12]

This is the power of literature, to break the moulds of habit and recapture the freshness of perception. Victor Shklovsky, who was writing in 1917, and was one of the first literary 'theorists' of the last century, argued that this was the dominant purpose of literature: to break through conventional ways of seeing the world. He wrote: 'Habitualization devours work, clothes, furniture, one's wife, and the fear of war . . . And art exists that one may recover the sensation of life; it exists to make one feel things, to make the stone *stony*. The purpose of art is to impart the sensation of things as they are perceived and not as they are known.'[13]

Musing allows us to feel the stoniness of the stone and to dwell upon its significance, 'to guess the unseen from the seen', as Henry James said, and 'to trace the implication of things, to judge the whole piece by the pattern'.[14] Musing also allows us to dwell upon the words we would use to convey our perceptions, to try them on the tongue. But musing alone will not teach us technique. For that we need to read.

Reading

> *The books you read are like the clothes in your wardrobe, they define your identity.*
>
>   Overheard remark at a writers' conference

> *The more aware we are – as readers, critics, or artists – of the fullness and breadth of the narrative tradition, the freer and sounder will be the critical or artistic choices we make.*
>
>   Robert Scholes and Robert Kellogg, *The Nature of Narrative*
>   (Oxford University Press)

All writers must read. It is, as Scholes and Kellogg say, the only way for a writer to appreciate the sheer richness of fiction, the numerous ways in which writers throughout history have created characters and told stories. Books open up imaginary worlds, they expand our creative experience, and like 'the clothes in our wardrobe', they shape our perceptions of style.

In this section, I don't want to focus on *what* books to read, I want to suggest *how* to read them. The only advice I have about what to read is that every writer should read books they enjoy (intellectually and emotionally) and books they know will challenge them (intellectually and emotionally). These might of course be the same books, but sometimes not. All writers have different ideas about what makes a book challenging to read (for some this might be *Emma*, for others *War and Peace*, *Finnegans Wake*, or the latest SF or romance blockbuster), but moving out of your literary 'comfort zone' broadens your horizons both as a reader and a writer.

Reading as a writer

The phrase 'reading as a writer' is something of a commonplace these days (it was first used in 1934 by Dorothea Brande in her book *Becoming a Writer*), but there is much less said about what that phrase actually means. Many people take their cue from Percy Lubbock who, in his book *The Craft of Fiction* (1921), suggested that the writer should ask two key questions about the way the books he or she reads are written: 'Is this proceeding of the author the right one, the best for the subject? Is it possible to conceive and to name a better?'.[15] But we can go back further, to Greek and Roman theorists who suggested that studying literature was a way for young writers to learn technique from: 'the imitation and emulation of the great historians and poets of the past'. For as Longinus said: 'Many authors catch fire from the inspiration of others.'[16] Drawing from these ancient and modern perspectives, I want to frame what I see as a critical-creative approach to 'reading as a writer'.

The Australian writer Kevin Brophy has suggested that when writers read they 'superimpos[e] the sensual and the intellectual', and I think this is where the critical-creative process begins: in the coming together of what we feel and what we think.[17] All readers read for pleasure: for the joy of story, the desire to explore imaginary worlds, the thrill of language used in new and startling ways. But for those who study fiction, who read books over and over, that initial pleasure is only the beginning of the story. Creative writers and literary critics are *active readers* who come back to their favourite books again and again. The reading strategies of these two groups of active readers, however, are not the same and I want to explore the differences here to show what I mean by the phrase 'reading as a writer'.

One of the fundamental differences between literary critics and creative writers is that critics read primarily for hidden or difficult meanings. They don't tend to focus on the 'surface' of the fiction because this is precisely what most readers already experience and understand when they read, and critics need to look beyond the easily accessible. As creative writers we also need to explore the deep places within fiction (and here we can learn from the literary critics), but it is more important, at least initially, for us to value the surface.

Reading with admiration

The first stage of active critical-creative reading lies in the transition from reading for pleasure to *reading with admiration*. This is when we think more closely about the ways we are being affected by what we are reading. We pause over our own responses (whether they be emotional, intellectual or sensual) and examine how the words on the page have produced this effect. How is the story constructed? How are the characters brought to life? How has the arrangement of seven ordinary words evoked such an atmosphere or setting? This is not a cold or clinical analysis. It is a personal exploration of the way fiction works by a reader who is moved by what he or she is reading. This gives us a very different perspective from most literary critics, because as writers we are deliberately connecting our critical awareness to our creative pleasure. (I say *creative* pleasure here because, as I want to show later in this book, readers are co-creators, 'creative conspirators', working with the writer to re-create the imaginary world.[18]) This type of active reading is intensely personal, in a way that literary criticism rarely is, and combines the critical and the creative to produce an emotional and intellectual 'map' of the surface of the fiction. This map is our guide to the technical complexities of the story world and begins to reveal just how intricate and well-wrought the 'surface' of fiction can be. As writers we should honour fiction's surface by giving it our intimate attention.

Reading as an editor

The second stage of active reading, *reading as an editor*, might seem wholly critical, but it too is a creative process. Reading as an editor means that you are again attentive to the way the fiction is affecting you, but this time you are looking for those moments that jar or fall flat or make you feel somehow unsatisfied. You might not immediately be able to put these feelings into words or pinpoint exactly what is wrong, but in the first stage of reading as an editor you simply give credit to your instincts. Listen to yourself when you feel that there is something not quite right about the dialogue, or a character's gesture, or a twist in the plot. Then you can begin to think about why. This is where the critical and the creative come together, in being able to identify and name what otherwise might remain a vague dissatisfaction. In identifying what doesn't work, you also need to think, as Percy Lubbock advised all those years ago, about how it could be changed. How would you rewrite this passage? What alternative gesture would you use? How would you re-structure the scenes? In other words reading as an editor is a critical-creative process that involves both identifying flaws in writing and creating alternatives.

Reading for the intention

The third stage of reading as a writer moves below the surface of the fiction to consider themes or meanings hidden beneath, and here I think writers can learn from the techniques of literary critics. The narratologist H. Porter Abbott suggests three ways of critical reading: intentional, symptomatic and adaptive, and I want to suggest that each of these is potentially useful for writers.[19]

Abbott quotes the novelist Paul Auster who said: 'in a work of fiction one assumes there is a conscious mind behind the pages,' and he argues that when we are *reading for the intention* we are trying to work out what this conscious mind is really trying to say.[20] For instance, if we have just read an adventure story about rabbits searching for a new burrow, we might think that the author *really* intended the story to reveal humanity's exploitation of nature, or the lost values of community, or the redeeming power of love. Now this type of intentional reading is often disparaged as naïve by critics who claim that no reader can ever know what an author *really* meant, and it has been labelled the 'intentional fallacy'.[21] And the critics are right, we can't ever know what writers *really* meant (especially when they're dead). But, however naïve, I still think that it is a useful way for writers to read, because what we are really talking about here is theme. We are asking what might have been the theme (or themes) in the author's mind when he or she wrote the book. We will never know if our guesses are right, but by asking the question we have begun to think about the fiction in a slightly different way. Reading for the intention makes us aware of how the story is held together: how symbols, assertions or asides weave in and out of the story binding the action to the core themes.

Reading for the intention in this way develops our sensitivity to theme both as readers and as writers, for if anyone needs to know what 'the conscious mind behind the pages' is trying to say, it's the writer him or herself. This doesn't mean that we can ever know all the potential meanings of our work, it simply encourages us to question what our fiction is about, what affect we are trying to achieve, and whether we need to revise further to achieve it. It makes us think about the underlying fabric of our fiction, the theme(s) that binds the story together. If the fiction is baggy, perhaps the underlying theme(s) is unfocused or unclear in our mind. Reading for the intention, then, like reading as an editor or reading with admiration, is something that we can practise on our own work as well as other people's. It is a way of reading that explicitly combines criticality and creativity: fusing our intellectual understanding with our emotional intuition.

Reading against the grain

Abbott's second type of reading, 'symptomatic reading', is perhaps the most difficult to perform when 'reading as a writer', but is still a useful strategy. This way of reading, that I call *reading against the grain*, is favoured by contemporary literary critics because it privileges what might be seen as extra-textual material (evidence from beyond the fiction itself). This might include information about the author's life; historical details from the time it was written; political or cultural arguments; psychoanalytical theories, or philosophies of language. In other words, it requires knowledge and study, and once critics have mastered these ideas they can read fiction to discern what it reveals about social anxieties, cultural change, repressed desires, and the nature of storytelling.

I am not suggesting that writers should also be literary critics, but I do think that reading texts against the grain can be revealing, potentially informing a writer's future work. It can also be a way of addressing our instinctual discomfort with certain authors. If we feel that there is a streak of mean-mindedness within a fiction that apparently celebrates generosity, then we can read against the grain to identify and unpick those moments that undermine the carefree surface. Another way to think about the power of reading against the grain is to focus on the idea of masterplots, familiar to many creative writers from numerous 'how to' books, and originally identified by literary theorists and mythologists.

The concept of masterplots can be very useful for writers, as I discuss in later chapters, but we should also be aware that they reflect cultural anxieties and desires that underpin profoundly held beliefs about the self, society and our place in the world. As such they play a major role in contemporary politics. For instance, liberal capitalism is supported by the 'rags to riches' masterplot, just as our current 'war on terror' draws on a whole series of masterplots: in some instances it's the 'revenge' masterplot, or the 'quest' masterplot; in others it's the 'enemy within' masterplot. And some have argued that the 'war on terror' is itself a 'conspiracy' masterplot or that the war in Iraq was the result of an 'oedipal' masterplot, in which the son (President George W. Bush) usurped the father's role (President George Bush) and finished what he could not (deposing Saddam Hussein). The point is that everyone draws on these familiar types, themes and plots to make sense of our world.

Frank Kermode has argued that these masterplots constitute 'the mythological structure of society from which we derive comfort, and which it may be uncomfortable to dispute'.[22] Historically, of course, it has often been the writers and artists who take on the uncomfortable task of disputing the masterplots, and many have been imprisoned – or even murdered – for their words. You may not be writing within a society that enforces its masterplots with secret police or violent repression, but becoming aware of culturally ubiquitous masterplots can make you more sensitive to the social significance of your own writing. If you 'read against the grain' to uncover the way a story implicitly reinforces certain culturally potent masterplots (perhaps racially or sexually loaded), you are more likely to recognise and manipulate these masterplots in your own work. In other words, just as we strive to avoid cliché and hackneyed phrases, so we could also read against the grain to avoid or re-work culturally embedded masterplots.

Reading for adaptation

Abbott's third type of reading, 'adaptive reading', is the most obvious reading strategy for creative writers. It accords with Longinus's advice to emulate the great poets of the past, which he makes clear, 'is not plagiarism; rather it is like taking impressions of beautiful pictures'.[23] More recently the critic Harold Bloom, in his book *The Anxiety of Influence*, has put this slightly differently. He has argued that all great works of art are simply powerful *misreadings* of previous works, and we can think of such misreadings in terms of *reading for adaptation*, the final stage of reading as a writer.[24] For if reading against the grain could be accused of 'reading too much into things', as literary criticism often is, then adaptive reading takes that as its mantra.

Adaptive readers take a story and remake it in their own image, either privately in their imagination, or, if they are writers, publicly in new fictions. There are a number of ways in which writers might engage in adaptive reading: from wholesale adaptation (Shakespeare's rewriting of *The Daughters of King Leir* and Jane Smiley's rewriting of *King Lear* in *A Thousand Acres*); to borrowing characters (Jean Rhys's *Wide Sargasso Sea* which rewrites Bertha from *Jane Eyre*); to mimicking or parodying plot structure (as Joyce did to Homer's *The Odyssey* in *Ulysses*); to affecting a voice or style (as Susanna Clarke has done with Jane Austen in *Jonathan Strange and Mr Norrell*); to simply redeploying a resonant phrase, detail or twist. Reading for adaptation, then, calls for a creative intervention into the text you are reading.

Active reading

To 'read as a writer' is to be an active reader, a reader who can return to a novel or short story after the initial burst of pleasure, and read it again in at least five different ways: reading with admiration, reading as an editor, reading for intention, reading against the grain and reading for adaptation. I've illustrated these different ways of reading by thinking about how we read fiction, either our own or another author's. But I think these ways of reading are equally important when reading non-literary texts: history books, newspapers, scientific theorems, cultural commentaries or literary theory. To take the example of literary theory: if a writer takes up Virginia Woolf's essay 'Modern Fiction', or James Frey's *How to Write a Damn Good Novel*, or Harold Bloom's *The Anxiety of Influence* or Terry Eagleton's *Introduction to Literary Theory*, then they could read with admiration (what makes this beginning so effective? what makes this voice so authoritative?); as an editor (what is wrong with the rhythm of this sentence? would it help if these adjectives were cut?); for the intention (what is this author trying to say?); for the symptoms of something hidden (what are the politics behind these ideas? what are the sleights of hand in this argument?), and for the adaptive possibilities (how can I use these ideas? how can this knowledge inspire new fiction?).

These different ways of reading allow us to engage more effectively with the words that we read and may already be considered as a form of research. But as creative writers our research is not confined to reading, it has much broader horizons.

Research

> *Research to me is as important or more important than the writing. It is the foundation upon which the book is built.*
> Leon Uris, *The Guardian*, 25 June 2003

> *Research is formalized curiosity.*
> Zora Neale Hurston, *Dust Tracks on a Road* (HarperCollins)

When most people think of research they think about libraries and archives, notebooks and scribbled findings – even in this era of the internet a layer of dust seems to cling to the very idea of research. And it is not hard to see the fiction writer as just such a dusty researcher, trawling the archives for details of fashion or historical facts that would give their stories verisimilitude.

During the prewriting phase of writing, authors may well engage in this process of accumulating information. Finding out about forgotten worlds can be a real pleasure, as Zora Neale Hurston suggests, and gaining knowledge about periods, places and people allows us to create what Leon Uris calls a 'foundation' for our fictional world. But this is not the only form of research, and in this section I want to break away from a concept of research that focuses purely on studying and note-taking. We need to stop characterising research as 'the gathering of facts' and begin to understand it as a creative and critical process: a process of discovery that embraces the chaotic musings, the leisurely observations, the struggle for words, and the search for story. All this is research, and only through this eclectic research process can we really discover the kind of 'foundations' we need.

We can think about this another way by saying that when we are researching our fiction we are not only looking for the facts of our story (although facts are necessary) we are looking the *feel* of our story.[25] We are searching for the form, for the style and for the language that will enable us to create a compelling imaginary world. We are searching for the people, the settings and the actions that will make it real. And we are searching for the ideas, the insight and the understanding that will make it true.

Our conception of research needs to embrace all this, as well as the doubts and uncertainties that characterise the critical-creative process. When a writer begins to research their story, either on the internet or by travelling to exotic locations, their notebook may not be filled with important dates or details, but with the kind of scribbling Frank Smith called disposable writing: rough charts and plans; freewriting exercises (non-stop writing of whatever comes to mind); dialogues with emerging characters, abandoned speculations and sketches. The shape of research during this prewriting phase might not be neat, it might even seem scrappy and shambolic, but it is a vital and energising part of the creative process.

Writing as discovery

When we begin to write the first draft we draw from this early research, whether written down or not. But that is not the end of the research process, it simply marks the beginning of a new phase, for the very act of writing is a form of research. This was recognised academically in the 1980s by teachers of composition who began to talk about 'writing as discovery', writing as a process of finding out about subject and form, but it had been recognised by fiction writers long before that. E. M. Forster's famous remark in *Aspects of the Novel*, 'How can I tell what I think till I see what I say?', is often seen as the catchphrase for such literary discovery, although Forster used the phrase ironically to describe those writers who 'will be enjoyed by all who cannot tell what they think till they see what they say'.[26]

The literary experimentalists that Forster joked about understood writing to be a process of discovery, and their work made twentieth-century writers re-think the traditional idea of fiction as *mimesis* – as an imitation of the real world – to uncover the process of discovery in all representation. The philosopher Richard Kearney gives a useful definition of mimesis. He says:

> Mimesis is invention in the original sense of that term: *invenire* means both to discover *and* to create, that is, to disclose what is already there in the light of what is not yet (but is potentially). It is the power, in short to re-create actual worlds as possible worlds.[27]

In writing fiction we create imaginary worlds that reflect upon, and thus reveal, the real world we live in. In Aristotelian terms we capture the essence (*eidos*), the shared universals of human life, the hidden truths about our existence. And through this re-creation we make discoveries about the world and humanity's wonderful, troubled, disastrous existence within it.

But the imaginary worlds of fiction do not simply reproduce the world as it is, as *mimesis*, or imitation, might at first suggest. Writers invent new worlds from the old, worlds that are possible rather than physical. Fiction writers, like scientists, are 'worldmakers', to use the term coined by the philosopher Nelson Goodman, and their research encompasses a dual process of discovery: of what is real and what is possible. This is perhaps why Paul Ricoeur sees fiction as 'an ethical laboratory' and why the poet Gary LaFemina sees his own writing as 'lab work'.[28] As fiction writers, our research circles back and forth between the 'real' and the 'possible' so that the nature of creative writing research becomes a spiralling process of discovery that leads us back to the very roots of the word 'research': the Latin words *circus* (a circle) and *circāre* (go round).

A short note on planning

Fiction, like sculpture or painting, begins with a rough sketch ... [and] an inadequate plan is better than none.
    John Gardner, *On Becoming a Novelist* (W. W. Norton)

Aldous Huxley said he had 'only a dim idea' of what he was going to say when he started writing. William Faulkner said he started with a memory or a mental picture. Isak Dinesen (Karen Blixen) started with a 'tingle', while Vladimir Nabokov had 'a clear preview' and didn't start writing until the whole book was planned on index cards.[29] The different ways in which writers prepare themselves to write their first draft pretty much demonstrates that there is no right way to plan. If you are not one of life's planners, then there is probably not much point in forcing yourself to make flow charts or scene sequences. But if you do not plan you have to be prepared to make mistakes, to throw away whole chunks of a draft that has gone in the wrong direction. You have to be prepared to find your story the hard way – through writing – until what began as an intuition begins to coalesce into fiction. In Jorge Luis Borges' story 'On Exactitude in Science', there is a map that is so detailed, it is the same size as the Empire it represents.[30] The danger of not planning, of refusing even Gardner's 'rough sketch', is that your first draft *becomes* your plan, and like Borges' map it covers the terrain rather than guiding you through it.

If prewriting is a process, we might think of the plan as its 'product', and after all the musing, reading and research, the plan can feel like a licence to write, an acknowledgement that at some level we have found our story. But the plan is not a product, fixed and unchangeable. It is part of the writing process, a map for a yet uncharted land, a map which may only reveal the first stage of the journey. And as the land becomes clearer so the map must change or be left behind. In the following chapters I address some of the theories that have attempted to define the structure and subject of fiction, theories that might well form the coordinates for this provisional map, and encourage you on your journey.

2   Form and Structure

Any work of art must first of all tell a story.

Attributed to Robert Frost

The idea that fiction must 'first of all tell a story' may seem rather obvious, but for years Modernist and Postmodernist writers dismissed the pleasures of story as a corrupt complacency, nothing short of escapism. Their literary experiments often focused precisely on the disruption of such bourgeois expectations, and attempted to find a new form for fiction. They approached 'story' in new ways, re-working myths from other eras to explore and expose the language of literature (as James Joyce did in *Ulysses*), or sabotaging the underlying structures of storytelling (as John Barth did in *Lost in the Funhouse*).

But in the twenty-first century attitudes have changed and there is a resurgence of storytelling within literary fiction (commercial fiction has always emphasised a good story). Deliberations over literary prizes, discussions within review pages, and many volumes of advice for writers all seem to conclude that the core of any good fiction is a damn good story. And although there are many things that might keep us reading (the richness of the atmosphere, the complexity of the characters, the beauty of the language, the ambition of the ideas) there is one question that's a guaranteed page-turner: 'what happens next?'.

Why we tell stories

Telling stories is as basic to human beings as eating. More so, in fact, for while food makes us live, stories are what makes our lives worth living. They are what makes our condition human.

Richard Kearney, *On Stories* (Routledge)

Why do we, as human beings, read and write stories? What does fiction do for us? I think these basic questions are worth pondering at a more personal level: why do *you* read and write stories? What does fiction (or film or TV) do for *you*? The answers you give to these questions might help you to understand why you want to be a writer. But they also might suggest fundamental principles that make storytelling universal. What is it about story that means we can still enjoy reading Homer's *Odyssey* or *Sir Gawain and the Green Knight* or contemporary novels about places and people with totally different values from ourselves? In these next two chapters I want to explore the structure and subject of fiction to find out if there are universal principles of storytelling, and if so, how we can use them to enhance our own writing.

For thousands of years, philosophers have debated the role of story in our lives, arguing, like Richard Kearney, that stories make us human. We can trace this impulse back to philosophers like Hesiod who, in *Theogony*, showed that stories of the gods offered 'a sense of the universe as an ordered whole, a cosmos rather than a chaos'.[1] In other words, stories have prevented our lives from feeling like a series of disconnected experiences, fractured and fragmented in time. Stories give us a framework for understanding ourselves, they give our lives a plot. We continually construct and re-construct our life-story: interpreting events (not always correctly); weaving memories together (not always accurately); anticipating the future (perhaps over-optimistically). We use this semi-fictional 'story' of our lives to understand who we are and how we fit into the world.

In *The Human Condition* Hannah Arendt argued: 'The chief characteristic of the specifically human life . . . is that it is always full of events that ultimately can be told as a story.'[2] And if we think about this as writers, we need to reflect not only on the narratives we tell ourselves, but also on the internal narratives of our characters. Whatever place they have in our story, we need to explore the (perhaps inaccurate or deluded) stories they are also telling themselves about their history and their world.

Reading Aristotle's *Poetics*

Aristotle was one of the first philosophers to attempt to dissect stories as a way of understanding them (this also makes him one of the first literary critics). He claimed that there were six parts to Greek tragedy: plot, character, diction, thought, spectacle and song, and in thinking about the form and structure of fiction I want to explore how relevant these distinctions remain for writers today.

According to Aristotle, plot – by which he meant 'an ordered arrangement of incidents' – is the most important element of any work, 'for tragedy is a representation, not of men, but of action and life'.[3] Many writers have argued against Aristotle's privileging of action over character, most notably Henry James who asked, rather exasperatedly, 'What is character but the determination of incident? What is incident but the illustration of character?'.[4] More recently, Milan Kundera has also underlined the interrelationship between incident and character, suggesting that action separates the character from the anonymity of the crowd: 'It is through action that man steps forth from the repetitive universe of the everyday where each person resembles every other person; it is through action that he distinguishes himself from others and becomes an individual.'[5]

If we are persuaded by these later revisions of Aristotle's thinking, we might see Aristotle's distinctions as hopelessly outdated and reductive. But they have been extremely influential, and the distinction between character-led and plot-led fiction is widely used in publishing to signal the difference between literary and commercial novels. So whilst acknowledging that Aristotle never read a novel or a short story, I still think we can read his age-old separations of narrative form in ways that are useful for fiction writers in the twenty-first century.

In *Poetics*, Aristotle argues that:

> In tragedy it is action that is imitated, and this action is brought about by agents who necessarily display certain distinctive qualities both of character and of thought, according to which we also define the nature of actions. Thought and character are, then, the two natural causes of action, and it is on them that all men depend for success or failure.
>
> (p. 39)

Action is the driving force of any story because it is the expression of character and thought. Action is not simply 'activity', nor is it defined by the kind of action we might now associate with 'action movies'. In fiction, the action itself may be quite mundane, but it can be given extraordinary power and meaning by thought and characterisation.

In Virginia Woolf's *Mrs Dalloway*, for example, when Mrs Dalloway hears about Septimus Smith's suicide, she remembers throwing a sixpence into the Serpentine (the lake in Hyde Park, London). The two actions (throwing away a coin and throwing away a life) are parallel, although clearly one is more dramatic than the other. But the simple act of throwing away a coin is given meaning and resonance through Mrs Dalloway's reflections on the death of a stranger. Both Mrs Dalloway and Septimus are 'agents' who display, in Aristotle's words, 'distinctive qualities of character and thought', which in turn give greater meaning to their actions. In the debates about which comes first, character or plot, Aristotle's emphasis upon the role of 'thought' is often overlooked. But in the example from *Mrs Dalloway* it is 'thought' that brings two very different actions into a new relationship, thought that 'defines the nature of [the] actions' for the reader.

The what and the how

The fourth point in Aristotle's list is diction, by which he means 'the expressive use of words' (p. 41) or 'the manner of representation' (p. 39). Plot, character and thought are, by contrast, 'the objects of representation' (p. 39). Here then is another distinction, between the 'what' of the story and the 'how' of the telling. And this is another way in which literary and commercial fictions are distinguished. Literary novels are often seen to privilege the 'how', drawing attention to the use of language as part of the pleasure of reading, whereas commercial novels privilege the 'what', specifically the plot, and use language as a transparent means of communicating the action. This does not mean that commercial novels are easier to write, for to make language 'invisible' takes as much skill as making it richly visible, and of course, the 'how' of the telling does not just simply *depict* the 'what' of the story. How we tell a story can fundamentally affect what the story is about, so that, as Wallace Stevens says, 'A change of style is a change of subject.'[6]

The distinction between the 'what' and the 'how' is also useful for another reason. It encourages us to think about fiction in terms of interrogatives, which can then become the building blocks for new stories. In prewriting, we can use interrogatives (what, who, where, when, why, how) to identify the subject of our story (the what), the characters (the who), the setting (the where and the when), the motivation (the why), the language and the form (the how). The content of the fiction (the what, who, where, when, why) and the form (how) are ultimately inseparable, but identifying them like this during prewriting

can help to refine them. Ask yourself about the 'how': would your
story work as a poem or a screenplay? What would it lose or gain in
those forms? Why must it be a short story (or a novel)? Could it be
told as effectively in first or third person or mainly through dialogue?
And if not, why not? These kinds of questions, which interrogate the
relationship between the 'what' and the 'how', help to clarify the story
and how best to tell it.

The difference between plot and story

> *Once upon a time there lived in Berlin, Germany, a man called Albinus.*
> *He was rich, respectable, happy; one day he abandoned his wife for*
> *the sake of a youthful mistress; he loved, was not loved; and his life*
> *ended in disaster.*
>
> *This is the whole story and we might have left it at that had there not*
> *been profit and pleasure in the telling, and although there is plenty of*
> *space on a gravestone to contain, bound in moss, the abridged version*
> *of a man's life, detail is always welcome.*
>
> Vladimir Nabokov, Laughter in the Dark (Penguin)

Nabokov's story is an amusing lesson in the distinction between the
'what' and the 'how'. All the content questions are answered here. We
know *what* happens (a man leaves his wife and ends up forsaken),
we know to *whom* it happens (Albinus), we know *where* it happens
(in Berlin), and we know *why* it happens (he falls in love with a
younger woman). But we crave detail. This telling is a summary. To
become meaningful as a narrative, to really affect us, we need to
know more. We might, as writers and readers, start filling in some
of the details ourselves. We might imagine Albinus's wife, his house,
his job, the routines of his life, the cold kisses on the cheek as he
left at the same time each morning for work. We might imagine his
first meeting with the young woman, running through a rainstorm
towards the plush comfort of his office, and his feelings as he rejected
bourgeois respectability for a bohemian life of drugs, sex and art.
Was he exhilarated by living on the despised fringes of society? Or
increasingly aware of his mistake as her friends laughed at him and
abused his wallet?

We try to make this skeletal story into a fully fleshed narrative, and
by doing so we highlight the differences between the bare facts of
the tale and the way they are told. This basic distinction between the

'what' and the 'how' is at the root of many contemporary theories about narrative. In the last century, a group of Russian theorists working in the 1920s, later known as the Russian Formalists, were some of the first to explore how fiction worked. They set up a divide between the basic story (what happened, which they called the *fabula*) and the way it was told (how the reader becomes aware of what happened, which they called the *sjuzhet*). In this way they were also following Aristotle who, two millennia earlier, had made a distinction between the *logos* (the events represented in the story) and the *mythos* (the rearrangement of those events in the plot).[7]

In simple terms we can understand this by thinking of a traditional murder mystery – the whodunit. The basic story goes as follows: Mr X has been having an affair with Miss Y; he ends the affair; she kills him; detective P and his sidekick Q investigate; after several false leads they solve the case; Miss Y is hanged as a murderess. But if we want to make this a mystery, this is not how we are going to tell it. We will start with the discovery of the dead Mr X, or with the arrival of detective P on the scene, or even with P and Q eating their early-morning bacon sandwich. In other words we will plot the tale, and plot (the way we tell it) is very different from story (things as they happened in the right order). But what if we began with the hanging – what sort of novel would we have then? Or what if we told it straight through as it happened? Then we might focus on Miss Y's fear of being found out and the lengths she goes to (perhaps seducing Q) to put detective P off the scent. We would have a novel of suspense (will she get away with it?) rather than surprise (who would have guessed it was *Miss Y* that did it?).

Prewriting, then, is an opportunity not only to devise the story in terms of what happens to whom, but to think about different ways of ordering the events. This may sound like a very obvious point, but I wonder how many of us (and I mean those of us not writing mysteries) simply tell our stories chronologically without first pondering the artistic and emotional effects of re-ordering the action. I'll come back to this point in Chapter 11.

The king died and the queen died

In the early twentieth century, there were many theories about fiction and what it should do, but these theories were not simply categorising literature for academic purposes, many of them were produced by the writers themselves: Henry James, E. M. Forster, T. S. Eliot, Ford Madox Ford, Virginia Woolf, George Orwell and many others all produced theories of writing. Forster's famous definition of the difference between a story and a plot still reappears today, although he was rather hard on the idea of story; he described it not as the backbone of the novel but as the 'tapeworm' that squirms through it, 'the lowest and simplest of literary organisms'. He said:

> When we isolate the story like this from the nobler aspects through which it moves, and hold it out on the forceps – wriggling and interminable, the naked worm of time – it presents an appearance that is both unlovely and dull.[8]

For Forster, story appeals only to our lowest instincts – to our curiosity – whereas plot engages a reader's memory and intelligence. But even he did not recommend flushing out the tapeworm of story altogether; for without it, he admitted, fiction is unintelligible. Instead he argued for recognising the difference between the two, and he gave this example: 'The king died and then the queen died' is a story, but 'The king died and then the queen died of grief' is a plot.[9] The difference between them is that in the second there is a relationship of cause and effect. One thing happened because another had already happened.

This simple example highlights two of the basic rules of storytelling: firstly, that narrative is about change, and secondly, that there must be some motivation for that change. So when you are musing on your plot, ask yourself what changes in the course of the story: what is the major transformation? Then consider the cause(s) and effect(s) of that transformation. Are the causal connections clear? If not, we might have lots of exciting and exhilarating action, but none of it will make any sense to the reader. For the narrative to cohere, action needs both motivation and consequence. If the king dies, the reader must be able to deduce a reason for the death and a response to it.

Forster is right to highlight cause and effect, but in working on our own fiction we must not underestimate the reader's role in constructing the plot. The narratologist Seymour Chatman argues that when readers see 'The king died and then the queen died' they *assume* that there must be some connection between the deaths, even if the writer withholds that information.[10] In other words the reader pieces the plot together from the fragments the author presents, just as we look at a couple of splodges on paper and see the outline of a face.

We are always looking to make sense of our world, and will impose a familiar pattern upon it, even where a pattern is not obvious. This relationship between the reader and the writer in creating meaning is vital to fiction, and is one that I will develop later in this book. But for now, we need to be aware of this mutual working: the writer must trust the reader to fill in the gaps. We need to understand the motivations and consequences in our fiction, whilst avoiding the temptation to over-explain.

Robert McKee's story values

Robert McKee's book *Story* is aimed at screenwriters and he doesn't distinguish between plot and story as Forster did, but his arguments about structure are useful for any writer. He insists that 'a story event creates meaningful change in the life situation of a character'.[11] So, to use our example from Forster, when the king died this was a dramatic change in the life situation of the queen. But McKee goes on to say that this change must be 'expressed and experienced in terms of a value'. Value for McKee is 'the soul of storytelling' and he uses this term to mean positive or negative aspects of our life experience. Hate and love are story values, one being negative, the other positive. Life and death are story values, and so are freedom/slavery, wisdom/stupidity, loyalty/betrayal, hope/despair and strength/weakness, to use some of McKee's own examples. So in the case of the queen, the event (the king's death) caused the change from life (positive) to death (negative). We might also imagine some other changes (from love to grief; hope to despair; perhaps even freedom to slavery) but then we would be fleshing out Forster's bare bones.

McKee adds one more condition to his exploration of change. He says:

> A story event creates meaningful change in the life situation of a character that is expressed and experienced in terms of a value and *achieved through conflict.*[12]

Conflict can be played out on a number of levels (personal, interpersonal, social or environmental), and for the queen we can devise several layers of conflict using McKee's model. If we imagine that the queen dies because religious leaders traditionally kill the king's consort one week after his death, then we can create personal conflict (her survival instinct against her religious duty); interpersonal conflict (her family's quarrel with the priests); social conflict (her people's rebellion against religious fervour); and environmental conflict (her confinement within the royal palace when she tries to escape).

So when prewriting, we need to think about the events of the story, the ordering of those events, and the way those events relate to each other. What changes do they cause and how are these changes experienced by the characters? How are they experienced by the reader? Does the story shift from a positive to a negative value (or vice versa)? Does the change respond to or engender conflict? Asking these questions during the time of prewriting can help to shape and strengthen the narrative you are yet to write. But even if you are nowhere near the stage of outlining the plot, even if you are just musing on the *feel* of your story, these questions can still be useful.

Philip Pullman said that before he devised all the adventures in *His Dark Materials*, he knew that the end should feel like a bruise, painful and yet sensuous.[13] To put this in McKee's terms, the value at the end might be loss or pain. If you can identify a feeling or sensation in this way, you can begin to shape your characters' journey in terms of the story values it reflects. Pullman's description of the bruise is interesting though, because at the end of *His Dark Materials* there is not just pain. There is love and there is hope. There is redemption and sacrifice. For the sake of clarity, McKee has stripped down the notion of value into simple binary oppositions, but novels do not often see the world in such stark terms. Values are tempered and compromised, even confused. After all a bruise signals both hurt and healing. So while these questions might prove useful during the prewriting process, allowing you to gauge the underlying changes within your story structure, they are not absolute. Story values do need to change, but the fiction might also question and challenge the values it rests upon.

The shape of the story

McKee's emphasis upon story values and the change in those values (from happy to sad; fearful to calm) focuses a writer's attention both the emotional shape of their story. This attention to structure prompts us to ask certain questions, such as: Where are the moments of tension and crisis in the story? Where are the moments of recuperation or deliberation? These questions, useful when prewriting, are vital when

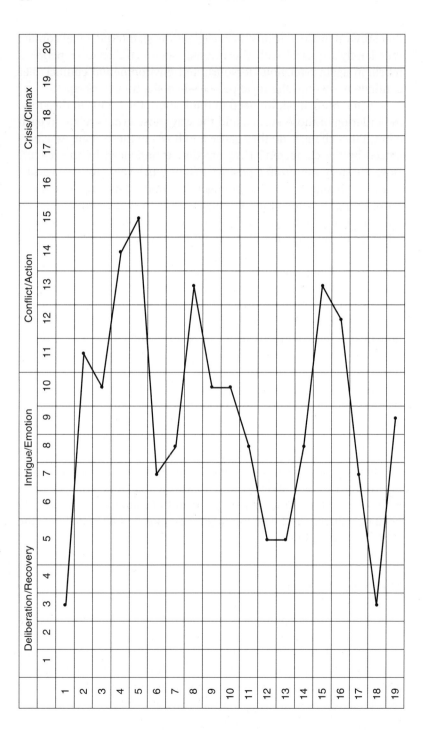

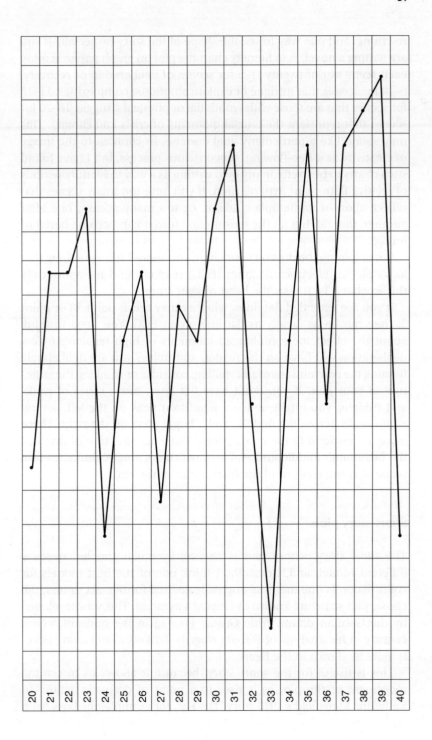

rewriting, and one way to see the shape of the story (especially if you are writing a novel) is to literally chart the plot on graph paper, scoring each scene out of twenty (1–5 for scenes of deliberation or recovery; 6–10 for scenes that intrigue or explore emotional complexities; 11–15 for scenes that are tense with emotional or physical struggle; 16–20 for scenes that represent the crucial moments of crisis and climax). This may sound like a particularly anal exercise, in contrast to the image of creativity as a free-flowing, subconscious process, but I have found such charts to be useful in my own writing as a way to identify periods of relative flatness or hypertension. If you have too many scenes that reflect upon or contemplate action, or too many scenes, one after another, that ratchet up the tension, the reader can become bored or inured.

When joining the dots on your chart, you should see something that looks like an electrocardiogram (ECG) readout, and metaphorically this is what it is. It tests the heart of your story.

If you see extended flat lines, whether they are at point 18 or point 2, they can be as deadly as flat line on an ECG. You need to think about the effect these prolonged moments of high tension or slow deliberation will have on the reader, and unless you are deliberately flouting the conventions of storytelling, consider re-thinking the structure of your plot. If you don't have flat lines, but a series of peaks and troughs, you might notice a significant peak on the left, several rising peaks across the middle, and a larger peak on the right. These peaks correspond to the conventional three-act structure of drama – the beginning, middle and end – in which each act culminates in a scene of rising crisis until the final climax at the end.

Short-story plots

The short story, whose plot is necessarily much simpler, needs a different model, and, ironically, I think one of the best models for short fiction is one that was originally devised for five-act drama: the classic plot structure known as Freytag's pyramid. This was developed by the German drama critic Gustav Freytag in the mid-nineteenth century in his analysis of five-act tragedy *Technik des Drama* (1863). It looks as shown in the figure.

This is useful for the short story, because it allows us to see the movement of the plot as it rises to a point of dramatic action. In Katherine Mansfield's 1923 story 'The Fly', for example, the boss (who

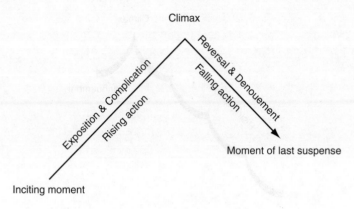

Freytag's pyramid

is not named) is visited by an old employee, Woodifield. Woodifield's daughters have been to Belgium to visit the grave of their brother who died in the First World War, and Woodifield tells the boss that they saw the grave of his (the boss's) son. When Woodifield leaves, the boss looks at the photograph of his son in uniform and tries to cry, but he is distracted by a fly falling into his inkpot. He drips ink onto the fly, watching it struggle for life, letting another drop fall every time it seems to recover, until eventually the fly dies. Then the boss flicks the body into the wastepaper basket, irritated, and unable to remember what he had been thinking about (I consider the symbolism of this story in Chapter 5). In terms of the pyramid plot structure, we can see that the 'inciting moment' is Woodifield's reference to the boss's dead son; the 'rising action' is the tormenting of the fly; the 'climax' is the death of the fly; the 'falling action' is the disposal of the body, and the 'moment of last suspense' is the boss's attempt to remember his grief.

Novel plots

The clarity of Freytag's pyramid works well here, but in a longer fiction, especially the novel, one point of crisis is not enough to sustain the weight of the narrative. In redrawing Freytag's pyramid, John Gardner suggested a more staggered build-up of tension that incorporated earlier moments of crisis as shown in the figure. This does not give us the detail of the ECG model, but in roughing up the edges of Freytag's pyramid, Gardner does show that the rising action cannot be too

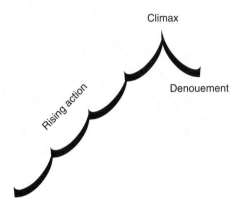

Climax

Denouement

Rising action

Gardner's building climaxes

smooth, it needs its own points of crisis and recovery on the way to the final climax.[14]

E. M. Forster warned that while 'the plot is exciting and may be beautiful . . . it is not a fetish, borrowed from the drama, from the spatial limitations of the stage'. He rejected the pyramids and other plot diagrams, with their inciting incidents, rising action, crisis and climaxes. Instead, he wanted to keep the possibility that the novel can grow into any shape it chooses. He asked: 'Instead of standing above his work controlling it, cannot the novelist throw himself into it and be carried along to some goal that he does not foresee?'.[15] My answer to Forster would be, yes, of course. A novelist can do anything he or she chooses. But Forster's notion of a goal here (foreseen or unforeseen) suggests that he does not want to do away with the notion of climax altogether. Writers have different ways of working: some (like Nabokov) prefer to organise the entire plot before they write; others (like Forster) want to see where it takes them. Most of us have a comfortable place within this spectrum of possibilities. But rather than rejecting the graphs and diagrams I think we need to think carefully about how and when we use them. If you are a writer who likes to see where the pen leads you, then use these models during rewriting, when you need an overview of your plot. If you are a writer who likes to know where you are headed, then use these models during prewriting as a way of structuring your plot before you begin writing.

For writers who want to break away from those conventional geometries completely, who want to experiment with circular or zigzag plots with no rising action, or allow their writing to find its own path, perhaps even the jagged, looped, back-tracking diagrams Laurence

Sterne draws to demonstrate the plot of *Tristram Shandy*, then it's important to know the conventions you are writing against, and why you're doing it.[16] As hard as it sounds, self-conscious cleverness or self-indulgent ambling are no less stultifying than over-worked conventions. If you want to achieve literary novelty, you need to know about the already existing 'novels in a box', the novels printed on roller towels, and the novels with fairylights through their pages waiting to be plugged in. If you want to find a new form, you need to know about the ways fictional conventions have already been warped or rejected by writers in the last century. But most important of all, you need to know that the fiction you are writing cannot be crammed into the conventional models because at its heart it is saying something completely new; its subject demands a new form. And it's to subject that I now turn.

3   Subject

Like me to write you a little essay on The Importance of Subject? Well the reason you are so sore you missed the war is because war is the best subject of all. . . . Love is also a good subject . . . Other major subjects are the money from which we get riches and poores. Also avarice. . . . A dull subject I should say would be impotence. Murder is a good one so get a swell one in yr. next book and sit back.
Ernest Hemingway, Letter to F. Scott Fitzgerald, 1925,
in *Ernest Hemingway on Writing* (Scribner)

What is the subject of fiction? What are all these stories about? Hemingway suggests some of the possible subjects for fiction writers, but I don't want to follow him by considering the relative merits of writing about marriage or mountain climbing. Instead I want to consider the claim that all the stories in the world can be seen as exploring the same fundamental subject: how to be a human being. This chapter focuses on the work of literary theorists who study folktales and myths to see how useful their ideas are for writers pondering the subject of their own stories.

Vladimir Propp and folktales

One of the most famous theories about story was developed in the 1920s by the Russian scholar Vladimir Propp. Propp studied over a hundred folktales to see if they shared a fundamental shape or, as he termed it, 'morphology of the folktale'.[1] And he concluded that in folktales there are only ever seven character-types (or roles) and 31 functions, by which he meant actions or incidents. Not all the folktales he studied included every role or function, but their basic subject and structure remained the same. This, somewhat paraphrased, is Propp's model of roles and functions.

Character-types or roles

Hero (a Seeker or a Victim)
Villain

Donor/Provider
Dispatcher
Helper
Princess (and her father)
False Hero

One character can play several roles, and many characters can appear in one role (such as donors or helpers).

Functions

1   A member of the family leaves or is absent (or a child is orphaned).
2   A restriction (a law or prohibition) is placed on the hero.
3   The hero goes against the restriction.
4   The villain tries to find the hero.
5   The villain gets information about the hero.
6   The villain tries to trick the hero into trusting him.
7   The hero falls for it.
8   The villain hurts the hero's family (injury) or one of the family desperately needs something (lack).
9   The injury or lack becomes known and the hero must act.
10 The seeker/hero decides upon action.
11 The hero leaves home.
12 The hero is tested (attacked, interrogated, etc.) and is then ready to receive a helper or magical agent.
13 The hero reacts to the actions of the future donor.
14 The hero can use the magical agent/helper.
15 The hero is led to what he is looking for.
16 The hero fights the villain.
17 The hero is wounded or marked.
18 The villain is defeated.
19 The injury or lack (in 8) is put right.
20 The hero returns.
21 The hero is pursued.
22 The hero is saved from this pursuit. (Propp notes that many tales either end here or repeat earlier functions.)
23 The hero returns home, unrecognised.
24 A false hero makes false claims.
25 A difficult task is set for the hero.
26 The task is resolved.
27 The hero is recognised.
28 The false hero or villain is exposed.

29   The hero is transformed (perhaps given a new appearance).
30   The villain is punished.
31   The hero is married and/or crowned.

At the heart of these stories is the growth or maturation of the hero. He (or she) has to face up to the possibilities of evil in the world (a threat to his family or the status quo) and, through courage, integrity and friendship, defeat it. As you were reading the list of functions, you might have recognised key stages in the stories of fairy tales like 'Little Red Riding Hood' or 'Jack and the Beanstalk' (you have to miss out some of the functions to find their structure) or games like *Super Mario Brothers*. But you can also see the basic stories of well-known novels here, such as J. K. Rowling's *Harry Potter and the Philosopher's [Sorcerer's] Stone* or nineteenth-century classics like Charlotte Brontë's *Jane Eyre*. I'm not proposing a perfect fit, after all Propp based his study on short tales that didn't have the complexity of a novel, and it's clear from his categorisation of functions and roles that he doesn't exactly have a Jamesian approach to character, but if we adapt and play with Propp's model, we can see how it might correspond to the stories of longer works.

Propp's functions in fiction

Consider *Harry Potter* in Proppian terms. The characters are relatively easy to identify (although as I write, the series is not yet finished and some roles may change).

Hero (seeker or victim): Harry Potter
Villain: Voldemort
Donor: Dumbledore (enabling him to use magic)
Dispatcher: Hagrid (taking him to Platform 9 3/4)
Helper: Ron and Hermione
Princess: Ginny Weasley
False Hero: Draco Malfoy (who may yet transform into a helper)

If we consider the 31 functions, we might begin with Harry's orphaned (1) and restricted (2 + 3) existence at the Dursleys' where he must stay because Voldemort is pursuing him (4). Harry learns that Voldemort killed his parents (8 + 9) and goes to Hogwarts (11). He fights Malfoy, trolls etc. (12) under the watchful eye of Dumbledore (13). He becomes skilled at magic (14) and realises that Voldemort is after the

Philosopher's Stone. With the help of Hermione and Ron he reaches the Stone's hiding place (15) and fights Voldemort (16). He is injured (he is already marked by the scar) (17) but defeats Voldemort (18) and protects the Stone. He receives an album of family photographs (partial 19) and returns to the Dursleys (20) but Voldemort is still after him (21). We then move into the second book, where the structure is played out once more (see Propp's note for 22).

But if *Harry Potter* might seem an obvious example, Propp's functions can also be applied and adapted for more classic texts like *Jane Eyre*. A list of the characters, drawn out in Proppian terms, might begin to illustrate some of the complexities.

Hero (seeker-hero: Jane Eyre / victim-hero: Rochester)
Villain: John Reed/Brockenhurst/Bertha
Donor: Uncle Eyre
Dispatcher: Helen Burns
Helper: The Rivers cousins
Princess: Jane/Rochester
False Hero: St John Rivers

Jane is orphaned (1) and living with the despicable Reeds (2 + 3). Mr Brockenhurst takes Jane to Lowood School (4, 5, 6, 7) where the conditions cause her friend Helen Burns to die of typhoid (8). Jane goes as a governess to Thornfield (9, 10, 11). Rochester chides her and they fall in love (12, 14). They arrange to marry (15). Bertha burns Rochester's room and the wedding is cancelled (16). Jane leaves Thornfield and wanders through the wilderness (11, 12). She finds her cousins, the Rivers (15), and discovers that she is rich (13, 14). She hears Rochester's call (15). He has been burned in the fire at Thornfield (16, 17, 18, 19). Jane finds him (20, 27). Rochester is mutilated (29) but Bertha is dead (30). 'Reader, I married him' (31).

Propp's functions in prewriting

Propp's schema very obviously reduces a work of fiction to its most basic elements, and if a writer tries to construct their plot using the 31 functions they may well imprison their imagination. But there are other ways to use such structuralist models of narrative. Prewriting is a time of experiment without risk, when narrative possibilities can be explored, developed, abandoned. We are not writing yet. We are not crafting phrases, or creating scenes that later we will be loath to cut. We can follow our impulses, and here Propp's schema can be a play-trail for the imagination, fuel for the 'what if?'. What adventure lies ahead of your character(s)? What restrictions are placed upon them? How do they violate them? Are they deceived by the villain? And who or what is the villain in this story? Are there a number of villains? Who are the helpers?

These roles don't have to be filled as Propp suggests. The villain could be the character's low self-esteem that must be defeated; the 'magical agent' could be love or money (as it was in *Jane Eyre*) as much as a mystical or scientific gadget. So Propp's functions could provide the spark of a more complex story and they are equally as useful for realistic fiction as they are for fairytales: stories about a child runaway, gangland murders, a battle with mental illness, thwarted romance or family drama could all be structured using Propp's functions, because the underlying subject (the struggle to become the person you should be) is fundamentally the same.

If you don't want to use Propp's model to inspire new story ideas, it may still help to focus already plotted or drafted fictions. If you can strip your narrative down to its 'functions' (for instance, 'Hero arrives at battle front', 'Hero meets rival', 'Hero has first test'), it might help to clarify the movement and subject of the basic story, and from this you can see how the narrative builds tension. You can also consider the effects of reversal and repetition, shifting chronologies, and withheld information.

In charting *Jane Eyre*, I went against one of Propp's rules: I re-ordered the functions. Propp argued that although many of the functions would not appear in a particular story, they would always appear in the same order. But what if we deliberately re-arranged them? Thinking of the functions again, consider 6–9:

6   The villain tries to trick the hero into trusting him.
7   The hero falls for it.
8   The villain hurts the hero's family (injury) or one of the family desperately needs something (lack).
9   The injury or lack becomes known and the hero must act.

What would be the emotional effect on the reader if (6, 7, 8, 9) were told as (8, 9, 6, 7) or (6, 8, 9, revealing 7 later)?

The narratologist, Michael Toolan, argues that Propp's character types can be mapped onto a surprising number of stories, from

Homer's *Iliad* to *Buffy the Vampire Slayer*, and he lists the characters from the first *Star Wars* trilogy to show that they are essentially Proppian types:

Villain: Darth Vader
Dispatcher: Luke's Uncle
Donor: Obi Wan Kenobi (magical power is provided by the Force)
Helper: Yoda
Hero (seeker or victim): Luke Skywalker
Princess: Leia[2]

It would not be difficult to map the story of the first *Star Wars* trilogy onto Propp's 31 functions, but perhaps more revealing would be to map the films' structure onto Joseph Campbell's theory of the 'monomyth' (a word he borrowed from James Joyce's *Finnegans Wake*). George Lucas has often acknowledged a debt to Campbell because after struggling with the second rewrite of *Star Wars*, Lucas read Campbell's book, *The Hero with a Thousand Faces*, and used it to help him construct a coherent plot within the galaxy far, far away.

Joseph Campbell's theory of the monomyth

> *Myths and fairy stories both answer the eternal questions: What is the world really like? How am I to live my life in it? How can I be truly myself?*
>
> Bruno Bettelheim, *The Uses of Enchantment* (Penguin)

> *It is just as deadly for the mind to have a system as to have none. It will thus be necessary to decide to combine both.*
>
> Friedrich Schlegel, Athenaeum Fragment 53, in *Philosophical Fragments* (University of Minnesota Press)

Like Propp's schema, Campbell's theory of myth, which he calls the journey of the hero, can help writers to draw upon the power of 'eternal questions' in their fiction. But we also need to be wary when using their morphologies. Lucas's success in plotting the hero's journey in *Star Wars* encouraged thousands of hopeful screenwriters to buy a copy of Campbell's book. The 'monomyth' became a Hollywood cliché, a formula, and the scripts that clung to it were trite and predictable. As Schlegel warned: 'It is just as deadly for the

mind to have a system as to have none.'[3] If the system domin-
ates the creative process, the results will be mechanical and flat.
But this does not mean that Campbell's research is no longer useful
for writers because, as Schlegel pointed out, it is equally paralysing
to have no system at all: the trick is to work both within and
beyond it.

We cannot grab at Campbell's model and force our imaginations
to subscribe to it, but his ideas might well inspire us during the
prewriting stage when we can adapt or pillage them as much for realistic fiction as for fantasy or SF. The title, *Hero with a Thousand Faces*,
reveals the model's flexibility, suggesting a hero with many potential
incarnations and numerous journeys to make.

Campbell's structure of the monomyth is worth our attention
because through his study he attempts to identify and define the roots
of our identity (and creativity) as human beings. Campbell invests
his study with psychological import, analysing ancient myths from
around the world to discover their shared patterns and emotional
resonance, and I am going to consider his model in some detail, illus-
trating it with reference to the first film in *The Matrix* trilogy (I'm
leaving *Star Wars* to you).

My reasons for choosing a film here are two-fold: firstly because
the story of a blockbuster movie soon becomes absorbed into wider
culture (so even if you haven't seen it, you probably know something
about it), and secondly because fiction writers can learn a lot from
screenwriters and visa versa. Another reason for choosing *The Matrix*
in particular is that it seems to be such a postmodern movie. The
Wachowski brothers, who wrote and directed it, deliberately played
on the uncertainties of Postmodernism, 'the desert of the real' as
philosopher Jean Baudrillard has called it (Keanu Reeves was made to
read Baudrillard's *Simulacra and Simulations* before filming began).
And yet beneath this postmodern surface, the story follows Campbell's
monomyth almost to the letter.

The psychology of the monomyth

At the heart of Campbell's study is the psychoanalytical notion of the
divided self, the separation of the conscious and unconscious, which
Sigmund Freud saw as the battle between the id (the pleasure principle: selfish instincts without social awareness); the ego (the reality
principle: the awareness of the self and its relation to the world), and

the superego (the guilt-inducing conscience). For Freud the id was buried in the unconscious, but the ego and the superego had both conscious and unconscious aspects. Carl Jung expressed the idea of self-division differently. After initially working with Freud as his friend and disciple, Jung's different theories caused a rift between them and they became enemies. Jung could not accept Freud's focus on sexuality as the key to unlocking repression, and whereas Freud focused on infancy and the development of the child from birth through adolescence, Jung was interested in the second half of life when we must confront and understand our mortality. As Joseph Campbell says, these two theorists take us full circle: 'from the tomb of the womb to the womb of the tomb'.[4]

Jung also theorised a 'personal unconscious' of repressed wishes and desires, similar to Freud's id, but argued that beneath this personal unconscious was a 'collective unconscious' which contained primordial images and archetypes. This shared psychic inheritance was comparable to our human genetic programming and represented humanity's unconscious submission to instinct. Jung saw our individual identity as being caught between the everyday preoccupations of the ego, and the deeper, psychic currents in the personal and collective unconscious. In his work, the separation of the ego (the 'I' that represents both our individuality and our selfishness) from the Self (our primitive instincts) was the primary division that needed to be healed. Freud also theorised our human desire to reclaim a lost wholeness: he saw it as underlying the desire to mate (Eros) and the desire for death (Thanatos).

Read psychoanalytically, the hero's search in the monomyth is a search for psychic wholeness and mature identity, and represents a universal struggle that we all experience. So it follows that every ordinary person has the capacity (in fiction as in life) to be a hero. Using this psychoanalytical perspective, it becomes clear that the donors and helpers, villains and dispatchers in Propp's schema are not just external figures, they are also aspects of the mind: attitudes and anxieties that enable and restrict us (and our characters). The donors and helpers might be love or education, just as the villains and dispatchers might be paranoia or curiosity. The subject of fiction is both psychological and physical: it is a battle with our inner demons as much as it is with the world's cruelties and injustices. Both must be overcome if we are to achieve self-knowledge and self-fulfilment.

Dreams and the monomyth

Campbell's argument is that 'dream is the personalized myth, myth the depersonalized dream' (p. 19). Following Freud and Jung he claims that myths and dreams symbolise the deep dynamics of the psyche – but whereas dreams are confused by the quirks of the individual, myths speak to everyone. In myth, the hero (or heroine) goes beyond their own personal, historical, physical limitations to reach into the 'primary springs of human life and thought' (p. 20). And if we think about John Gardner's description of fiction as a 'vivid and continuous dream', we might argue that the stories we write are also part of this continuum.[5] For Jung, dreams and myths reach down into the archetypes of the collective unconscious: archetypes which teach us how to be human, to think and understand as humans do. And this, from a Jungian perspective, is also the purpose of fiction. Even though realist contemporary novels and short stories may seem a long way from the strangeness of dream or tribal myth, a Jungian would argue that they share the same subject and they serve the same vital purpose: they teach us how to live.

In a recent lecture on Jung, Tom Davis asked some provocative questions about the nature of children's play and dream experience. He said:

> What do children dream about? All sorts of things, but one odd thing. They have a tendency to dream, and play, about monsters. Wild animals. Fear of darkness. Falling from trees. Jungles. Fighting. Being eaten. And traditional children's stories reflect these dreams. Why? My children were brought up in Moseley, Birmingham [UK]. No monsters, no jungles, no serious danger of being eaten by wild animals. This is not part of the work of being human now, not for most of us. But of course it was, a very long time ago. Are these ancient fears and survival skills part of the package of images that we are born with? Do we inherit our dream images?[6]

Jungians often point to the behaviour of animals to support their argument that we are born with a package of images. For example, if a hawk flies over a newly hatched gosling, the gosling immediately ducks and runs. In the first minutes of its life, before it has experienced anything of its strange new environment, it instinctively knows it must hide. The same effect can be achieved by the cardboard shape of a hawk, but not by the shape of any other bird. How does the gosling know what to fear?

Recent research has also shown that foetuses engage in more REM (dream) sleep than adults. Are these dreams full of images and symbols from our collective unconscious? Do they prefigure the themes of ancient myths and contemporary stories? Joseph Campbell argued that the reason myths exist, why they are continually recycled and why they continually fascinate us, is because they are archetypal: they contain the secrets of life, the outline of the journey we must all take towards enlightenment. For writers, this breaking down of myth to find a 'deep story' that speaks across cultures and histories may present an exciting way to tap into the 'collective unconscious'. Alternatively, you may want to reject the monomyth as culturally homogenising, because it seems to obliterate social and contextual differences, and as psychologically essentialising, in that it assumes that human beings have a true nature that is ultimately unchanging. That's fine. Intellectually, culturally, politically we can adopt, adapt or reject the monomyth, like any other story-telling model.

The writer's journey

The criticisms of Christopher Vogler's *The Writer's Journey*, which successfully simplified Campbell's detailed study of mythology into an accessible 'how to' for writers, is a case in point. Vogler, who worked for the Disney corporation, produced a summary of character-types and a model of the hero's journey as a three-act screenplay. But in doing so, he firmly put the Hollywood stamp upon an otherwise eclectic study. In the second edition of his book, which responds to criticisms of the first, he makes some interesting points about the cultural distinctions that influence the fictional conception of the hero. He suggests that 'Australians distrust appeals to heroic virtue' due to a colonial legacy that saw many young 'heroes' fight in British wars. Germans, he says, have also seen the concept of hero 'tainted', in this case by the pernicious rhetoric of Nazism. And he acknowledges the subtle 'cultural imperialism' that led him to stress a 'preference for happy endings and tidy resolutions, the tendency to show admirable, virtuous heroes overcoming evil by individual effort', which is not always the case in Campbell's original work.

I think Campbell's monomyth is far more flexible than Vogler's rewriting initially suggests, because, like Jung's archetypes, the mono-myth is really only a potential subject, one that can conclude in many different ways, and one that only becomes meaningful when it embodies the specific cultural and social environments of its readers and listeners.

In this way Campbell's mythic model offers potential inspiration for widely different and unexpected stories, and in the prewriting phase of composition we will almost certainly be confronted by its ubiquitous power and persuasiveness, even if this only unconsciously shapes our writing. The critical-creative approach to this dilemma is to identify the structure of those myths that hover under the surface of our culture (and reappear in so many books and movies), so that, even if we reject them, we are better able to respond to them in our fictions. In working through Campbell's theory, I'm going to follow his use of the word 'he' to signal the hero (as the hero of *The Matrix* is male) but I want to stress that the hero can also be female.

The structure of the monomyth

Campbell's fundamental argument was that myths from around the world shared the same underlying subject. He said: 'the successful adventure of the hero is the unlocking and release again of the flow of life into the body of the world' (p. 40). He called this adventure the hero's journey and divided it into three phases: *Departure, Initiation* and *Return*, each with their own function. But like Propp, Campbell stressed that not every element needed to happen, and that it was even possible for the hero to fail.

The Departure

The first stage, the Departure, can be understood as the journey from the safety of the ordinary world, the hero's status quo, into the unknown and frightening world of the adventure. The hero (or heroine) encounters a call to adventure (witnessing a crime; receiving a message, request or proposition; uncovering a secret; falling in love). His own anxieties, fears and weaknesses may hold him back at first, so that at first he refuses to act, but he is helped by a more exper- ienced guide or mentor (a teacher, friend, neighbour, or stranger) who gives him wise advice and may also equip him with the things he needs (ID, money, education, magic potions, weapons). With this help he defeats the threshold guardian (this may be an authority figure, a lesser villain, a demon spirit, or his own fear) and enters the world of the adventure (the city, the desert, the workplace, space, the front room). All the imagined pleasures and fears of this realm now begin to be played out as the hero has reached the point of no return. He cannot go back. He will be transformed by the experience he is about to have. The beginning is over and the story now gets underway.

Campbell divides the Departure into five elements (the call to adventure, the refusal of the call, supernatural aid, crossing of the first threshold and the belly of the whale), and we can see these working clearly in *The Matrix*. The *call to adventure* occurs when Neo's computer tells him to 'follow the white rabbit', and again when he receives instructions via a mobile phone. When the Agents come for him, however, Neo refuses to obey those instructions and fails to escape. Campbell argues that this *refusal of the call* reveals the emotional immaturity of the hero, showing that he is 'bound in by the walls of childhood' (p. 62) and remains dependent on the relationships and conventions of his juvenile world. Neo then receives *supernatural aid* which further prepares him for adventure. Trinity removes the 'bug' from his stomach, and although she does not conform to Campbell's traditional image of an old man or woman providing the adventurer 'with amulets against the dragon forces he is about to pass' (p. 69), her actions accord with the mythic structure of the adventure and she becomes Neo's first guide.

Neo *crosses the first threshold* when he takes the red pill. For Campbell this threshold crossing marks the turning point in the story, when the hero passes beyond the safety of the tribe and enters the regions of the unknown, regions which present 'free fields for the projection of unconscious content . . . suggesting threats of violence and fancied dangerous delight' (p. 79). The fifth and final element of the hero's departure comes when he enters *the belly of the whale*. The womb-like imagery here underlies the symbolism of the hero's journey as both self-annihilation and rebirth, and this is explicitly referenced in *The Matrix* when Neo's body is violently expelled from the mechanical womb and rescued by the crew of the submarine Nebuchadnezzar.

The Initiation

The next phase of the hero's journey is the Initiation, which is also divided into several elements: the road of trials, meeting with the Goddess, woman as temptress, atonement with the father, apotheosis and the ultimate boon. The Initiation stage begins with a series of trials that may develop in intensity and complexity and only when the hero has been tested, has confronted his fears, beaten his enemies, and established the trust of his friends (who may have accompanied him from the Ordinary World or be a part of the Adventure World) will he face the ultimate wonder and terror at the heart of the adventure: the love/temptation of the feminine principle and the strength/power of the masculine.

This may be expressed quite literally in the story as sexual love/temptation followed by the battle against and reconciliation with a powerful masculine figure (the father or other authority). Or it may be worked through more symbolically, so that the hero faces the death of his old self (either by risking physical death or allowing the death of his old personality) and achieves a new balance between the masculine and feminine aspects of his own character (strength, intellect, love and intuition). This is the true achievement of the quest, although the hero might also receive or steal a more physical prize, which in some way represents his achievement and enables others to share in it.

Campbell describes *the road of trials*, the first element of the Initiation, as a favourite phase of the myth-adventure, calling it 'a dream landscape of curiously fluid, ambiguous forms, where [the hero] must survive a succession of trials' (p. 97). In *The Matrix*, the road of trials begins with Neo's training in the 'construct', and moves through his meeting with the Oracle and survival of the 'glitch' in the matrix. For Campbell these trials have a psychological function which he expresses through a single question: 'Can the ego put itself to death?' (p. 109). Can the hero turn away from his self-centred or self-serving perception of the world and acknowledge something more profound? In other words, can Neo let go of his previous concept of himself and accept that he was living in the Matrix?

The next three elements of the Initiation (meeting with the Goddess, meeting the woman as temptress, and atonement with the father) may follow from one to the other, or represent different fates for the hero, and they are best understood in symbolic terms. In *The Matrix*, Neo *meets with the Goddess* through his love for Trinity, and it is Cypher, not Neo, who *meets the woman as temptress*. He betrays his friends for the sake of illusionary material comfort, and shows the way in which the Goddess/temptress binary represents more than physical or sexual desire.

Psychologically the marriage with the goddess represents the marriage of the feminine and masculine aspects of the self (the reaching of maturity), in which the positive aspects of the feminine (love, nurture and emotional understanding) and the positive aspects of the masculine (strength, power and order) come together. The meeting with the temptress represents the lure of the negative aspects of these terms (power and ego) in which the feminine represents guile and self-serving temptation, and the masculine represents tyranny and oppression.

On first reading, this stage of the Initiation, which presents women as either goddess or temptress, seems to evoke the Madonna/Whore binary that feminists have successfully critiqued, revealing how it positions women as symbolic dumping grounds for cultural hypocrisy. And although this movement from good/bad woman to good/bad father seems to uphold and even reinforce binary oppositions such as male/female, good/bad, life/death, for Campbell these myths ultimately work to resolve them into unity. He writes that 'the hero may derive hope and assurance from the helpful female figure ... only to find, in the end, that the father and mother reflect each other, and are in essence the same' (p. 131). Campbell's father and mother figures represent the Jungian principles of the feminine and the masculine (distinct from individual men and women) and unless they 'reflect each other' in each person (regardless of their sex) they will become warped, and the negative aspects of each principle will come to the fore.

The final elements of the Initiation stage are the atonement with the father, the apotheosis and the ultimate boon. For Neo, the *atonement with the father* comes when he rescues Morpheus from the military base. Campbell describes this time as an 'ego-shattering initiation' (p. 131) in which the hero must confront and atone with the terrifying force of the father. Importantly the father is seen as both an ogre-figure and a figure of wisdom and mercy, and the two sides of the father, Father-as-Mercy and Father-as-Ogre, are represented by the two characters of Morpheus and Agent Smith, both of whom have created, and will be surpassed by, Neo.

If the hero wins through the atonement, as Neo does, he can achieve what Campbell calls *apotheosis*, in which he is ranked among the gods. Here the oppositions of masculine/feminine in the previous elements are reconciled and the hero overcomes his ego, achieving true spiritual growth. He has understood what Morpheus describes as the 'difference between knowing the path and taking the path'. This is the *ultimate boon*, in which the hero glimpses the power that lies beyond our limited human world, and Neo begins to believe that he is 'the One'.

The Return

The final phase of the hero's journey is the Return, and again, there are several stages: refusal to return, magic flight, rescue from without, crossing the return threshold, mastery of two worlds and freedom to live. The Return from the adventure is not easy, and is often the most dangerous time. It may involve pursuit, or further trials that risk all that has so far been gained. This is the moment when the possibility of the hero not making it is strongest, the time of greatest uncertainty. But once the hero has crossed back into the ordinary world this moment is full of import, a moment of rebirth which constitutes the emotional climax of the story. The hero may wander unrecognised in the ordinary world, or live uneasily unable to thrive, or he may find a new happiness. What is most significant is that his adventure will benefit his community and his world. The elixir he has brought back, which may be a physical or emotional treasure (riches, medicine, freedom, peace, love) has given his society the freedom to live.

In *The Matrix* Neo at first *refuses to return*, fighting Agent Smith single-handed when Trinity and Morpheus leave the Matrix. When he does attempt to return he uses *magic flight* (the ringing phone) to escape. Campbell points out that this stage of the journey is often perilous and can be undone by the small errors of human frailty: as when, in the Greek myth, Orpheus looked back and Eurydice was lost in the Underworld. The danger of failure and death is ever-present and the hero may have to be *rescued from without*, helped by friends when all seems lost, just as Trinity brings Neo back from the dead with a kiss. Neo survives, *crosses the return threshold*, waking up in the besieged Nebuchadnezzar, and is again re-born.

Neo is now *master of two worlds*, he understands about Zion and he has gained control of the Matrix by entering and shattering the chimera of Agent Smith. His actions are the first step towards giving humanity the *freedom to live* and in the final moments of the film, Neo promises to show us 'a world without rules and controls, without borders or boundaries, a world where anything is possible'.

The monomyth and prewriting

I could have chosen many different stories to illustrate Campbell's vision of the monomyth, stories which might have given new emphasis to the different elements and stages of the hero's journey and shown the flexibility of the model. *Harry Potter and the Philosopher's [Sorcerer's] Stone*, for instance, condenses the Return to the very last page: Harry doesn't want to leave Hogwarts (refusal of return), but travels on the Hogwarts Express (magic flight) to Platform $9^3/_4$ (the return threshold) joking that he can always threaten the Dursleys with magic (master of two worlds) even though they have no idea that he has saved the world from Voldemort's return (freedom to live). But this shift of emphasis does nothing to lessen the power of Rowling's novel. Rather, it illustrates that models can be adapted. The story you wish to tell has its own integrity and should not be contorted to conform to an external set of rules.

As writers, we can use the work of theorists such as Propp and Campbell to inspire possibilities, perhaps even to give archetypal resonance to our own writing, but we must remember that in the abstract these models lack the particularity that makes a story powerful. Like Jung's language archetype, which provides the potential for language rather than language itself, and might find expression in English, French or Cantonese, these models provide only the potential for story. Only when they are infused with the specific details of culture and environment, details that give a vibrancy and particularity to your story, will they lend resonance to your writing. For as Edith Wharton once said: 'The value of a subject depends almost wholly on what the author sees in it.'[7] Every author will see different things in every subject, and it's these differences of vision and 'voice' that I consider in the next chapter.

4   V o i c e

Every story has its own voice, just as every person does.
Kate Grenville, *The Writing Book* (Allen & Unwin)

We all have our own voice, and if we were talking together now, instead of writing and reading, our different voices would be very clear. We could hear how high or low they were, whether we shrieked when excited or murmured when nervous. But this isn't the only way we would 'hear' our voices. Our voices would be distinct in terms of the way we used phrases, repeated ourselves, paused or babbled; they would be marked by what we chose to talk about: people or ideas, sport or shopping, even fiction writing. For anyone listening to us, our voices would provide clues about our personal histories, not only telling them where we came from and what social group we belonged to, but allowing them to glimpse our experiences, our beliefs and our desires.

Within this book we cannot hear each other's voice. We are not speaking, but reading and writing. The words on these pages are all that connect us. But in some ways you can 'hear' me – by reading these pages, you recreate my voice in your own mind, or at least the voice of a person you think would write this type of book. If we ever meet you might be surprised by the difference between the voice you imagined and my 'actual' voice, but that perhaps shows how much my writer's voice is brought to life by your reader's ear. Voice is not simply created by the author. It is produced by a cacophony of voices: the author's, the characters', the narrator's and the reader's. This chapter will think about 'voice' in all these ways: firstly by considering the writer's voice, then by thinking about what Kate Grenville has termed the story's voice, and finally by imagining the voice of the reader.

Finding an individual voice

In fiction, writers rarely 'speak' to their readers in the way I'm addressing you now, but authors are still seen as having individual and distinctive voices. And new writers are often urged by books and teachers to 'find their voice' without being told what this really means. It's a frustrating and intimidating demand. How does anyone 'find' their voice? The instruction to look for it (as if it were somehow lost) seems to me to create an anxiety that might actually silence a writer altogether. And the anxiety is compounded when we're told that the way to find our voice is to 'be natural', just to 'be ourselves'. There's nothing harder than 'being natural' on demand. And that's perhaps because our 'natural self' is intensely complex, constructed as it is not only by biology or instinct, but by family and culture, language and history.

I want to defuse the anxiety about 'voice' by offering critical-creative strategies for overcoming the difficulties of 'being natural', and I want to begin with an assertion: every writer already has their own voice, because every writer has their own perspective on the world. As Dorothea Brande put it over seventy years ago: 'No one else was born of your parents, at just that time of that country's history; no one underwent just your experiences; reached just your conclusions, or faces the world with the exact set of ideas that you must have.'[1] Your social, cultural, political, psychological and biological history make you individual, and so within every one of us there is the raw material for original work. There is much to be done to make it good work, of course, but the potential is there.

This might be a surprisingly romantic idea to place at the heart of a critical-creative approach to writing, echoing as it does that hackneyed phrase, 'we're all individuals', but I think that it's an important one for fiction writers. Even in the teeth of a theoretical tradition that has torn such humanist ideas to pieces I still want to claim that 'human life is not (essentially) a fiction, and that fictions are (essentially) about human lives.'[2] Theorists who argue that identity is constructed by political ideologies and unconscious repressions still have to recognise that each finite individual is uniquely positioned (historically, geographically, biologically, socially) in relation to those external or internal forces. And even if our identities are total fictions, as many theorists claim, then each one will be telling a subtly different story. There will always be individual differences – as well as species and social sameness – for that is what makes us human.

The ideology of the individual

To begin to understand the difficulties of finding a 'natural' voice, I want to think through some of the theories that have challenged such an easy notion, and begin to respond to them from a writer's perspective. Louis Althusser is one of many theorists who have claimed that we only believe ourselves to be individuals because we are steeped in ideologies that tell us so. And believing ourselves to be socially free and independently minded, we then live according to the rules and rituals of society: we work as we are supposed to; spend our money as we are supposed to; bring up children as we are supposed to and eventually die to be replaced by them. In other words all our ideas about individuality (and the writer's individual voice) are ideological fictions. We represent ourselves and our world in ways that are prescribed and normalising.

According to Althusser, it really doesn't matter that *you* are reading this book (you could easily be replaced by another reader), just as it doesn't matter that *I* am writing it (if not me, there would be another author to write another book for you to read); we are all cogs in a (capitalist) machine that would keep turning without us. It is only because we believe in a fantasy of ourselves as 'unique individuals' that we can continue to behave like automata. Althusser's model is provocative and in some ways persuasive, but we need to remember that even if we do only have a *subjectivity* because we are *subjected* to an ideological system, as he says, it does not mean that we should devalue the significance of our own identity, memory or experience, any more than we should devalue the significance of the people around us.

As writers, we might well want to explore the kind of questions that Althusser tackled from his Marxist perspective (he was really dealing with the unbridgeable gap between the psychic/social narratives of everyday life and its unknowable reality). We might, for example, want to explore the tension between conformity and resistance in the inner lives of our characters, or show the way they are *subjected* by schools, religion, the media or other 'Ideological State Apparatuses' as Althusser called them.[3] But if we lose the idea of individuality, however compromised or tenuous it might be, however mired in ideology, then we cannot be writers. For without a sense of human value and individuality, there is no fiction. And I am not only thinking of Henry James' *Portrait of a Lady* or Flaubert's *Madame Bovary* here. Even novels that present inhuman dystopias, like Orwell's *Nineteen Eighty-Four* or Brett Easton Ellis's *American Psycho*, only achieve their effects because they anticipate and evoke the reader's profound belief in the value of the individual (it is, after all, part of our ideology).

If Althusser is right, and we have come to know only an 'imaginary version of ourselves' then perhaps this is why we struggle to find our own voice. To explore this idea further though we need to trace it back to Freud.

Freud and Althusser

Freud was one of the first theorists to set out a view of the mind in which a large part of who we are is lost to us (in the unconscious). For Freud, the unconscious wasn't just like a wastepaper basket, storing all the thoughts, fears and desires that we couldn't handle – it was dynamic. It was a wastepaper basket with a mind of its own. And it continually threw back all the rubbish – all those terrible, unbearable fantasies – for everyone to see. Every slip of the tongue (or the pen), every gesture and dream revealed what we had hidden, or repressed, in our unconscious. So to overcome this deeply embarrassing aspect of our human nature, we deny that it exists. We invent 'imaginary versions of ourselves' that are stable and in control, and we all pretend not to notice the way our unconscious spews up repressed desires at every turn.

Althusser was very influenced by Freud (or rather Jacques Lacan, the man who transformed Freud's work by putting language at the centre of his theory rather than sex), and he took seriously the idea that we can never really know our 'self'. But Althusser gave this idea a specifically Marxist twist. He took the concept of 'ideology' and transformed it from something that meant propaganda, a set of lies that produced 'false consciousness', lies that we could easily see through if we knew the facts, into something that meant common sense. Ideology as common sense is not something we can easily shake off if we know the facts, because now the facts look ridiculous and wrong, counter-intuitive.

If we consider the revolutions in thinking over the past five hundred years (Copernicus, Darwin, Freud) you might see how this evolving 'ideology as common sense' might work. How could it be that the earth goes around the sun when we see the sun moving every day? How could it be that a human is just an ape when we have created vast civilisations? How could it be that we have an unconscious when we clearly all know who we are? Ideology may change, as these examples show, but it changes slowly through endless and arbitrary struggles over power. We can never get beyond ideology to see the 'real' world or our 'real' selves beyond the imaginary versions we have created, because our very sense of the real is created within ideology. But, as writers and people, we can begin to grasp that we do not know the whole truth.

Of course, these ideas did not originate in the twentieth century. Many ancient religions reflect upon similar concepts: mistrusting everyday experience, doubting common-sense assumptions about the world, believing that ordinary life limits the potential of the mind. Think of Buddhism for example, and the rituals of meditation and yoga. One of the purposes of these spiritual practices is to silence the inane chatter of the everyday in order to contemplate a higher reality, a reality that's lost in the habitual babble of ordinary life.

So when critics say, as Trevor Pateman does, that it is 'the task of the writer ... to find a voice, in which his or her subjectivity is engaged ... a human subjectivity liberated from both personal repression and ideological distortion' they are asking for a great deal, as Pateman himself recognises.[4] To acknowledge this difficulty does not mean that, as writers, we should unquestioningly accept the 'imaginary versions of ourselves' produced by the dual pressures of personal repression and ideological distortion, any more than it means that we must all go into psychoanalysis. As human beings living in this world we can never be entirely free from delusion, and if we try to 'find our voice' by first liberating ourselves from all psychic and social repression we might just be incarcerated as mentally incompetent (as Althusser himself was after murdering his wife) before we ever get to write our great fiction masterpiece. It is only by acknowledging the power of the 'imaginary self' that we can begin to subvert it.

Finding the story's voice

So how does a writer 'find' their voice? I think that a critical-creative approach must begin by acknowledging that deliberately *trying* to find your own voice as a writer is a recipe for excruciating self-consciousness. And the more self-conscious we become, the more we exacerbate the effects of psychic and social repression. To really find our own voice we need to develop strategies to overcome the painfully constructed awareness of ourselves *being writers*. The way to do this is to re-envisage the idea of voice: the writer does not need to find their own voice, instead we need to find the story's voice. And a story's voice is not uni-vocal; it is multi-stranded, weaving the writer's voice, the characters' voices and the reader's voice together.

To find the story's voice, the writer must do three things: relinquish the *search* for their own voice; work with and for the reader, and welcome into their minds and words the competing voices of their characters.

This chapter explores some of the ways a writer might begin to do this. Firstly it suggests that the initial step to finding our own voice is, rather ironically, to find ways of silencing ourselves: to stop that internal, infernal self-commentary and remove ourselves from the idle chatter of the everyday – the commonsensical ideologies and the straining, restraining ego – to find a more expansive stillness. Secondly, it focuses on language itself to think about the way we might re-imagine the writer's voice as not one 'voice' but as the sum of all the different voices and languages that are in our fiction. And thirdly, it re-considers the writer's relationship with the reader, seeing the reader not as a passive consumer waiting to be impressed, but as a 'co-conspirator' eager for the experience of the fictional world and ready to work together with the writer to produce it.

Silencing the imaginary self

Dorothea Brande recommended that writers close their eyes and attempt to hold their mind as still as possible, without being distracted by their own thoughts. It is worth attempting, putting this book down and simply allowing your mind to be still and silent for a minute. Do it now. Close your eyes and keep your mind quiet for one whole minute. It's not so simple, is it? In fact it's extremely difficult. Even a few seconds of complete quietness can be overwhelming, perhaps even a little frightening. You probably noticed that as your mind quietened, the (panicky) thoughts rushed in, like air into a vacuum, providing a running commentary on your attempt at silence; throwing up things you must remember to do; things you must tell friends when you next meet. It's an interesting experiment, and one that shows how continually we re-affirm the 'imaginary versions of ourselves' through the oppressive everyday chatter of 'normal life'.

Brande saw this exercise as a way to find our own genius, a word we don't often use now, perhaps a word that has been replaced by the more democratic sounding 'voice'. For Brande, though, genius was something we all had, and it didn't matter how great our genius was, for, as she said: 'its resources at the feeblest are fuller then you can ever exhaust.'[5] She was most interested in showing that when we relinquish conscious control, our unconscious would still work for us, our imagination still produce results. To demonstrate this she reprinted a psychology experiment that goes something like this:

> Take a piece of paper and draw and circle on it (drawing round a mug will be about the right size), then draw a cross through the circle, like so:

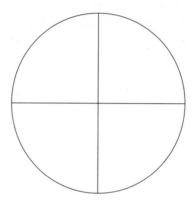

> Find a piece of string about ten centimetres long and tie something heavy to the end (a ring, a piece of blutak, etc.). Now hold the string over the shape with your finger and thumb, and keep it absolutely still. Think about the vertical line, follow it with your eyes and imagine going up and down that line. What you begin to notice is that, without you moving your fingers, the string starts to follow the line of your thought, moving back and forward like a pendulum. Try the same thing with the line going across the circle, and then try the circle itself, imagining going both clockwise and anti-clockwise and watch what happens to the string.

The experiment can be a little weird the first time – but it reminds us that there is more going on in our minds and our bodies than we can consciously control by force of will. Our imagination constantly produces ideas that we are too busy to notice. Perhaps the reason that people puzzling over a problem think that inspiration strikes them out of the blue, like the proverbial thunderbolt, is that their minds are so rarely quiet they don't 'hear' the answer that is already there.

The idea that the unconscious is 'creative', while the conscious mind is 'critical', is a convenient but clumsy fiction that disguises the fact that the imagination is both critically creative and creatively crit-ical. We, as writers, are all aware that we cannot *tell* our imagination to work, but that is not because our 'creative side' resists critical inter-vention. It is because when *telling* we are not *listening*. As Malcolm Bradbury argued: 'the writer's problem is to turn the creative and critical skills of the imagination onto those elements the imagination has, within itself, already begun to create.'[6] By practising quietness, we learn to *listen* to the silent language of our own imagination.

In this way, a writer can silence all the empty phrases of habit, all the ready-made opinions of the world, all the familiar clutter of living. And by doing this we can potentially reconnect with aspects of ourselves that are otherwise buried beneath the bland expectations of common sense and the anguished lies of the ego. By listening, we allow our 'voice' to emerge. This doesn't mean that we 'hear' it as such, but that, hopefully, when we read our own work, we can detect a new sense of integrity and resonance.

The raw material of fiction

There are other benefits from these moments of quietness. For by disconnecting from the world's idle chatter, even momentarily, we are able to see it anew. It allows us some critical distance upon the voices and languages that, after all, are the raw materials for our fiction. For if we are word-smiths, the words we craft are as likely to come from the shopping mall as from Shakespeare. Language is our medium and our minds are filled with the many voices and languages, ways of thinking and speaking, that we have absorbed from life. Italo Calvino casts the question of the 'self' and our relation to the hubbub of ordinary life in rather different ways from Althusser. He sees the self as a kind of literary patchwork that is able to be constantly re-imagined: 'Who are we, who is each one of us, if not a combinatoria of experiences, information, books we have read, things imagined? Each life is an encyclopedia, a library, an inventory of objects, a series of styles, and everything can be constantly shuffled and reordered in every way conceivable.'[7]

Calvino allows us to shift perspective. The voices around us are no longer seen as a threat to our own voice (as either ideologically distorted or stylistically contagious). They do not confine us as writers, any more than the 26 letters of the alphabet confine us. Instead our particular configuration of experience and words, knowledge and imagination gives a particular resonance to our voice. And this is the case even though the words we use have all been used before.

As writers, we deal in second-hand goods, second-hand words – for as the Russian theorist Mikhail Bakhtin said, the writer is 'not, after all, the first speaker, the one who disturbs the eternal silence of the universe'.[8]

As writers it is not for us to pretend that each word comes into our fiction new-minted. It is for us to understand that all the well-worn words we use trail their history behind them. All language has already been spoken and all language already belongs to other people. To take some very obvious examples: no writer could use the word 'humbug' without trailing the ghost of Charles Dickens and Ebenezer Scrooge, just as no writer can use the phrase 'I have a dream' without evoking Martin Luther King. When trying to find our voice, it is important, and ultimately liberating, to recognise that the very words we use are not really our own.

Writing as ventriloquism

Bakhtin argues that 'the word in language is half someone else's . . . every word is directed towards an *answer* and cannot escape the profound influence of the answering word that it anticipates.'[9] On an immediate level this recognition that language is caught between the speaker and listener, or reader and writer, has two implications for the way we think about our writing. Firstly, the struggle for meaning, in which the speaker and listener wrestle over the meaning of words, can add vibrancy to dialogue, and this is an idea that I'll develop in Chapter 10. Secondly, if the language in our novels and short stories is 'half someone else's . . . directed towards an answer' then perhaps we also need to think about what kind of answer we anticipate and how this recognition changes the concept of a writer's voice.

To think this second point through we need to consider some of Bakhtin's ideas about writing. Bakhtin was one of the first theorists to argue that prose fiction was more interesting and important than poetry. And he believed that what made the novel a distinct and valuable genre (we could include the short story here too) was that it contained not just one voice but many, and many different languages too. He was not talking about languages like French or Spanish here, but the different languages we use in different circumstances in our lives. So, for instance, for Bakhtin our social group (class, gender, ethnicity, age, family) would influence our language, as would our geographical location (dialect) and our job (lawyer, doctor, politician, factory worker). What was wonderful about prose fiction for Bakhtin was that it could incorporate all these different languages in a way that no other genre had before.

He used the term 'heteroglossia' to describe this and argued that in fictional texts the author uses and reworks these different languages for artistic affect. The important thing for Bakhtin was that language was not just a 'system of abstract grammatical categories' but 'a world view'. He said that all languages were 'specific points of view on the world, forms for conceptualising the world in words ... As such they encounter one another and co-exist in the consciousness of real people – first and foremost, in the creative consciousness of people who write novels' (p. 292).

When we bring these languages, this heteroglossia, into our work we are not only manipulating voices, speeches and dialects, we are also manipulating ideas about the world and the way we should live. In other words we are crafting ideologies. Our writing is populated by different and competing voices, gleaned perhaps from literary traditions or city streets, and these voices have different values and status. Our own 'voice' (shaped as it is by the language of our social group, geography or profession) is only one voice among these others, perhaps not one that even speaks directly to the reader. For Bakhtin, the writer's voice is like a ventriloquist's voice. It can only be heard through the voices of others, and the more perfectly those other voices are realised, the more effective is the writer's voice. Again, we are in a paradoxical position: to find our voice, we must lose it – not in silence this time, but in the voices of others.

As writers we take our words not from a dictionary, but from other people's mouths, and they still have the 'taste' of these other people on them. The author's voice in fiction is, for Bakhtin, a 'double-voiced discourse', not a singular voice, but a voice that mimics and echoes other voices. For him, all words 'taste' of the ways they are used and the people who use them, whether that be: 'a profession, a genre, a tendency, a party, a particular work, a particular person, a generation, an age group, the day and hour'. And all words are 'populated by intentions' (p. 239). When we place these stolen words into the mouths of our characters their 'taste' lingers, but we now force these clashing flavours together to create new meanings.

For Bakhtin, a writer's style (or voice) is found in the way they orchestrate this conflict between words. He says: 'The prose writer does not purge words of intentions and tones that are alien to him, he does not destroy the seeds of social heteroglossia embedded in words, he does not eliminate those language characterizations and speech mannerisms (potential narrator-personalities) glimmering behind the words and forms, each at a different distance from the ultimate semantic nucleus of his work, that is, the centre of his own personal intentions' (p. 298). The key for Bakhtin is that the writer should use the diversity of language to express the singularity of their creative intention: in other words, to find their voice, the writer must know, at whatever level of conscious or unconscious imagining, their own intentions as an artist.

Dialogues within fiction

When we create fiction, our intention as a writer is 'refracted' through these alien words which appear to be saying something else, and this is what Bakhtin meant by 'double-voiced discourse', a concept that is worth exploring in a little more depth. Double-voiced discourse is most easy to see when our characters speak. Bakhtin says that their words 'serve two speakers at the same time and express simultaneously two different intentions: the direct intention of the character who is speaking, and the refracted intention of the author' (p. 324). He sees this as central to a fiction writer's art, because here the reader can experience the resonance of language as a living thing.

We can think of this double-voiced discourse occurring in every word we write, because every word is caught between the conventions of the literary, the languages of the world, and our own 'voice'. Bakhtin argues that 'the style of a novel is to be found in the combination of its styles; the language of a novel is the system of its "languages"' (p. 262). And using his theories, we can also say, the voice of the novel is to be found in the managed medley of its 'voices'.

Bakhtin uses the term 'dialogism' to suggest how different languages are always interacting, and it's worth highlighting the three most significant ways that we can manipulate these interactions within our own writing.[10] The first is the 'dialogue' with other novels or stories. We might paraphrase or misquote phrases, echo ideas, characters, or styles in ways that make a connection to other texts. Literary critics argue that this happens anyway, whether the author is aware of it or not, and it's true that we cannot always recognise when we have absorbed the languages of others. Our language is, as Calvino showed, a patchwork. But if we become more attuned to this interaction with other texts (through reading), we can potentially use these dialogic relations more deliberately to give our own writing more scope and power.

The second dialogue takes place between the characters' different languages, with their different points of view and values, different quirks and idiosyncrasies. For Bakhtin these voices represent the soul of fiction writing. A writer's voice, as he saw it, was not to be found in the authoritative statements of the narrator (and such nineteenth-century style narrators are, anyway, a rarity in twenty-first-century fiction), but in the representation of self-conscious, autonomous characters who are able to argue back.

The third form of dialogism is the dialogue between the writer and the reader. And this is the kind of dialogue I want to consider in more detail in the final part of this chapter.

The voice of the reader

[N]o author, who understands the just boundaries of decorum and good-breeding, would presume to think all: The truest respect which you can pay to the reader's understanding, is to halve the matter amicably, and leave him something to imagine, in his turn, as well as yourself. For my own part, I am eternally paying him compliments of this kind, and do all that lies in my power to keep his imagination as busy as my own.

Laurence Sterne, *The Life and Opinions of Tristram Shandy*
(Penguin)

Laurence Sterne's characteristically tongue-in-cheek treatise on the reader's role makes a point that no writer should forget: the reader does half the work. And without the work of the reader there is no fiction. So when people talk about 'the writer's voice', as if the writer is totally in control, simply telling their tale to a silent and impassive reader, they have mistaken the very essence of fiction. It is not a one-way conversation. The writer's voice does not exist in glorious isolation: it only exists in the reader's mind. It is 'refracted', to use Bakhtin's term, like a ray of light through glass, and 'heard' through the reader's own repertoire of voices. In other words, the reader is also a ventriloquist and the writer can only 'speak' through them.

If we think about fiction as a dialogue between writer and reader, then it can change the way we think about our writing. For now the reader becomes, as the narratologists say, our 'creative accomplice', our 'co-conspirator', working with us to create the story.[11] As writers we must allow space for our readers, leave them 'room for the imagination' as the saying goes. Practically, this means that we must resist the temptation to over- or under-explain, for the reader's involvement will be lessened if: 'the text makes things too clear or, on the other hand, too obscure: boredom and overstrain represent the two poles of tolerance, and in either case the reader is likely to opt out of the game.'[12] We must trust that the reader will fill the silences, without allowing them to fall through the gaps in our story.

If we think back to E. M. Forster's example of a story: he argued that 'The king died and then the queen died' is a merely a story, but 'The king died and then the queen died of grief' is a plot, because in the latter version there is a relationship of cause and effect. But how many of us, when we read, 'The king died and then the queen died', don't assume that the queen's death is in some way related to the king's? Almost without thinking, we begin filling the gaps and looking for the connections – was it the same illness, food-poisoning, accident? We are prepared to do our share of the imaginative work in creating the story. This is what Jean-Paul Sartre called the 'pact' between writer and reader, a pact which acknowledged that writing and reading are 'two interdependent acts requir[ing] two differently active people. The combined efforts of author and reader bring into being the concrete and imaginary object which is the work of the mind. Art exists only for and through other people.'[13]

We can take this idea even further. Paul Ricoeur argues that 'Finally it is the *act of reading* which completes the work, transforming it into a *guide* for reading.'[14] This approach to fiction demands that we radically revise our perception of our own work. Instead of thinking of our completed manuscript as a finished product ready for the reader to consume, we must think of it as a 'guide' for the reader, a set of detailed instructions for the DIY creation of an entirely new and imaginary world: a world that can only exist in the reader's mind. Our job as a writer, then, is not to present the reader with a ready-made imaginary world; it is to persuade the reader to create a world within their own imagination, using the materials we provide. This in no way allows the writer to shirk their craft. But it changes the dynamic: instead of worrying about the originality of our own voice, we must focus on the ways we encourage the reader to imagine.

Nearly 2,000 years ago, Longinus argued that it was better for a storyteller to address not the whole audience but a single member of it: 'you will affect him more profoundly, and make him more attentive and full of active interest, if you rouse him by these appeals to him personally.'[15] Interpreting this from a twenty-first-century perspective doesn't mean that we must actively speak to our reader like a Greek poet or nineteenth-century novelist ('Reader, I married him') – in most contemporary fiction the writer remains an invisible presence behind the characters. It means that we must recognise the way our words address our readers individually, and the way that, as Bakhtin said, they anticipate an answer, even if we cannot be entirely sure what that 'answer' will be.

Michael Toolan points out that 'Real readers can apprehend stories in quite unpredicted ways, seeing a different point to them, and picturing quite dissimilar authors of them.'[16] If we accept that our fiction is a dialogue between us as a writer and our individual readers, then we have to accept that we don't have ultimate control over the meaning of our words (although we can craft them to avoid unnecessary ambiguity). For Longinus the reader responds to (or answers) our words not only because those words carry meaning, but because they carry force: they electrify our conspiring reader. And so the emphasis on craft is newly stated: not in terms of *finding our own voice*, but in terms of *finding the voice of our reader*.

Fictionalising the reader

But who is this reader? And how can we imagine them? Walter Ong suggests that the reader is a 'fiction' in the writer's mind, an imaginary person, a character we invent.[17] Many writers write for a particular person they know (although even here, as Ong points out, they must fictionalise the mood of the person reading); others think in publishers' categories (women in their thirties; children aged 9–11); others write for themselves or an imaginary reader so attuned with their thinking that they will understand every nuance and smile at every joke. It's perhaps one of the ironies of writing that we write in solitude in order to communicate with a host of strangers.

One way of thinking about the relationship between the writer and the reader is to turn to the models produced by critics such as Seymour Chatman. Chatman charts several stages between the actual writer (in this book, me) and the actual reader (you). His diagram looks like this:

Narrative text

Real author - -> Implied author → (Narrator) → (Narratee) → Implied reader - -> Real reader

To begin in the middle – the narrator and narratee are characters in the text (even if we don't see them).[18] Laurence Sterne's character-narrator, Tristram Shandy, often addresses a narratee, even going so far as to have the narratee answer back: 'How could you, Madam, be so inattentive in reading the last chapter? I told you in it, *That my mother was not a papist.* – Papist! You told me no such a thing, Sir. Madam, I beg leave to repeat it over again, That I told you as plain, at least, as words, by direct inference, could tell you such a thing.'[19] We know, as readers of *Tristram Shandy*, that *we* are not being addressed as 'Madam'. 'Madam' is another reader, one who is inside the story itself. We are the reader who is supposed to enjoy this conversation, looking over her shoulder from a safe distance. We, as 'real readers', step into the role of 'implied reader', and sit more or less comfortably in the position the fiction has allocated for us.

The 'implied reader' was a term first coined by Wayne Booth in the early 1960s as a way of describing (or imagining) the kind of reader the author had in mind when they were writing, and it remains a useful term for writers.[20] There may be a real difference between the readers we hope or assume will read our fiction and our actual readers (some of whom may have not yet been born). But, if we have a clear notion of our 'implied reader' this will give a focus to our stories. If those fictions are published, we will never know even a fraction of our real readership, but if we know our implied reader (creating them like a character) then we will have provided a 'role' for the real readers to assume.

On the other side of Chatman's diagram sit the 'real author' and the 'implied author'. The 'real author' is the physical person who *writes* the fiction, and the 'implied author' *is* a fiction: an imaginary being the writer creates in dialogue with the reader. The 'implied author' is the reader's impression of the writer: their answer to the question, 'what kind of person would write this book?'. As you read, you are forming an impression of me as a writer, one that I contribute to, but cannot ultimately control. Just as when you read a slasher novel, a fluffy romance, or experimental Metafiction, you will make judgements about the 'implied author'.

Sometimes these judgements would please the 'real author', some-times appal them, and sometimes the 'real author' might fabricate an 'implied author' to deliberately mislead. The science fiction writer James Tiptree Jr, for example, whose 'lean, muscular, supple' stories were hailed for years in SF circles as the most masculine writing since Hemingway, turned out to be 'a medium-sized old lady in jogging shoes' called Alice Sheldon.[21] But Sheldon still insisted that beneath the pseudonym, and with the exception of 'deliberate male details here and there', she was writing in her own voice, 'writing like myself'.[22]

The 'implied author' is, in other words, the writer's voice. And the writer's voice, like everything else in fiction, can only be 'heard' and brought to life by the reader. But just as the reader is inventing the author, so the author is inventing the reader, and for Walter Ong this 'fictionalising of readers' is what makes writing so difficult. He says: 'It is not easy to get inside the minds of absent persons, most of whom you will never know. But it is not impossible if you and they are familiar with the literary tradition they work in.'[23] And so he brings us back to reading. For Ong, the literary tradition is not a threat to the writer's voice, an influence that contaminates our inherent originality, but a way of understanding 'the tradition they [our readers] work in'. For only when we really understand what it takes to be a reader can we understand what it means to write.

5   Style

About style, the less said the better. Nothing leads to fraudulence more quickly than the conscious pursuit of stylistic uniqueness.
                                        John Gardner, *The Art of Fiction* (Vintage)

With characteristic directness, John Gardner argues that when it comes to style, 'the less said the better'. But I want to dedicate a whole chapter to style, because I think that if we understand what style is about, we will stop trying to contrive 'stylistic uniqueness'. We will begin to recognise that style is not about surface decoration, and does not bloom during the final polish of the narrative. It grows up from the roots.

Style is fundamental to fiction writing because it is found in the balance between observation and imagination; the balance between the world we see and the world we write. Traditionally, this has been called *mimesis*, or imitation, but as we have seen, fiction does far more than imitate the world, it also discovers and invents it. For in its 'imitation' of the world, fiction must use language, and language can never be an invisible window onto reality – words will always construct, distort and transform. In this chapter I want to think about how we can begin to find our own style as writers by considering this relationship between the language we use (our technique) and our vision of the world.

Émile Zola said that 'at the bottom of all literary quarrels there is always a philosophical question'.[1] And if we think about the changes in fictional style that have occurred over the last few centuries, the philosophical question at the root of fiction would seem to be this: 'What is the nature of reality?'. Such philosophy may seem beyond the reach of our own writing, but every time we represent the world in fiction, we cannot help but put forward another version of reality. Every novel or story we read expresses its own view of the world: sometimes so explicitly it feels like propaganda, sometimes so implicitly it masquerades as common sense. Historically, these different perceptions of reality have driven revolutions in literary style (as well as revolutions of a more politically violent kind). And if we think about the labels we use to identify historical changes in style – Realism, Modernism, Postmodernism – we realise that they do not simply describe changes in the use of adverbs (as important as adverbs are), they describe changes in the cultural conception of reality.

A short history of the novel

Fiction itself only emerged as a distinct genre when in the late seventeenth century people began to see themselves and their world differently. It developed out of particular political, philosophical and religious changes. Before the birth of the novel, seventeenth-century poetry and drama concerned itself with the comic or tragic exploits of the aristocracy and nobility, with a healthy splash of low-life thrown in for laughs. But in the eighteenth century there was a new merchant class, a middle class, who wanted a form of literature that would reflect and shape their own emerging identities. And so the novel was born. It was a new form of literature (the word 'novel' still retains that sense of newness), one that focused on the stories of middle-class individuals whose values and beliefs would be tested and perhaps even changed by dramatic social experience.[2]

But as a genre, the novel had yet to negotiate its relation to reality. Were these early novels individual histories or were they simply lies? Writers like Daniel Defoe and Samuel Richardson passed off their stories as 'histories', pseudo-memoirs, and used first-person narratives (as in *Moll Flanders*, supposedly 'Written from her own Memorandums' and *Robinson Crusoe*, 'Written by himself'), or used letters (as in *Clarissa*, which was subtitled 'The History of a Young Lady'). The novel was part confession, part rogue's gallery, part letter, part moral tract. It had yet to find its form.

In the mid-eighteenth century, Henry Fielding began to divide his narratives into Chapters and Books, a formal structuring which revealed the distance between life and art, and showed the way fiction shaped and distorted the reality it represented. At the same time, Fielding insisted (with comic glee) that his novel was an accurate portrayal of reality: 'there is one Reason, why a Comic Writer should of all others be the least excused for deviating from Nature . . . Life every where furnishes an accurate Observer with the Ridiculous.'[3]

The eighteenth century was a time of experimentation and consolidation, when the foundations of new fictional genres were laid down. But just forty years after the publication of *Robinson Crusoe* (often seen as the first novel), a book was written that exploded all the newly formed conventions before they could even become conventional. Laurence Sterne's literary experiments in *The Life and Opinions of Tristram Shandy* would be hailed as decidedly postmodern were it not for the fact that they are more than two hundred years too early. His novel has a black page (when a character dies); squiggly line diagrams to show narrative digressions; a blank page for the reader to write their own description of a character; lost chapters that turn up at the end, and a hero who isn't even born until nearly half way through the book. And all these jokes at the expense of convention show up one thing: the difference between literature and life, between reality and representation.

Style as balance

When we think about our own style, the reason we might try to contrive 'stylistic uniqueness' is that we are responding to the pressure to be original, without really understanding what such a concept can mean in the twenty-first century. Many people in the eighteenth century predicted that Sterne's novel was a faddish success that would disappear from history. They were wrong. Its humour and humanity have given it staying power. But, nevertheless, it's true to say that many texts that strive for novelty do not survive. As John Gardner puts it, they are 'intellectual toys' that engage us only for a moment.[4] I tend to agree with Trevor Pateman when he says that 'real imaginative achievements – the things which are brilliant, just right and deserve our applause are closer to what we might call the banal than to what we might call the fantastic.'[5] His opposition between the 'banal' and the 'fantastic' does not refer to realist or fantasy fiction. It refers to an opposition in style: between stylistic balance and stylistic cartwheels.

The way I have been describing style, as a balance between the world we see and the world we write, could be visualised as a seesaw, where style is the pivot under the plank. And if you see it in this way, you can see an important thing happening. If you put more emphasis on one side, you change the position, and thus the nature, of the other side. Stressing certain techniques, as in Metafiction, does not just alter the *representation of reality* in your fiction, it alters the *understanding of reality* in your fiction; insisting on the exact reproduction of reality, as in Naturalist fiction, does not just curtail the *possibilities of literary representation*, it changes the *nature of literary representation*. Pateman's idea of brilliance is rooted in this sense of balance: it calls for imaginative techniques that respond to specific visions of the world, and specific visions of the world that produce their own imaginative techniques. He calls this 'banal' because this stylistic balance does not call attention to itself. It calls attention to the fiction.

Realism, Modernism, Postmodernism

If we return to Zola and the 'philosophical question' at the root of literature, we can see how stylistic changes in the fiction of the last two centuries represent a shift in this balance between the interpretation of reality and technique. Consider the three major movements within fiction of the last 200 years and the questions they asked about reality:

Realism: How can we represent objective reality (what is 'out there' in the world) without literary distortion?
Modernism: How can we represent reality when all reality is subjective, created by an individual perspective?
Postmodernism: How can we represent objective or subjective reality when neither exists?

The styles that we associate with Realism, Modernism and Postmodernism may be talked about in terms of the presence or absence of metaphorical flourishes and chronological narratives, but ultimately they represent different ways of imagining the world. Three quotations from three very different writers might illustrate the point, as we move from Zola's insistence that the writer 'believe only in facts' in *Le Roman Expérimental* (1880) to D. H. Lawrence's rejection of 'the superficial unreal world of fact' in *Women in Love* (1921) to John Barth's claim in *Chimera* (1972) that 'the truth of fiction is that Fact is fantasy'.

As we move away from the Realist conception of the world, that there is a reality 'out there' that we can describe, towards the Modernist and Postmodernist view that there is no 'reality' beyond what we perceive and describe, we need to refine our description of style. Originally, I suggested that style was like a see-saw balancing our observations of a concrete, distinct reality against our literary representation of that reality. But what we learned from writers in the twentieth century is that the very act of observation is itself an imaginative act, an act of perception that blurs the subjective and the objective. Style, then, can be understood as a balance between the *possibilities of perception* and the *possibilities of expression*. And to understand more about these possibilities we need to think about our personal and cultural contexts, our awareness of literary traditions, and our anticipated relation to our reader.

Reading and the reader

If we think for a moment about the reader: the reader is the stranger who must re-construct our fiction's world-view. And all the reader has to go on, as they begin to read the first pages, are their own perceptions of the world (which might be very different from ours – after all this reader might live in 2307) and their expectations of what a short story or novel should do (their knowledge of the literary tradition). In other words what connects you to your reader are other books. The reader's expectations of your story will be shaped by their personal experience of reading and by their particular culture's assumptions about literature. If we work in a literary vacuum, striving after 'stylistic uniqueness', we risk becoming either incomprehensible or unoriginal (unaware that it's all been done before). But if we know the traditions of fiction, and write with that awareness, then our style becomes our own. A writer's ability to express their originality comes from an understanding of the conventions and innovations within their chosen form.

T. S. Eliot advocated just such an approach to style, and argued that a writer must have an 'historical sense', which is only gained by reading the work of other writers. He said that writers needed to be aware of both contemporary works and the writing of the past. He argued that the writer 'is not likely to know what is to be done unless he lives in what is not merely the present, but the present moment of the past, unless he is conscious, not of what is dead, but of what is already living.'[6]

For us as story writers (Eliot was speaking about poetry) the 'already living' are those works of fiction that have contributed to the evolution of our genre and are 'living' not only because they are read themselves, but because their influence still affects new writing. This does not mean that you cannot write until you have read your way through several thousand novels and short stories. It means that you must be open to writing from the past and the present: that you must become aware of the way in which your own style both conforms to and reacts against what has gone before. And by saying 'conform' I don't mean that it will be the same. It cannot be the same, for we live in different times. Our 'reality' has changed. Contemporary writing is neither better nor worse than work from the nineteenth or twentieth century, it's simply different. In 'Tradition and the Individual Talent', Eliot argues that it is an 'obvious fact that art never improves, but that the material of art is never quite the same'.[7]

The philosopher Paul Ricoeur makes a similar point when he says that 'the work of the imagination does not come out of nowhere. It is tied one way or another to the models handed down by tradition.' He goes on: 'Whatever could be said about this or that work, the possibility of deviance is included in the relation between sedimentation and innovation which constitutes tradition.'[8] Sedimentation and innovation characterise the literary tradition, however narrowly or widely we define that body of work (every writer constructs their own tradition, those works which they value above all others). And sedimentation and innovation also characterise our own style, made up as it is of a slow accumulation of experience (of life and writing) that gradually shapes our perceptions, and reveals new possibilities for change.

The legacy of realism

We no longer see fiction as Zola did (as a transparent screen that displays the world 'out there' exactly as it is), but that does not mean that it's not useful for us as writers to think about his ideas, if only as a way of honing our own perceptions. Writing in the 1880s, Zola wanted a new fiction that rejected the imagination as a distortion (a clouding of the screen). He said: 'The highest praise one could formerly make of a novelist was to say: "he has imagination". Now that praise would almost be regarded as a criticism. This is because the conditions of the novel have changed. Imagination is no longer the novelist's most important faculty.'[9]

We might reject Zola's extreme Realism (known as Naturalism) and his 'abasement of the imagination', but contemporary writing has nevertheless taken some of its key principles from the French Realist tradition. If you open any 'how to' book you are guaranteed to find a section on the importance of details, on 'finding the significant detail', on 'using all five senses', on being 'concrete not abstract'. This is a legacy of Realism, of its insistence on portraying the world as it is, including all the ephemera. In 1861, the artist Gustave Courbet made a claim for painting that equally describes the Realist movement in fiction. He said: 'painting is an essentially *concrete* art and can only consist in the representation of real and existing things.'[10] In their focus on the everyday and the commonplace, on ordinary people doing ordinary things, writers like Balzac and Zola, and many others from their time, have firmly put their stamp on contemporary writing.

Their influence has not only been felt in terms of the subject matter of fiction, but also in terms of the language, or rather languages, it is written in. For Realism didn't only portray ordinary people doing ordinary things, it portrayed them in ordinary language. There was a turn against the poetic, which was seen as elitist, and a new exploration of vernacular dialects. Courbet went so far as to argue that it was 'dishonest to write poetry, pretentious to express yourself differently from other people'.[11]

The confrontational tone of these pronouncements is worth noting, for it reveals two important things about Realism. Firstly it shows that although we now take Realism for granted as the most conventional way of writing, writers (and painters) in the nineteenth century saw Realism as a discovery, a way of writing that rebelled against the norm of their times (which was the idealism of the Romantics). The novelist Champfleury, for example, ridiculed his contemporaries whom he saw as ignoring the issues of their own times, 'in order to dig up corpses from the past and dress them up in historical frippery'.[12] Secondly, by revealing the way Realism was born in polemic, it reminds us that however convenient such a label is, we cannot use it to categorise the work of an entire era. Many French writers rejected the label, even Gustave Flaubert, who was praised as one of the great writers of the movement. He spoke instead, with characteristic acidity, of his desire to detach himself from the reality of the Realists: 'I have always tried to live in an ivory tower, but a tide of shit is beating at its walls to undermine it.'[13]

Realism, then, was contested in France throughout the mid- and late-nineteenth century, even as it was being exported to America and England by writers such as William Dean Howells and George Eliot. Other nineteenth-century writers had a more difficult relation to the Realist style, both in the way they saw the world and the way they expressed it (think of Charles Dickens or Mark Twain) and some proclaimed their resistance to it. Feodor Dostoevsky, for example, asserted that he had 'quite different conceptions of reality and realism than our realists and critics. My idealism is more real than their realism.'[14]

Modernism looks within

Dostoevsky's disdain exposes the chinks in the Realist philosophy and shows that the idealism of the Romantics was not to be stamped out so easily. Realism claimed to emphasize the truth of life and writers such as Theodore Dreiser urged fiction writers to 'tell the truth' in this way. But what was the truth? By the beginning of the twentieth century the nature of the 'truth' was no longer self-evident. Freud had published his work on dreams, sexuality and the unconscious; Einstein and Heisenberg had published their work on relativity and uncertainty; Nietzsche had claimed that God was dead, and Darwin's theories of natural selection had been widely accepted. The world was changing.

New inventions such as the aeroplane, the telegraph, the telephone, the radio, the motor car, moving pictures and the box camera were all changing everyday life. Changing technologies allowed people to communicate more easily, travel faster, reproduce new images of themselves. The world seemed to be trembling on the brink of a new era, both terrifying and liberating, in which the old Victorian certainties would be swept away. Technology was revealing new possibilities for humanity, new visions for the future, even as the Great War showed just how vulnerable humanity was to the power of the machines. Old models of Realism seemed outdated, unable to represent the reality of this fast-changing, uncertain world. New movements sprang up all over Europe and America: Cubism, Futurism, Surrealism, Imagism, Expressionism. They were searching for a new 'truth', one that was found in 'the core of the eddy', to use Samuel Beckett's words, rather than in 'worshipping the offal of experience'.[15]

Fiction shifted its gaze, to 'look within'. Instead of focusing on the external detail of ordinary life, Modernist writers focused on the internal, the psychological. They weren't giving up on the real, so much as re-defining it: dreams, memories, fantasies were now all seen as part of 'reality', just as they were for the Romantics. Another painter, Paul Klee, sums up the change. He said that the purpose of art was not to 'reflect the visible, but to make visible' that which wasn't ordinarily seen.[16] And this act of 'making visible' rather than reflecting the visible, changed literary style. The act of perception became more important than the 'thing' perceived. The emphasis fell on imaginative vision, on language and on technique (think of James Joyce's *Ulysses*).

In 'Modern Fiction', Virginia Woolf wrote a manifesto for Modernist writing, disparaging the Realist writer whom she saw as: 'constrained . . . by some powerful and unscrupulous tyrant who has him in thrall to provide a plot, to provide comedy, tragedy, love interest, and an air of probability embalming the whole'.[17] Her objection to Realist fiction was that it made life conform to a predetermined model, rather than making fiction conform to life. She wanted a new kind of fiction that represented the extraordinary life of the individual mind as well as the more ordinary life of the social body. She asked:

> Is life like this? Must novels be like this? Look within and life, it seems, is very far from being 'like this'. Examine for a moment an ordinary mind on an ordinary day. The mind receives a myriad of impressions – trivial, fantastic, evanescent, or engraved with the sharpness of steel. From all sides they come, an incessant shower of innumerable atoms; and as they fall, as they shape themselves into the life of Monday or Tuesday, the accent falls differently from of old. . . . Life is not a series of gig lamps to be symmetrically arranged; but a luminous halo, a semi-transparent envelope surrounding us from the beginning of consciousness to the end. Is it not the task of the novelist to convey this varying, this unknown and uncircumscribed spirit, whatever aberration or complexity it might display, with as little mixture of the external or alien as possible?[18]

Woolf was arguing against 'plot' as it would be expressed in diagrams and charts, against 'story' that in its neatness was false to the reality of human experience, and against 'subject' where that meant the externally verifiable world of social and historical actions. The novels and short stories of the 1920s tended to, as she said, 'look within', focusing on the characters' perception of themselves and their world. Often the structuring principle was not the 'plot' as it was in, say, the Sherlock Holmes stories by Conan Doyle, or the 'idea' as it was in some of the new science fiction stories, it was the 'epiphany'. James Joyce coined this new phrase for literary criticism, stripping it of its religious meaning, and used it to signify a moment of profound real-isation within fiction. The epiphany was the moment when everything became clear, when the character suddenly understood his or her self in the world. Other writers, like Katherine Mansfield, toyed with this idea of the epiphany as fictional resolution, and created comprom-ised epiphanies (as in the story 'Bliss') where the endings are more ambivalent.

The Modernists still focused on the details of ordinary life, but now these details did not just exist as evidence of 'the real', they were infused with more symbolic, sometimes ambiguous, significance. We can return to Mansfield's story 'The Fly' (discussed in Chapter 2) as an example. When the boss remembers the death of his son in the First World War, he feels he must cry but the tears won't come. Then he notices that a fly has fallen into his inkpot. Slowly he drips ink onto the creature, admiring its struggle to survive, until the drops of ink eventually kill it. He flicks the body into the wastepaper basket and realises that he has forgotten what was on his mind. As readers we realise that the fly is highly symbolic, but its symbolism is not entirely clear. Does it represent his son and the other young men sent to their deaths by the 'Old Men', the bosses (in which case the story plays out the boss's guilt); or does the fly represent the boss's own suffering (in which case the story plays out the boss's – and hence authority's – suppression of grief)? Does the ink represent blood, tears, ammunition or amnesia? And so on. The reader must keep interpreting the symbols, making the literal become figurative, to give the story 'meaning'.

Modernists like Woolf, Mansfield and Joyce argued against *mimesis* as a reproduction of the external world and argued for *mimesis* as a subjective or linguistic interpretation of the world. What inter-ested them most was perception itself, that moment when the subjective (self) and the objective (world) collided. And because of this, they were accused of wanting a *psychological* revolution in artistic thinking while effectively ignoring the *political* revolutions that were taking place all around them. George Orwell lambasted writers such as Woolf and Joyce because he thought that in 'cultured' circles, 'art-for-art's-saking extended practically to a worship of the meaningless. Literature was supposed to consist solely in the manipulation of words.' For Orwell, fiction writers seemed to be directing their readers to 'Rome, to Byzantium, to Montparnasse, to Mexico . . . to the subconscious, to the solar plexus – to everything except the places where things are actually happening'[19] (this was, after all, the era in which Russian communism and German and Italian fascism emerged). Orwell rejected the Modernist style, but didn't just argue for a return to pure documentary Realism (his two most famous novels, *Animal Farm* and *Nineteen Eighty-Four*, are fantasies). He argued for fiction with social and political purpose, and his style reflected that principle.

The self-consciousness of Postmodernism

After the horrors of the Second World War, especially the Nazi Holocaust and the use of the atomic bomb on Hiroshima and Nagasaki, there was another shift in the cultural conception of reality, a reality that we now knew could be utterly devasted by human technology. There was also a shift in the perception of art. Commandants in concentration camps, who had overseen unspeakable atrocities, listened to music and read poetry and fiction. What did this say about our civilisation? What did it say about literature and the moral aspirations of fiction to make its readers more compassionate and empathetic? Writers began to wonder about the implicit messages within the fictional form itself: did the 'willingness to suspend disbelief' encouraged by fiction correspond to an equal willingness to overlook atrocity? Many writers responded to these anxieties by writing fiction about fiction. Old models, whether they be Realist or Modernist, were seen as inadequate, unable to represent the radically unstable, uncertain world of the late twentieth century.

John Barth described this new fiction as the 'literature of exhaustion' and wrote about 'the used-upness of certain forms'. For him, the Modernist emphasis on technical inventiveness had degraded into intellectual game-playing: 'Somebody-or-other's unbound, unpaginated, randomly assembled novel-in-a-box and the desirability of printing Finnegan's Wake on a very long roller-towel.'[20] He wanted a new form of fiction that wasn't just about novelty. He wanted a fiction that broke away from the idea of the 'vivid and continuous dream' and flaunted its own construction, its own fictionality. He writes in 'Lost in the Funhouse':

> You who listen give me life in a manner of speaking.
> I won't hold you responsible.
> My first words weren't my first words. I wish I'd begun differently.
> . . . I must compose myself.
> Look, I'm writing. No, listen, I'm nothing but talk; I won't last long.

And in 'Life-Story':

> The reader! You, dogged, uninsultable, print-oriented bastard, it's you I'm addressing, who else, from inside this monstrous fiction. You've read me this far, then? Even this far? For what discreditable motive? . . . Can nothing surfeit, saturate you, turn you off? Where's your shame?[21]

Metafiction, or fiction about fiction, became associated with Postmodernist writing. It was a writing that distrusted old certainties, and broke apart conventional notions of Truth, History and Progress to replace them with competing truths, histories, and quirky progressions. And although experimental Metafiction is associated with the last third of the twentieth century, the sense of self-awareness within fiction persists in much contemporary writing. Even writers who are not considered explicitly or wildly experimental (think of Toni Morrison, Brett Easton Ellis, J. M. Coetzee, Salman Rushdie, Don DeLillo, Zadie Smith) often draw attention to the constructed-ness of their narratives. Like Realism before it, Metafiction has entered the mainstream, and what once was considered stylistically radical has become the norm.

Alain Robbe-Grillet, one of the most experimental and theoretically motivated of recent novelists, has argued that 'we . . . who are accused of being theoreticians, we do not know what a novel, a true novel, should be; we know only that the novel today will be what we make it, today, and that it is not our job to cultivate a resemblance to what it was yesterday, but to advance beyond.'[22] No one can know the shape of fiction in the future. As writers, though, we cannot advance beyond 'yesterday' if we don't know what yesterday was. And neither should we feel that good fiction 'today' must be a radical departure from what has come before. Rather we should look to the past to see where our sympathies and sensibilities lie, perhaps within the philosophies of Realism, Modernism or Postmodernism, and re-make these models for our own times. We should remember Pateman's conviction that brilliance was more likely to be found in the banal than the fantastic, in stylistic balance rather than stylistic cartwheels.

Advice about style: a blast from the past

If we look to the past, we might also find writing, and advice about writing, that remains stubbornly and resolutely contemporary. Longinus, writing in the third century, lists three stylistic faults that we should still heed and avoid. The first is tumidity, or swollen writing, whose style is over-blown. 'As in the human body', he says, 'so also in diction swellings are bad things, mere flabby insincerities that will probably produce an effect opposite to that intended; for as they say, there is nothing drier than a man with dropsy.' The second offence is frigidity, or mean-spirited writing, which is calculated without any real emotional investment: 'Writers slip into this kind of fault when they strive for unusual and well-wrought effects, and above all attractiveness, and instead flounder into tawdriness and affectation.' The third is false sentiment, 'misplaced, hollow emotionalism where emotion is not called for, or immoderate passion where restraint is what is needed. For writers are often carried away, as though by drunkenness, into outbursts of emotion which are not relevant to the matter in hand, but are wholly personal, and hence tedious. To hearers unaffected by this emotionalism their work therefore, seems atrocious, and naturally enough, for while they are themselves in an ecstasy, their hearers are not.'[23] This advice reminds us that fiction writing is not a monologue, but a dialogue between writer and reader. Indulgent self-expression has no place.

When you consider the advice of one of the fathers of Realism (Gustave Flaubert) and compare it to one of the fathers of Modernism (Ezra Pound) and one of the fathers of Postmodernism (Italo Calvino) you might be surprised by the similarities. This is the advice Flaubert gave to Guy de Maupassant:

> Whatever one wishes to say, there is one noun only by which to express it, one verb to give it life, one adjective only which will describe it. One must search until one has discovered them, this

noun, this verb, this adjective, and never rest content with approx-
imations, never resort to trickery, however happy, or vulgarisms, in
order to dodge the difficulty.[24]

This is Pound's advice in, 'A Few Don'ts for an Imagiste':

> Use no superfluous word, no adjective, which does not reveal some-
> thing. . . .
> Go in fear of abstractions. . . .
> Use either no ornament or good ornament.[25]

And this is Calvino's lament about the loss of exactitude:

> It seems to me that language is always used in a random, approx-
> imate, careless manner, and this distresses me unbearably . . . It
> sometimes seems to me that a pestilence has struck the human
> race in its most distinctive faculty – that is, the use of words. It is
> a plague afflicting language, revealing itself as a loss of cognition
> and immediacy, an automatism that tends to level out all expres-
> sion into the most generic, anonymous, and abstract formulas, to
> dilute meanings, to blunt the edge of expressiveness, extinguishing
> that spark that shoots out from the collision of words and new
> circumstances.[26]

All three are concerned with what Flaubert termed the *mot juste*, the
writer's search for the perfect word. And this was a theme that the
anti-Modernist George Orwell repeated in his political writings. In
'Politics and the English Language', Orwell argued that poor language
can disguise poor thought and he illustrated this with the concept
of the 'dying metaphor', one which I think is especially useful for
writers. He argued that new metaphors evoke a visual image in the
reader's mind, and dead metaphors (like 'iron resolution') are no
longer metaphors but have become ordinary words and are therefore
safe. But the 'huge dump of worn-out metaphors which have lost all
evocative power and are merely used because they save people the
trouble of inventing phrases for themselves', these are the ones to be
avoided.[27]

Here are Orwell's rules for writing:

1 Never use a metaphor, simile or other figure of speech which you
   are used to seeing in print.
2 Never use a long word where a short word will do.

3   If it is possible to cut out a word, always cut it.
4   Never use the passive where you can use the active.
5   Never use a foreign phrase, a scientific word or a jargon word if you can think of an everyday English equivalent.
6   Break any of these rules sooner than say anything outright barbarous.

He acknowledges that 'one could keep all of them and still write bad English' (p. 359) but these are good rules to keep in mind as a writer, because if you flout them, you must justify it to yourself when you are editing, asking yourself if it is stylistically vital or simply laziness.

Gardner versus Gass

Nearly thirty years ago, the writers John Gardner and William Gass engaged in a debate about what fiction should do, and their differences illustrate the importance for writers of finding their own style, rather than relying on the zeitgeist. For Gass, an experimental writer, fiction is about 'transforming language ... disarming the almost insistent communicability of language'. He wants his fiction to be an 'object in the world', an object made of signs (language) that he has put together like a sculpture. The individual meaning of those signs (words) is not important, only the shape they have been given by the sculptor. He explains his point using the metaphor of road signs: 'I've gone down the road and collected all sorts of highways signs and made a piece of sculpture out of these things that say Chicago, 35,000 miles. What I hope, of course, is that people will come along, gather in front of the sculpture, and just look at it – consequently forgetting Chicago.'[28] As readers we are not meant to worry about what his book 'means' (where the 'signs' point to), we are only meant to admire the construction, the object he has made from the signs (words).

   Gardner, on the other hand, argued that fiction was a continuous dream shared with the reader. He objected to what he saw as the subservient position of the reader in Metafiction, where the writer was 'a manipulator as opposed to an empathiser' and said that 'if the novelist follows his plot, which is the characters and the action, if he honestly and continuously proceeds from here to here because he wants to understand some particular question, the reader is going to go with him because he wants to know the same answers.'[29] For

Gardner, then, the signs do point somewhere, and the reader should
be able to follow them.

We might respond to this debate in rather traditional terms by
saying that for all the innovations of the last two hundred years, the
argument rests on the age-old principles of Truth and Beauty. Gass
argued for the Beauty of fiction, but was suspicious of its appeal to
Truth, whereas Gardner argued that Beauty only has significance if it
also conveys Truth. These terms (terms I have avoided until now) are
as slippery as the fly in the ink, meaning as much and as little, but
they nevertheless symbolise the parameters of stylistic convention and
innovation. Truth and Beauty, botched and bloated as they are from
years of claim and counter-claim, are ultimately the emblems of every
writer's style. Not because they contain any secret or lost wisdom, but
precisely because they don't. They are faded, empty signs that every
writer must re-shape in his or her own image. Every writer must ask
him or herself, 'What is Truth? What is Beauty?', and the answers you
give to these questions, answers shaped by your life, your reading,
your aspirations, will teach you the nature of your style.

6   Foundations of Fiction

Every human existence is a life in search of a narrative. . . . This is not simply because it strives to discover a pattern to cope with the experience of chaos and confusion. It is also because each human life is always already an implicit story.

Richard Kearney, *On Stories* (Routledge)

A text cannot be created simply out of lived experience. A novelist writes a novel because he or she is familiar with this kind of textual organisation of experience.

Walter J. Ong, *Orality and Literacy* (Methuen)

To explore the foundations of fiction, I want to think through some of the oft-repeated advice to writers to 'write what you know' and 'write what you read'. I want to see how useful such advice is, and whether there are better ways for writers to approach their fiction. John Gardner, for example, insists that writers should simply ask themselves: 'What can I think of that's interesting?'.[1] I'm going to approach these questions through Paul Ricoeur's philosophy of narrative, and specifically what he has termed 'the triple circle of *mimesis*'.

Ricoeur has been called a 'philosopher of human possibility' and one of the things that interests me most about his work is his exploration of the way fiction relates to the world, through both the writer and the reader. He argues that fiction is born out of, or rather prefigured within, the experience and understanding of a particular person (the writer). This experience and understanding is then re-worked, or configured, to provide plot, characters and actions (the fiction), which is then read and affects, or refigures, the experience and attitudes of another person (the reader). This is 'the triple circle of *mimesis*' as it moves from the life of the writer to the text of the fiction to the life of the reader: from the prefiguring to the configuring to the refiguring of experience.

Ricoeur's version of *mimesis* develops the traditional idea of fiction as an imitation of the world that has been taken from Aristotle. For

Ricoeur, if fiction is imitation then it is creative imitation, or as he puts it, a creative re-telling.[2] And he sees this creative re-telling as having three parts, which we can compare to the advice writers so often receive: the first part is the understanding of experience (write what you know); the second is the understanding of emplotment (write what you read), and the third is the understanding of effect (write what interests you). He calls these three aspects of writing *Mimesis I*, *Mimesis II* and *Mimesis III* and I want to think about each of these in turn as a way to explore our relation to our own writing.

Firstly though, we need to consider Ricoeur's challenge to the idea that life and literature are fundamentally different ways of experiencing the world. He argues that the opposition between stories and life is a false one, and he suggests that by reading (and writing) stories we effectively 'live' in the story world, or as he puts it, '*in the mode of the imaginary*'.[3] In other words, life and fiction intersect. We bring life into fiction, and fiction into life, because, as Richard Kearney argues, our lives are 'always already an implicit story'. We shape our lives according to the 'plots' in our culture (rags to riches, forbidden love, rivalry) and vicariously 'live' the lives of characters in the fiction we write and read (or watch), 'trying on the different roles assumed by the favourite characters of the stories most dear to us'.[4] Sadly, however, there is one key difference between life and fiction for a writer. For although we can be the narrator and hero of our own story, we cannot, as Ricoeur says, 'become the author of our own life': we can't plot ourselves a lottery win or draft our immortality.[5]

Mimesis I, or write what you know

So how can we use Ricoeur's model to think about writing? Let's consider the phrase 'write what you know'. If we connect it to Ricoeur's concept of *Mimesis I* then 'what we know' would be characterised not only by the places and people that we have seen and heard, our memories and our emotions, but by the sense of mortality that makes them so significant. Ricoeur asks us to think about the way we understand ourselves in time: how our lifetimes, which on a cosmic scale are so insignificant, become so filled with meaning and possibility. For as Hayden White argues: 'The universal human quest for meaning is carried out in the awareness of the corrosive power of time, but it is also made possible and given its distinctively human pathos by this very awareness.'[6] Ricoeur argues that something as simple as a calendar brings out into the open our half-submerged awareness of the terrible disparity between the temporal span of our human lives and our universe, in that it 'cosmologizes lived time and humanizes cosmic time'.[7] In fiction we do something similar: we humanise time by creating a narrative.

Ricoeur's explanation of *Mimesis I* focuses on action and the way we understand it. When we experience the world we don't simply see a random series of movements, or people doing arbitrary things: we see actions. We see actions that have motivation and consequence. In other words, we see actions that are rooted in time (where motivation came before and consequence after). And if in our writing we are to present *action* rather than simply movement or activity, we need to be clear about why it is happening (why the character acts in that way) and what the effect will be upon others (how others characters will respond). Ricoeur said that every action is meaningful only because it is some specific person's doing at some particular moment, but he also stressed the role of interpretation in making that action comprehensible. For example he pointed out that if someone raises their hand then we only know whether they are voting or hailing a taxi or saying hello if we look at their surroundings.

The question of interpretation also leads onto a wider context, which we might paraphrase in terms of our 'world-view'. For instance if we see striking workers, we might interpret this action as the seed of revolution, or as an abdication of responsibility, or as a symptom of social greed. And we might interpret it differently if these people were disrupting the Stock Exchange, the local cemetery or a Drive-Thru McDonald's. If we 'write what we know' without questioning the way in which 'what we know' is itself an interpretation then we might find ourselves limiting our fictions. For although it is true that if you live in Houston or London, you will probably be better placed writing about Houston or London rather than the experience of growing up in Papua New Guinea, it is also true that what you 'know' about Houston or London is rooted in your own social, personal and political point of view, and might not be what your character would 'know'. We need to find some distance between our own point of view and our character's: and this can only come through the deliberate work of critical-creative imagination: exploring our own perceptions, cultural prejudices and social ideologies and thinking and feeling beyond them.

When Arthur Golden wrote his first novel *Memoirs of a Geisha*, he had to 'cross three cultural divides – man to woman, American to Japanese, and present to past'. Or rather, he crossed four divides, because, as he said, 'geisha dwell in a sub-culture so peculiar that even a Japanese woman of the 1930s might have considered it a challenge to write about such a world.' He researched for many years, reading about the 1930s, visiting Japan, talking to geisha, but after all this work, he ended up writing 'a dry [third-person narrative] precisely because of [his] concerns about crossing four cultural divides'.[8] It was only when he moved beyond what he knew, and dared to use his critical-creative imagination to write a first-person narrative as the geisha Sayuri, that he brought the book to life.

As we saw in Chapter 5, Émile Zola championed the idea that a writer should write what he knew. He argued that fiction should be about 'observation and analysis', a transparent screen that depicted the world just as it was. He advocated close scrutiny of place and people and copious note-taking. The actual writing was then a process of piecing the notes together like a jigsaw so that they revealed the picture without distortion. He said: 'the story builds itself up from all the observations gathered together, from all the notes taken, one leading to the other . . . You can easily see, in this work, how little part the imagination has in it all.'[9] And I think this is the problem with the advice to 'write what you know'. For although it is vital that we draw from our experience, our emotion, our research, our 'practical sense' as Ricoeur put it, of how action works and is interpreted, if we limit ourselves to 'what we know', without questioning how and why we know what we do, then we can become locked within our experience rather than inspired by it.

Mimesis II, or write what you read

Ricoeur saw *Mimesis II* as 'opening the kingdom of the *as if*' (p. 64). For Ricoeur this was different from the 'what if?' formula we all know. The 'as if' is an imaginary world that is experienced 'as if' it were real, as if we ourselves could live there. It is a version of John Gardner's 'vivid and continuous dream'. I see this second stage of *mimesis* as corresponding to the school of thought that says that writers should 'write what they read,' in that Ricoeur is primarily concerned with the way emplotment mediates experience. I think we can understand this better by returning to Walter Ong's point that in the literate world we are 'familiar with this kind of textual organisation of experience'. We have 'text-bound minds'. In his study of oral literature and oral cultures, he argues that:

> The present day phenomenological sense of existence is richer in its conscious and articulate reflection than anything that preceded it. But it is salutary to recognize that this sense depends upon the technologies of writing and print, deeply interiorized, made a part of our own psychic resources. The tremendous store of historical, psychological and other knowledge which can go into sophisticated narrative and characterization today could be accumulated only through the use of writing and print (and now electronics). But these technologies of the word do not merely store what we know. They style what we know in ways which made it quite inaccessible and indeed unthinkable in an oral culture.'[10]

It is the way that writing 'styles what we know' that interests Ricoeur in *Mimesis II*. Emplotment stops fiction from just being a related series of events (and then and then and then . . .); it pulls all the events together into an intelligible whole. Emplotment enables us to make sense of events (in fiction as in life), so that we can ask what the story is 'about', what is the thought behind it. Ricoeur argues that fiction is 'discordant concordance': it is discordant in that it contains all sorts of different, possibly clashing, ideas, characters and impulses; and it is concordant in that the work of emplotment holds all these elements together as one story.

When we are advised to 'write what we read', it is primarily for two reasons. Firstly because our reading has given us an understanding of emplotment – of the way a series of events becomes meaningful as a narrative, and how different genres make themselves 'intelligible' to their readers. If we read romance, for instance, we understand how to interpret the actions of the characters. So if the heroine fights with the hero, we know that their anger only increases their passion, and we interpret this as a symptom of repressed desire. We know that for the romance to 'make sense' the heroine has to fall in love with the hero; if she continues to hate him, the fiction becomes unintelligible within that genre. Secondly, when we 'write what we read' it gives us a way to bring the endless possibilities of fiction into focus. 'What we read' makes up our own mini-tradition and so it offers us a way to understand the complexities of the form: in other words, it allows us to find a sense of 'concordance' in the overwhelming 'discordance' of millions of books, and to explore these different possibilities within our own writing.

This is true even if you write in opposition to what you read. Terry Pratchett, for instance, began the *Discworld* series 'as an antidote to bad fantasy'. He played with the conventions and stereotypes of the genre, imitating the themes and techniques of other writers. He says: 'The first couple of books quite deliberately pastiched bits of other writers . . . I was rapidly stitching together a kind of consensus fantasy universe.' This consensus, or 'concordance' in Ricoeur's words, was made up of all the familiar fantasy elements that readers expect. But the success of Pratchett's books lies in his particular celebration of 'discordance' within this concordant fantasy world. He says: 'I remember a description *Mad* magazine did about *The Flintstones*: "dinosaurs from 65 million years ago, flung together with idiots from today." I tried to do something like that with Discworld.'[11] Pratchett used his reading to create something reassuringly familiar and comically bizarre.

If you write 'what you read' you will find it easier to create your 'implied reader' because, as Walter Ong says, you will be familiar with that particular 'textual organisation of experience'. You will know the expectations of the reader. But what if your reading is eclectic? What if you read as much poetry as fiction? Or if you study medical textbooks? If we 'write what we read' we need not feel limited by one particular genre. We might even create new fictional possibilities by combining these different forms as Italo Calvino did in *Cosmicomics* (combining physics and geology with fantasy) or as J. G. Ballard did in *The Atrocity Exhibition* (combining the short story with anatomy). Sometimes it might be the case that what you read, perhaps crime or science fiction, isn't what you write at all. But in the act of reading itself, you have engaged in the process of emplotment that seals the relationship between writer, text and reader.

The advice to stick to what you know or to keep to what you read is, it has to be said, sensible advice. And it remains a good starting point for writers. But it doesn't capture the real spirit of writing. Because ultimately fiction is about pleasure: the pleasures both of imaginary worlds and finely wrought words. We need to be invested in our fictions, emotionally and intellectually. And if that is to happen then the question all writers should start with is not 'What do I know?' or 'What do I read?' but, as John Gardner said: 'What can I think of that's interesting?'. Fiction, as Ricoeur says, offers us a new world, and 'new possibilities for being-in-the-world'. The question for us as writers, with the blank page in front of us, is: 'What possibilities can I explore, what new worlds do I want to create?'. For the world of our fiction is the 'world' we will 'live' in, at least in our dreams, for weeks, months or years to come.

Mimesis III, or write what you like

Ricoeur argues that by creating imaginary worlds we do not just invent new possibilities for living, we 're-make' reality itself. He goes on:

> the more imagination deviates from that which is called reality in ordinary language and vision, the more it approaches the heart of the reality which is no longer the world of manipulable objects, but the world into which we have been thrown by birth and within which we try to orient ourselves by projecting our innermost possibilities upon it, in order that we *dwell* there.[12]

In other words, fiction 'projects our innermost possibilities' and allows us to see a reality beyond the mundaneity of the material world: it allows us to live, to *dwell* in the brittle shell of conventional reality. This is what Ricoeur means by *Mimesis III*. It is the interaction of text and life, when fiction changes, or refigures, the reader's world. This change might be extremely subtle, but it is still significant (and of course the phrase 'that book changed my life' is so ubiquitous it has become a cliché).

Ricoeur's triple circle of *mimesis* changes the nature of fiction from an art form that imitates reality into an art form that re-makes it. Fiction not only draws from our experience (what we know), it provides ways for us to interpret that experience: and this for Ricoeur is what makes us human. For him a life that has not been interpreted is 'no more than a biological phenomenon'.[13] The triple circle, then, becomes a kind of spiral, as a writer creates a fiction that changes a reader who creates a fiction that changes a reader who creates a fiction and so on: 'fiction is only completed in life and . . . life can be understood only through the stories we tell about it.'[14] This means that fiction is not secondary to reality, as lies are to truth, but rather that fiction and reality are constantly interacting. In fact Ricoeur goes further. He argues that 'works of fiction are not less real but more real that the things they represent, for in the work of fiction a whole world is displayed.'[15]

Umberto Eco makes a similar point. He argues that fiction presents finite, enclosed worlds, 'small worlds' as he calls them, and since we cannot wander outside this world's boundaries, we are 'led to explore it in depth'.[16] Such depth allows us to know characters, witness human relationships and explore human emotions in ways that might even surpass our lived experience. Eco argues that 'we know Julian Sorel (the main character of Stendhal's *Le Rouge et Le Noir*) better than our own father. Many aspects of our father will always escape us (thoughts he kept quiet about, actions apparently unexplained, unspoken affections, secrets kept hidden, memories and events of his childhood), whereas we know everything about Julian there is to know.'[17] When Eco's father died he lamented that he was 'left to draw feeble conclusions from lackluster memories'.[18]

The imaginary worlds of our fictions not only interpret our existence, they also supplement our existence, offering a glimpse of our humanity in its naked vulnerability. Fiction thus gives us the pleasure of story and an understanding of what it means to be alive. This pleasure and understanding are the foundations of fiction.

Foundations:
Exercises

Ballet dancers practice technique. Pianists wear down their black and white keys with hours of daily practice. Actors rehearse, and rehearse again. Painters perfect still-life objects at various angles . . . By practice one learns to use what one has understood. Only writers, it seems, expect to achieve some level of mastery without practice.

Sol Stein, *Stein on Writing* (St Martin's)

Sol Stein compares becoming a writer to learning how to ride a bicycle: you can watch others doing it; you can find out how to steer and turn the pedals, but eventually you have to sit on the saddle and risk the fall. You have to practise. These exercises are designed to help you do just that, to work through the ideas in this book in a practical way – because it's one thing to read about something, quite another to integrate it into your own writing.

Chapter 1: Establishing Practice

1 Make some time each day (on the train, in the supermarket, in the office, at college) to step back from your own everyday preoccupations and soak up what William James called the 'blooming, buzzing confusion' of life.

2 'Use the fiction maker's eye on yourself' (Dorothea Brande). Consider yourself doing the washing up, walking up stairs or sitting in a room and imagine how you would look in a stranger's eyes. What interpretations would a stranger make of your appearance, expressions, and body language?

3 'The books you read are like the clothes in your wardrobe, they define your identity.' Make a list of the novels and stories in your 'wardrobe' (at least twenty). Make a separate list of all the stories and books you would like to read and work your way through them.

4 Read a short story five times: firstly with 'admiration' (for how it achieves its effect), then again as an 'editor' (for what doesn't

quite work), then for the 'intention' (what you think the writer was trying to say), then 'against the grain' (asking what it reveals about social anxieties, cultural change, and repressed desires), and finally for 'adaptation' (in what ways might you adapt aspects of this story to make a new work).

Chapter 2: Form and Structure

5 James Joyce rewrote Homer's *The Odyssey* in *Ulysses*. Plan how you would update and recast Homer's story if you were to rewrite it today. (If you haven't read these books, consider putting both on your 'to do' list).

6 Invent a simple story (as I did with Mr X and Miss Y on p. 32). Note down three different plots for the story and consider the effect of these changes on the tone of the tale. What are the artistic and emotional effects of re-ordering the action?

7 Read through a story or novel you have written (or the plan) and work out where the climax(es) is/are. Attempt to chart the highs and lows of the story on paper to see the 'shape' of your story (see pp. 36–7). Do the tensions rise? Is there a balance between drama and release? Are there flat lines (either high or low)? Consider the implications of your chart for the pace of your story. How might you review and rewrite to improve it?

Chapter 3: Subject

8 Plan a story using:

   (a) Propp's 31 functions and seven roles
   (b) Campbell's stages of Departure, Initiation and Return

Feel free to miss out, rearrange or condense the various functions or elements within these models.

9 Try to identify the 'functions' of your fiction-in-progress to clarify the movement of the basic story. Write a numbered list. Now, working from the list, consider the effects of shifting chronologies, withholding information, or re-arranging functions.

10 Take a character from a story you have written. Imagine that this character is to be the hero of a new story and devise ten different ways in which this character could receive a 'call to adventure'.

Chapter 4: Voice

11 Study a page from the work of three different writers (for example Jane Austen, Raymond Carver, Gertrude Stein) noting the rhythm of the words they use, the construction of their sentences, the characterisation of the narrator/characters:

(a) write a sentence or two that describes each different 'voice'
(b) write a single paragraph about a woman looking at the sea mimicking the voice of one of these authors. Repeat for each author. Then consider which author you found it easiest to imitate and which the hardest. Ask yourself why. Read through each paragraph. Which is the most effective? Why?

12 Using the same three writers as in 11, consider your role as a reader when reading their work. Were these authors writing for someone like you? If not, did that make you uncomfortable? What imaginative work did you do when reading? Now write a paragraph for each author that describes your feelings as a reader.

13 Write a short short story about a child escaping a house fire in three different ways:

(a) using words of only one syllable
(b) using only five long sentences (with words of any length)
(c) using the words and sentences you think work best

Read the three versions through and consider the 'voice' in each story. Pretend for a moment you hadn't written them and ask yourself what kind of person would have written each story.

14 As Bakhtin said, when we write we are not the first speaker, 'the one who disturbs the eternal silence of the universe'. All words trail meanings behind them like a comet's tail. Choose a word you like and find out as much as you can about the word's origin and previous meanings. Then write sentences (including dialogue) that explore the subtleties of these different meanings. How would different characters use this word?

Chapter 5: Style

15 Read a novel and a story from three different eras (perhaps for example, George Eliot's *Middlemarch*, Virginia Woolf's *To the Lighthouse* and Italo Calvino's *If on a Winter's Night a Traveller* or Nathaniel Hawthorn's 'Young Goodman Brown', Katherine Mansfield's 'Bliss' and James Alan McPherson's 'Elbow Room'. Consider the ways the different styles might correspond to different views of reality.

16 Write a short short story in which a character watches a dying bird. Write the same story three times in the following ways:

(a) The character describes the dying bird as an objective reality.

(b) The character describes the dying bird as a subjective reality (focusing on their own perception of the bird and how the scene affects them).

(c) The character describes the dying bird as an uncertain reality (focusing on the uncertainty of perception, self-identity and language).

17 This exercise examines Courbet's claim that it was 'pretentious' and 'dishonest' to write poetry. Take a passage from an old poem, such as Spenser's *Faerie Queene*, Wordsworth's *Prelude*, Keats' *Ode to a Nightingale*, and rewrite the poetic language into simple, concrete prose. What is gained and/or lost in this rewriting?

18 Write a story in which an ordinary thing (such as a shoe, an insect, a coin, a hat) plays a vital role in the plot and also has an implicit symbolic meaning (as the fly did in Mansfield's 'The Fly').

Chapter 6: Foundation of Fiction

These three exercises build upon each other:

19 Writing what you know: stand outside your house and look at your street. Notice the people, the houses, the cars, the dogs, the bicycles, the litter. Imagine how you must look to the people around you. Now write a sketch in which a character (who does

not know what you are doing) describes you standing on your doorstep.

20 Writing what you read: choose a story that you enjoy reading. Work out how the plot is constructed, how the characters are represented, how the voice of the story is achieved. Now take the sketch you have written for exercise 19 and rewrite it as if it were a scene from a similar story.

21 Writing what interests you: ask yourself what you find interesting (family secrets, criminality, alien life-forms, unexpected kindnesses, and so on). Now take the scene you have written for exercise 20 and build a story around it.

Part II

Speculations

7 Exploring Possibilities

I don't give a hoot what the writing's like, I write any sort of rubbish which will cover the main outlines of the story, then I can begin to see it.

Frank O'Connor, 'The Art of Fiction No. 19', *The Paris Review*

To begin this chapter, and the second part of this book, I want to return once more to Frank Smith's ideas about the stages of writing. His three-part model for writing can be summed up in this way: prewriting is 'the most mysterious, variable, and frustrating aspect of writing'; writing is an 'intangible activity . . . the words just come (if they come at all)', and rewriting is 'the writer's own response to what has been written'.[1]

For Smith, writing is the hardest stage to identify and talk about; he calls it 'the slim and elusive filling in the sandwich'.[2] He cannot pin it down. Even when he identifies the three-stage process, the actual moment of writing itself slips away, unable to be fixed. But this is the nature of writing. A critical-creative approach doesn't mean putting creativity on the slab, ready to dissect. We can acknowledge the role of criticality without denying the intangible nature of creativity, just as we can acknowledge the way critical ideas might influence prewriting, writing and rewriting without denying the spontaneity of storytelling.

The ideas in Part II of this book are focused on rewriting, rather than the time of writing itself, because during this stage (as during prewriting) you are more conscious of structure and style. That's not to say that the ideas in the following chapters won't affect your writing. They will, but these influences will be more subconscious. When we draft we should allow ourselves to simply write, in whatever way is most productive and comfortable for us. And if as Frank O'Connor says that means writing 'any sort of rubbish' to get to the outline of the story, then so be it.

Ernest Hemingway once said that any writer 'should have read the dictionary at least three times from beginning to end and then have loaned it to someone who needs it'.[3] In other words, a writer should fill their mind with words and ideas before they put pen to paper and then close the books. When you write you are simply following your instincts, following the story that is playing out in your head as it moves through your fingertips and onto the paper (or screen). Everything you've read and thought about when prewriting will already be there in some disguised, adapted or rejected sense. Your job at this stage is to follow your urges, containing and limiting them only because new directions become clear to you. This is the time when your focus is on the *experience* of the world you are creating, and the people within it, not upon the finer points of word choice.[4]

Writing and 'felt sense'

We can approach the writing stage through the philosophy of Eugene Gendlin, who created the concept of 'felt sense'. 'Felt sense' describes the way we understand our environment through feelings and sensations before we can translate this understanding into words. Gendlin argues that 'a felt sense is not a mental experience but a physical one. A bodily awareness of a situation or person or event. An internal aura that encompasses everything you feel and know about the given subject at a given time – encompasses it and communicates it to you all at once rather than detail by detail.'[5]

The concept of 'felt sense' has been used to describe a writer's initial experience of the storyworld: they may have impressions of characters, settings and events without necessarily having words to express them.[6] When we write, we focus our attention onto aspects of this felt world, trying to draw them into focus through language. If, for instance, we write about a character, we have a 'felt sense' of that character as well as thoughts about that character – just as we have about the important people in our life. To give an example, think for a moment about your mother. If I asked you, you could no doubt tell me about her physical features, behaviour, attitudes; and if you thought very hard, you could probably remember thousands of incidents from your childhood. But that kind of thinking takes time, and before you articulated any of those thoughts, you probably experienced a vague 'felt sense' of your mother that captured something fundamental about your relationship. As Clayton E. Tucker-Ladd argues: 'Vague and non-specific as it is, you will never confuse the "felt sense" of your mother with a "felt sense" of someone else.'[7]

'Felt sense' applies not only to people, though, it also applies to events and situations. If you witness a car accident you have a 'felt sense' of that event. If you go through a divorce, you have a 'felt sense' of that experience. And when you write about such events, you will also have a 'felt sense' about your creations (whether or not you have directly experienced anything similar). When we write fluently, we talk about the words 'just coming to us', as Smith does, without conscious thought. For Gendlin, this sense of spontaneity reveals the way that our writing responds not only to our thoughts but also to the internal rhythms, moods and inchoate sensations of our bodies, as the 'felt sense' is 'focused' through language.

For the writer, 'focusing' involves two processes: firstly, the gradual focusing of the overall fictional world or story in our imagination, and secondly, the detailed focusing on particular aspects of that world in our writing. These two processes are constantly interacting, so that when we write about a particular detail, say the opening of a door, it helps us to bring more of the felt world into focus in our imagination. And the more we bring that imaginary world into focus, the better able we are to choose those precise details that illustrate or symbolise the wider world. As John Gardner said: 'Getting down one's exact meaning helps to discover what one means.'[8] Allowing ourselves to be absorbed by the 'felt sense' of our imaginary world lets the richness of the experience find its way on to the page. Consider Hemingway's metaphor of the iceberg:

> If a writer knows enough of what he is writing about he may omit things that he knows and the reader, if the writer is writing truly enough, will have a feeling of those things as strongly as though the writer had stated them. The dignity of movement of an ice-berg is due to only one-eighth of it being above water. A writer who omits things because he does not know them only makes hollow places in his writing.[9]

We do not need to describe every detail in order to bring our world into focus; we need to bring our world into focus in order to describe the details that count.

The process of focusing does not all happen at once. It can be weeks, months or years until the vague ideas of prewriting are focused and refocused through writing and rewriting. Every writer works to their own rhythm. I have days where I can invent and want to do nothing but mull over ideas, drawing on my felt sense, noting any scraps that seem promising (prewriting); and I have days when I want to get it all down onto paper, bringing the imaginary world into being (writing); and then I have days when all I want to do is refocus that vision, re-working the words I have written (rewriting). I do not do each in turn; I follow my mood. Sometimes the blank page is too intimidating and I take comfort in editing. Sometimes I want to get away from words altogether and lose myself in creative possibilities. And sometimes I cannot type fast enough to catch the story in my head. These choices mean that I do not force myself to write when my instincts tell me not to, because I can always work at prewriting or rewriting, and this means that it is easier to avoid writer's block.

Writer's block

When I speak of 'writer's block' here, I want to think beyond the initial rather clichéd sense of the writer sitting impotently in front of the typewriter, wastebasket full, empty page in front of him (in the cliché it's always a man). For if we are to avoid writer's block, we need to understand it both critically and creatively. I want to argue that just as writing has three aspects (prewriting, writing, and rewriting), so writer's block has three aspects, and although the first two are quite obvious to the suffering writer, the last can sometimes be missed. The first kind of block is a lack of ideas (prewriting block); the second is the inability to get words on paper (writing block), and the third is the inability to edit (rewriting block). If you ever suffer from writer's block, the first step in overcoming it is to identify which of these you have. Each stage of writing requires a balance of the critical-creative imagination, but the way we use our imagination is different at each stage.

Prewriting block: waiting for inspiration

The first step in overcoming block is to think about each stage of the writing process and understand what it involves. When we are prewriting we do not need to have the entire draft of the story worked out. Neither do we have to tell anyone what we are thinking about or expose our tender young shoot of an idea to the harsh winds of other people's opinions. All we are doing in prewriting is playing with the possibilities. Think of yourself as an experimenter or a child obsessed by the 'what if?', a child who is not interested in the rules and routines of the adult world. Do not feel oppressed by the pages you have to write to make this idea into a story. You simply do not have to worry about writing at this stage of the process.

In prewriting we are doing several things that might not be connected to a particular story or idea:

(a) observing and note-taking
(b) musing, thinking, feeling
(c) reading and researching

Every writer can do these things, although often they might be missed as 'optional', and this might well lead to block. Other aspects of prewriting include:

(a) inventing characters and situations
(b) exploring ideas and models
(c) piecing together a plan

And it is here that writers most often feel themselves to be 'blocked'. They feel lacking in inspiration. They need an idea.

In *A Technique for Producing Ideas*, James Webb Young suggests that an idea is 'nothing more nor less than a new combination of old elements'.[10] This is echoed by Arthur Koestler in *The Act of Creation* when he argues that the creative act 'does not create something out of nothing; it uncovers, selects, re-shuffles, combines, synthesizes already existing facts, ideas, faculties, skills. The more familiar the parts, the more striking the new whole.'[11] This definition in itself can be helpful, in that it reminds us that nothing comes from nothing, and that as writers we are not trying to invent stories from scratch. We are taking the elements of our life experience, our reading, our imagination and bringing them together to create 'a new combination'.

There are many things you can do to help with a prewriting block; some psychological, some practical. You might take up mediation or yoga to silence the imaginary self (so that you can listen to your imagination; or focus your felt sense); or you might simply change your attitude to prewriting. In *How to Get Ideas*, Jack Foster suggests that the first thing you should do is to stop telling yourself that you will never come up with a good idea. For Foster this is a self-fulfilling prophecy. He insists that: 'The ones who come up with ideas *know* that ideas exist and *know* that they will find those ideas; the ones who don't come up with ideas *don't know* that ideas exist and *don't know* that they will find ideas.'[12] For writers with prewriting block, the methodologies of other creative professions may offer new ways to think about inspiration, and one of the best models I have found was developed over fifty years ago by the advertising executive James Webb Young.

Five steps to new ideas

Young's five-step model for producing ideas draws closely from the methods of the famous fictional detective, Sherlock Holmes. Holmes was renowned for his almost supernatural powers of observation, and the first step in Young's model involves observation and study to allow the mind to 'gather its raw materials' (p. 20). Young warns us, however, that in practice this can be hard work, and he complains that instead of studiously observing, reading, or listening, 'we sit around hoping for inspiration to strike us' (p. 21). To overcome this inactivity he suggests that advertisers follow the advice given to de Maupassant when he was learning to write: 'Go out into the streets of Paris . . . and pick out a cab driver. But study him until you can describe him so that he is seen in your description to be an individual, different from every other cab driver in the world' (p. 22).

This kind of observation and description gives the writer specific knowledge of people and places, and if as writers we shirk the task, we cannot expect our ideas or our writing to flourish. But to create new ideas we need more than specific knowledge, we need general knowledge too. We need to read about archaeology and astrophysics as well as literature. For, as Young says, creative people are like cows: 'no browsing, no milk' (p. 24). You might even take up an old-fashioned hobby and keep a scrapbook of ideas, news-clippings, quotes and facts, just as Holmes did. You never know when it might reveal a 'new combination of old elements'.

In Young's second step, the mind goes through a 'process of masticating those materials', chewing over ideas, thoughts and experiences, a process which, in Chapter 1, I have called 'musing'. He advises that you write down all your ideas, however incomplete, because this keeps the process flowing. This is a form of 'disposable writing', but with Young's method, the musing is concentrated. You keep writing down ideas, however feeble, without stopping; writing beyond tiredness and despair. Only when you've reached what Young calls the 'hopeless stage' (p. 31) are you ready to move onto the third step, which is to 'drop the problem completely and turn to whatever stimulates your imagination and emotions' (p. 33): Sherlock Holmes would take Watson to the opera.

After gathering our 'food', relentlessly chewing it over, and at last allowing it to quietly digest, we are ready for step four, the moment of inspiration: 'Out of nowhere the Idea will appear' (p. 34). If this does not happen, you need to go back over the first three steps, making sure you have enough 'food', that you 'chew' it well and allow it to settle. But if you do find inspiration, Young's fifth step is to 'take your little newborn idea out into the world of reality' (p. 38), where you'll realise that it is not as fine as you thought and will take 'a deal of patient working' (p. 38). This is a danger time when you might reject your idea as worthless, but Young, as an advertising man, recommends sticking with it, exposing it to the criticism of others, and allowing that criticism to stimulate new growth.

Personally I think that for many writers, such brutal exposure might be too early. We have much work to do inventing characters and situations, exploring ideas and models, piecing together a plan. It may be that as a writer you thrive on criticism and need something to react to when forming ideas, in which case share your thoughts with friends and people whose advice you trust. But if you are not such a writer, I would repeat Young's first three steps, developing and enriching your initial idea, building the storyworld in your imagination, before sharing it with anyone else.

Writing block: facing the blank page

Often writer's block is fear: either fear that your words will be awful or fear of the amount of work ahead. For the first fear, remember Hemingway's famous dictum: 'all first drafts are shit.' For the second, change your focus: don't think of novels or stories, think of chapters, pages and paragraphs. Focusing on what you plan to do that day or that week (especially with a novel) can help you to overcome the idea that writing is a momentous task. To overcome writing block we need to think about what this stage of the process involves. The writing stage:

(a) explores the characters and their relationships
(b) follows motivations into actions and consequences
(c) establishes the general shape of the story

It is not about finding the perfect words. It is not even about writing the *actual* story you hope to publish. You don't have to worry about that yet – that comes later. The writing stage simply allows you to develop *a version of the story* through the act of putting words onto paper. And that is all. No one need see this first draft. And if you keep focused, critically and creatively, on what you want to achieve from this stage of writing (a rough draft) it will help you to avoid getting blocked.

But what if you still find that you cannot write? Perhaps you should not fight the block – but accept it, welcome it in fact, because it is telling you that you are not yet ready to write this part of your story. You need to do more prewriting. It might be that you are not confident enough of your characters, or that you need more information about a situation. In this case the block is a positive guide, leading you on to the next phase of writing via the necessary musing, researching, reading, and observing of prewriting.

If the block is not guiding you to prewriting, however, but is simply undermining your confidence in yourself as a writer, Damon Knight suggests a way to overcome it. He argues that blocked writers should invent a writing persona.[13] Imagine this persona to be a writer who is confident, skilled, fearless, and fluent. This is who you are when you write – not someone who despairs of ever writing a decent sentence and cringes when they glance at the famous titles on their bookshelf. You can practise writing in your new persona by completing writing exercises (perhaps using the exercises in this book) or simply writing without stopping for ten minutes every day.

Another negative writing block can be caused by the confusion of the writing and rewriting stages of the process. There is a flow between these two stages, and some writers revise previous chapters as a way of generating creative energy before writing the rest of the draft (I do this). Some writers also tinker with the draft as they go, trying to express the story in the way that feels most right. But this tinkering is not rewriting. There is a huge difference between writing and rewriting: for when we rewrite we start thinking about other people reading our fiction, and when we write we simply get down the story *for ourselves* in the best way we know how. This is a crucial difference.

Confusion between the writing and rewriting stages is perhaps the most common form of block, often underlying what seems to be a simple lack of confidence. It also underlies the mistaken assumption that a writer's critical awareness detracts from their creativity, causing the 'critical' to be seen as a negative, judgmental, undermining faculty. But I want to turn this false assumption on its head. It is not the writer's critical awareness that causes this kind of writer's block – in fact the writer's critical awareness offers the solution – the block is caused by the writer's creativity, by their fearful imagination. The blocked writer's despair is fuelled by the anticipated and *imagined* criticism of others – friends, family, editors, reviewers, readers – who become characters in another story playing out in the writer's head: the story of their own humiliation and defeat. In other words, the writer is creating two stories: one *within* their novel or short story, and another *about* their novel or short story. A critical-creative approach might help the writer to recognise this other story *as a story* and shut the anticipated audience out of the room until the next stage in the process: rewriting.

Rewriting block: messing with the manuscript

Rewriting block is not as obvious as a block at the prewriting or writing stages, after all we have had the ideas and written the story – how can we possibly be blocked? But if we cannot bring ourselves to rewrite or revise, this block can be just as damaging to our fiction. In rewriting, a writer needs to:

(a)   revise the plotting of the story
(b)   define the individuality of the characters
(c)   strengthen the pace and momentum of the story
(d)   find the perfect words

If, as a writer, you cannot face returning again and again to your initial drafts, then you leave much of the process of writing undone.

There are several reasons for rewriting block, including tiredness, excitement, and fear. Finishing the first draft of a story, especially the first draft of a novel, is a moment for celebration. And we should celebrate – but we should not confuse the completion of the writing stage with the completion of the novel or short story itself. Neither should we let the excitement of writing out the story, or the fear of more work, or the uncertainty about what to do next, persuade us to send the work to an agent or editor (or tutor) without first rewriting. Even if you read the novel or story through and think it's great, enjoy that feeling but don't send it out. Keep it in a drawer for a month and then look at it again. And if, having overcome your tiredness and initial excitement, you still feel blocked, then perhaps the problem is simply an uncertainty about what rewriting entails. If that is the case, the next section of this chapter might help, but before we move on to approaches to rewriting, there's one final block that deserves mention.

Publication block

This last kind of block is perhaps the opposite of rewriting block. For in this case, the fear of rejection is so strong that the writer is simply unable to accept that a piece of writing is finished. For this writer, there is always another change to be made before the novel or story is ready to be shown to another reader. This compulsive rewriting may actually be dis-improving the work, making it worse. One way to avoid falling into this trap is to keep records of previous drafts. If you are rewriting using a computer, copy the chapter or draft into a new document (named Chapter X draft Y) and revise it afresh. This allows you to compare different drafts to see if parts of an earlier version were better. Likewise in longhand – keep drafts legible. But if you want to publish, and your work never seems ready, force yourself to plunge your work into the outside world by sending it to a small magazine, a lesser-known agency or an independent publisher (therefore not exposing yourself too broadly). Don't touch the piece until you hear back (normally three months), and then if it is rejected you can go over the work again with fresh eyes and send it out to another magazine, agent or publisher. And remember the words of Samuel Beckett: 'Ever tried. Ever failed. No matter. Try again. Fail again. Fail better.'[14]

Approaches to rewriting

> *First drafts are for learning what your novel or story is about. Revision is working with that knowledge to enlarge and enhance an idea, to reform it . . . Revision is one of the true pleasures of writing.*
> Bernard Malamud, 'The Writer at Work', in *Talking Horse: Bernard Malamud on Life and Work* (Columbia University Press)

> *Proofread carefully to see if you any words out.*
> Anonymous

As Bernard Malamud says, rewriting is potentially the most exciting stage of writing. It can also be the most demanding. You have

completed a draft of your fiction, and you are now ready to transform it. Rewriting, of course, may well begin long before the final
draft is complete (especially if you are writing a novel) but the
method of revising I want to explore here presupposes that you
are working with a substantial (if perhaps not complete) manuscript. I want to draw from Sol Stein's method of revision that
he calls 'triage' after the system of treating battlefield casualties.
Basically this method tackles the major issues (character, structure,
scenes) before working closely on more particular imperfections
(word choices).

As most books about writing will tell you, the best way to begin
revising is to put your work away for at least a couple of weeks and
focus your attention on other projects. This is Stage 1. If you are
tempted to ignore this stage and 'just get on with it', remember that
during this time you are developing a critical distance which will help
you to be more discerning when you 'read as an editor'. Only when
you have completed Stage 1 should you move on to Stage 2, print out a
hard copy of your manuscript and read through as if it were someone
else's work. This helps to strengthen your critical distance. Sol Stein
even recommends creating a title page with another author's name
on it. This could be someone you admire – or perhaps an author you
dislike if you think it would give your revising a critical edge!

When you read through you are concentrating on the big picture.
This doesn't mean that you can't highlight sentences or passages
where the writing simply doesn't work – but don't get bogged down by
them. Don't be distracted into rewriting individual sentences. There
will be time for that later. On this first reading you are concentrating
on structure and character. Ask yourself some hard questions and use
them to decide whether your characters or your plot need more work:

The major characters:

1 What makes your characters interesting?
2 Do your characters have a mixture of good and bad qualities?
3 How well do you know your characters?
4 Are all your characters distinct from each other?
5 Can you imagine your characters doing something that you have
   written not about?
6 What makes your characters different from you?
7 Why should a reader want to get to know your characters?

8   Do your characters (in a novel) change as a result of their experience?
9   Do the characters act from their own motivation (or for the author's convenience)?
10 If you write from one of your characters' point of view, is this consistent?

Plot:

11 Is the beginning you've chosen the most interesting place to start?
12 Does your mind wander at any point during reading?
13 Does the tension in the story build?
14 Is the main character in an enthralling predicament?
15 Is there sufficient conflict between the characters?
16 Do moments of suspense collapse too soon?
17 Do sub-plots disappear for too long?
18 Is the main plot line sufficiently strong?
19 Are plot surprises contrived or do they emerge from the depths of the story?
20 Is the ending emotionally satisfying?
21 Are there any plot-lines unresolved (or characters forgotten) at the end?

One way of tightening the plot of a novel is to work at the level of scenes (remember a chapter in a novel might contain a number of scenes). Sol Stein recommends that after reading through the draft, you should decide which scene is the most memorable – which stays in your mind? Then flick through the draft to find the least memorable scene. Ask yourself what makes one scene memorable and another not. How could the least memorable scene be revised to make it more effective? Could it simply be cut? If it contains vital information, how else could this be slipped into the story? Stein goes on: 'Once you've revised or done away with your least memorable scene, you now have a *new* least memorable scene! You need to subject it to the same tough scrutiny. Would the book be stronger without it?'.[15]

When you are confident that your characters and plot are sound, you can begin to work on the more detailed revisions. Still pretending that this story was written by another author, read it with admiration and read it as an editor. If something works think about why it works. If something doesn't work consider how you might change it. Mark all the sentences, words, phrases, metaphors that clang. In a different colour, mark the ones that please you. Mark all the dialogue that is stilted or flat or slow, and in a different colour, mark the dialogue that grips you when you read it. Remember Longinus's advice (see Chapter 5) and cut the flabby insincerities and emotional outpourings. Very often understatement evokes more emotion in the reader. If there is a line or word that is not needed, cut it, for as C. S Lewis said: 'Whatever in a work of art is not used, is doing harm.'[16]

Think of the rhythm of your sentences. Are there passages where the sentences are all of uniform length? Or does the mix of long and short sentences create a monotonous rhythm that needs breaking up? Do you begin sentences with participles ('Looking out of the window, Jake noticed that . . .)? If so consider cutting them. Do you over-use adverbs and adjectives? Again consider cutting them. Many writers, from Gabriel García Márquez to Stephen King, avoid adverbs, considering them to be signs of lazy writing.

Once you have completed your first rewrite, put it away for a few weeks before repeating the whole thing on a clean draft. It is up to you how many times you rewrite, but when you have reached the point where you feel that you have produced the best work you can, that the characters are fully realised, that the plot is coherent and pacy, that the writing is tight and polished, then you are ready to send your manuscript out into the world.

The chapters that follow explore many of the features that play a key role in rewriting (as well as writing and prewriting), building upon this basic guide to help you to develop your own approach.

8   Forms and Structures

A story should have a beginning, a middle, and an end ... but not necessarily in that order.

Attributed to Jean-Luc Godard

This chapter addresses some of the key issues writers face when deciding how to structure their fiction and focuses upon the traditional model of 'beginning, middle and end'. Like Godard, many writers have rejected this easy temporality, corrupting or warping time and consequence in their writing: William Burroughs attempted to find spontaneity in his 'cut-ups'; Alain Robbe-Grillet rejected novelistic expectations with his *écriture labyrinthine*; Marc Saporta put his loose-leaf, unpaginated *Composition No. 1* into a box with the following instructions on the cover: 'The pages of this book may be read in any order. The reader is requested to shuffle them like a deck of cards.'[1]

But even Saporta, who so deliberately rejected the ideological, common-sense structure of 'beginning, middle and end', acknowledged the significance of time in fiction. In his introduction to the novel printed on the box, he said: 'For the time and order of events control a man's life more than the nature of such events.' When the reader shuffles *Composition No. 1*, the events will not be changed, only the order in which they occur. The shuffling introduces a random, spontaneous element to the representation of time. It also means that the reader will have to piece together the 'story' by recreating the 'real' order of the action – just as they must do with an Agatha Christie. If, in your writing, you also wish to reject the formality of beginning, middle and end, you are free to experiment. But I still think that it is important to be aware of the underlying significance of this formal structure.

Traditionally one of the functions of story has been that it humanises time; allowing us to see the relentless march of days, months, years, centuries, in terms of the human experience of birth, growth and death; in terms of remembered ancestors and new generations; of the past, present and future. As human beings we conventionally understand ourselves as having a beginning (birth, infancy, childhood, adolescence), a middle (adulthood, middle age), and an end (old age, death). And though this has been challenged by everything from belief in the afterlife to postmodernist theories of the perpetual present, it remains the fundamental structure of what Paul Ricoeur calls 'our narrative understanding of ourselves'.[2]

As writers we may want to disturb that sense of narrative identity, after all the easy mapping of life-structure onto story-structure was abandoned in the nineteenth century. But when we contemplate the role of beginning, middle and end in our fiction we need to understand not only the mechanics of this conventional structure, but its significance for all storytelling. Oakley Hall argues that in fiction beginnings, middles and endings can be re-conceived as 'situation, complication, resolution'.[3] This re-naming allows us to see the naked structure of story. The beginning establishes the fictional situation (the characters, the setting, the motivation for change), the middle complicates the fictional situation (exploring the relationships, exacerbating tensions, creating suspense) and the ending resolves the fictional situation (revealing character change, addressing uncertainties, relieving suspense).

Of course there are differences between novels and short stories. The middle of a short story may simply illustrate the situation introduced in the beginning and the ending may resolve nothing, leaving the reader unsettled and questioning. But as a model, the beginning, middle and end structure represents the conventional rhythm of fiction, and it's one that I want to explore further in this chapter.

Beginnings

> *You are about to begin reading Italo Calvino's new novel,* If on a winter's night a traveller. *Relax. Concentrate. Dispel every other thought. Let the world around you fade.*
>
>   Italo Calvino, *If on a winter's night a traveller* (Vintage)

In thinking about beginnings I want to address the vexed question of when and where a story should begin, considering and debating the different opinions and theories that abound in books about writing. Calvino breaks all the rules in his novel, beginning with a direct appeal to the reader: 'Adjust the light so you won't strain your eyes. Do it now, because once you're absorbed in reading there will be no budging you. . . . Try to foresee now everything that might make you interrupt your reading. Cigarettes within reach, if you smoke, and the ashtray. Anything else? Do you have to pee? All right, you know best,' and it is several pages later, after several digressions about reading positions and book-buying that we reach the line, 'The novel begins in a railway station, a locomotive huffs, steam from a piston covers the opening of the chapter, a cloud of smoke hides part of the first paragraph.'[4]

Calvino's fiction exemplifies Paul Ricoeur's idea that writing is simply 'a guide for reading' (see Chapter 4), a set of instructions for the creation of imaginary worlds. By making the reader a character, Calvino plays with our expectations, telling us that we will be absorbed by the story while delaying the moment when the 'story' will actually begin. Instead, our attention is directed towards the act of reading itself, how we choose a book, how we sit, how we assess the author, how we desire the tale to begin.

His experimental fiction both defies and obeys the conventions of storytelling. By addressing the reader, he becomes the traditional tale-teller who prefaces each recital with the words 'Are you sitting comfortably?', and by tempting us with the promise of a story, he arouses our curiosity even as he refuses to consummate it. In thinking about beginnings I want to follow Calvino and consider how writers position their readers and how they stimulate their curiosity, but first I want to consider the different 'beginnings' writers experience when prewriting, writing and rewriting.

Prewriting, writing, rewriting

The beginning is not the story. The beginning is the *motivation* for the story. This is a key difference, and we must be critically, as well as creatively, aware of the role of these early pages. We must not try to cram in too many characters, too much information, or too many sub-plots in our eagerness to get the story moving. We must remember the dual function of any beginning: to engage the reader in the story world and to trigger the story itself. And we must focus our energies on doing just that.

The question of where to begin, and how to trigger the story, is often fraught, but if we think critically about the differences between prewriting, writing and rewriting, we can see that the 'beginning' of a story will be different at each of these stages. In *prewriting*, the 'beginning' of the story might be a snippet of conversation, an idea, a character. This is the thread that guides you as a writer into the story world. The route you take is not one that any reader could follow. It's a difficult, tortuous route with many wrong turns. It's a route marked 'Writer Only'.

When we come into the *writing* stage, and begin to write the first draft, we need to find a new beginning, a more conventional way into the story. But here again, we are looking for our own way into the story, another 'Writer Only' route. The reader will not follow this path. The only question you should ask when you first begin writing Chapter 1 is this: 'Will this path lead me into the story?'. Do not ask: 'Is this the best way to start?' or 'Will this beginning grab the reader?'. These are questions for a different stage in the process. In the writing stage all you need to do is find your own way into the story. And if Chapter 1 allows you into your own story world keep writing. Only in the final stage, *rewriting*, do you need to find a beginning that will tempt readers to follow you.

We can visualise these different beginnings if we think about our fiction as a labyrinth, a traditional hedge maze. In the *prewriting* stage, we are in the dark, fumbling for a way into the maze-like story world. We stumble upon a hole in a hedge and scramble through, getting scratched and caught up on the branches as we go. Then we crawl through the maze, gradually working out which paths lead to dead-ends and which lead us further into the story. In the *writing stage* we come to the maze again. It's lighter now and we have some sense of direction, perhaps even a map of sorts (our plan). This time we want a more comfortable way into the story world. So we walk round and round the edge of the maze until we slide through a bigger hole and find ourselves running along familiar paths. In the *rewriting stage*, things are different. Now we have to prepare the maze for others, people who have no time to meander around or squeeze through gaps in hedges. We have to make a snazzy entrance. We have to impress.

The advice in this chapter is aimed at this final stage of the writing process: rewriting. It might also be useful in the prewriting stage, when we are pondering on ideas and structures. But as writers we must remember that we cannot prepare the way for others until we have first found the way ourselves. In other words we cannot rewrite the beginning until we have drafted the beginning. And if we confuse these two stages we are in danger of becoming blocked. This is not to say that we cannot alternate between writing and rewriting as we work. But I would advise that you don't rewrite your beginning until you are at least half way through your story. Only then can you recognise the point where you stopped walking around the edge of the maze and placed your feet firmly on the path.

There is a rather ironic rule called the 'Chapter 3 rule' which states that you should scrap the first two chapters of your draft and start with your third (for short stories we might call this the 'page 3 rule'). When drafting this might seem impossible, but more than once I have spent weeks and months polishing early chapters only to realise that the real story began in Chapter 3. All the background detail in Chapters 1 and 2 (that once seemed so vital) could be condensed into two or three paragraphs. The first chapters allowed me as a writer to get into my story, but for the reader they were an unnecessary preamble. So if you find yourself explaining who your characters are, or why they are in a particular place, or what makes that setting so important, then ask yourself if these pages or chapters are the writer's or the reader's way in to the story. And, when it comes to rewriting, don't be afraid to cut.

If we are critically and creatively engaged with each stage of the writing process, we can decide what the beginning needs to do, and when and how it needs to do it. We can allow ourselves to explore different possibilities, in prewriting and writing, in notes and drafts, without fearing rejection by an imaginary reader. These stages are 'Writer Only' stages, and they establish a safe space for creativity. Only in the final stage, rewriting, do we invite the imaginary reader (or perhaps ourself *as a reader*) to look over our shoulder as we work.

Where to begin?

John Gardner argues that just as a marathon runner and a sprinter will not set off at the same pace, so a novelist and a short-story writer will not begin their fictions with the same impact.[5] But how do we interpret such advice when many of the 'how to' books for writers insist that novels as well as short stories should grab, grab, grab from the very first page?

The question of where and how to start is a vexed one for fiction writers, and when we turn to 'how to' books for help, we often have to navigate our way through contradictory advice. If we take two 'how to' books as examples, James Frey's *How to Write a Damn Good Novel* and Jack Bickham's *The Thirty Eight Most Common Fiction Mistakes (and How to Avoid Them)*, both written by writer-teachers, we can begin to see the problem.

James Frey advises beginning the story just before the beginning. He says: 'Events can only be understood within the context of the character's situation at the time the events occur; therefore it's important to the reader to know the *status quo situation.*'[6] Jack Bickham, on the other hand, says that 'every good story starts at a moment of threat.' He advises writers to 'start your story with a mountain climber hanging from a cliff by his fingernails, and I guarantee that the reader will read a bit further to see what happens next.'[7] For Frey, character and situation are foremost; for Bickham action, and specifically threat, comes first.

Both writers agree on several key points, including the assumption that every story begins with a moment of change. But where they differ is crucial. Frey argues that to understand the significance of the change, you need to begin your story or novel *just before* that change happens, and Bickham contends that from 'page 1, line 1' the story should begin with the change itself. To make sense of these differences, and to figure out the best approach for our own writing, we need to understand the different traditions that Frey and Bickham represent.

Frey can be seen as arguing for the structure Joseph Campbell explored in the monomyth (see Chapter 3), which placed the first stage of the hero's journey, the 'call to adventure', in 'the world of common day'.[8] For Campbell, and those who followed his mythical model, the story begins with the seeds of adventure in the ordinary world. These seeds (disturbed characters, precarious situations, ominous rumblings of discontent) are firmly planted in the reader's mind in the opening pages. Beginning in this way, with the *status quo* as Frey recommends, allows the writer to establish what is at stake for the characters: what motivates them to act, and what they risk by their actions.

Bickham can be seen as following Horace's dictum in *Ars Poetica* that stories should start *in medias res*, in the midst of the action. Horace claimed that: 'All the time he [the good writer] is hurrying on to the crisis, and he plunges his hearer into the middle of the story as if it were already familiar to him; and what he cannot hope to embellish by his treatment, he leaves out.'[9] Beginning in this way, *in medias res*, allows the writer to start with a bang, to make the maximum impact on the reader's emotions. Essential information about characters and their situation is held back to be slipped into later scenes (of course, avoiding chunks of exposition that would slow down the story after such a gripping beginning).

Both approaches have advantages and disadvantages for writers. If you begin before the change, there is a risk that the opening of your story will seem slow. That's why Frey advises beginning *just before* the change, to strip out all unnecessary build-up. But if you begin with the change (or threat), there is a danger that the event will have only minor, rather sensationalist, impact on the reader. In fiction as in life, if we know someone, a small incident will have more emotional significance for us than the high dramas of a stranger.

There are two fundamental questions about your beginning that you have to ask as a writer. Firstly, a question that applies to both Frey's and Bickham's approach: 'Is this moment of change dramatic enough to interest my reader?'. This requires a harsh and honest answer. Secondly: 'Does the tension of this moment rely on an understanding of the character?'. If the answer is no, then follow Bickham's approach. If the answer is yes, you need to identify precisely what the reader needs to understand. Make a list of characteristics and circumstances that are important, and then cut everything that is not vital. Now devise the shortest possible dramatic scene that would communicate those features.

Curiosity, Introduction, Affect (CIA)

Sol Stein says that the goals of the opening paragraphs are: 'to excite the reader's curiosity, preferably about a character or a relationship; to introduce a setting and to lend resonance to the story.'[10] This seems a long way from Jack Bickham's emphasis on threat, but I think the key features that Stein develops should be found in any beginning. We can think of them as *Curiosity, Introduction* and *Affect* or *CIA* for short, and I want to consider each of these aspects in turn.

E. M. Forster saw curiosity as 'one of the lowest of the human faculties', rating it far below intelligence and memory, which he saw as vital for reading.[11] But without curiosity, without the desire to find out what happens next, the reader will simply stop reading. Curiosity is a page-turner, and Bickham's contention that a story should begin with threat just elevates it above the other faculties. However, curiosity is not only aroused by the climber hanging by his fingertips. As Sol Stein says, curiosity can be focused on a character or relationship. Curiosity can be stimulated by the arrangement of words on the page. Toni Morrison's novel *Beloved* begins with the words: '124 was spiteful. Full of baby's venom.'[12] The curious reader may question what these strange sentences mean, and read on to find out. Readers might also be intrigued by ideas. Yann Martel began his novel *Life of Pi* with a debate about sloths and religion, and millions of readers kept reading.

In my first comic novel, *Around the Houses*, I was so keen to rouse the reader's curiosity that I made the very first words a question: 'Anna, what the hell are you doing?', hoping that what it lacked in subtlety it would gain in immediacy.[13] By the time I wrote the next book in the series, *Back Around the Houses*, I was more confident about what I was doing as a writer and less prone to beat the reader about the head with my first sentence. The second novel began: 'Naked and shivering in the early morning light, Gordon Gates knelt awkwardly on the damp grass.'[14] I would probably re-order that sentence now to avoid the comma breaking it in two, but when I was writing that novel, I wanted 'Naked' to be the first word. This beginning also raises questions, and my readers, especially those who already knew Gordon from the first book, might wonder about his unlikely predicament. But it is not quite so in-your-face as the previous one. In the novel I am working on at the moment, I have moved yet further from the urgency of my first beginning. This novel (a pre-teen fantasy) begins with character-focused description:

Elsa Mist sheltered her eyes from the July sun and looked down at Old Shastonbury Street. She could see the roofs of the tumble-down houses sagging under tatty thatches, or worse still, sheets of rusted tin. Rows of stone cottages, all shapes and sizes, all crammed together. Elsa thought the whole street looked like it had been dropped from a great height. Just thrown onto the road, like clay onto a potter's wheel, and squeezed together by giant hands.

In my own writing, then, I seem to be moving slowly from Jack Bickham's advice to 'grab, grab, grab', to James Frey's assertion that character and situation should come first. But I don't think that's quite the case. Each story has its own style, a style established in the very first lines, and as I gain more confidence in my writing, I simply feel more able to explore those possibilities.

The second aspect of CIA, Introduction, is not only about setting, as the quotation from Stein suggests. The beginning introduces the setting, the characters, the tone, the genre, the language, and the point of view of the fiction. When a reader starts reading, it is as if they are sitting in front of a stage that is completely dark. When we are rewriting, we know everything that is on that stage, and everything that is about to happen, but the reader will only see what we show them. Our sentences are like spotlights, our tone like a filter over the lens, changing the mood and colour of the light. Little by little our words illuminate the stage, gradually revealing the story world to the reader, and one of the hardest tasks for a writer is to decide what the first sentence (or spotlight) will reveal and how: What are the characters doing when the lights go up? Which details will bring the scene to life?

The third aspect of CIA, which Stein terms resonance, I have named Affect. Affect is a psychological term for emotional response, and I'm using it to emphasise that writers need to do more than address their readers at an emotional level, they need to *affect* them emotionally. In other words, you do not want your fiction to simply *represent* emotion, through the characters' actions or relationships, you want your writing to *induce* emotion in the reader. You want your reader to feel for your characters, to feel involved in their actions, to feel pleasured by your writing. The beginning needs to *affect* the reader by creating emotional tension (either between the characters, or through their situation), and not allowing that tension to be released (either through aggressive/pitiful outpourings, or through a break in the suspense).

I argued in the first part of this book that the foundations of fiction were pleasure and understanding, and when we begin any fiction, this is what we offer to our reader: a particular kind of pleasure and understanding. The pleasure might be the Aristotelian kind (an emotional purging of pity and fear), or it might be more sentimental (love conquering hardship). Understanding can be emotional or intellectual; but as most fiction takes humanity and human behaviour as its subject, this understanding will usually involve insight into human relationships (even if the characters are aliens, animals or machines). The beginning of your fiction rouses the reader's curiosity, introduces character and setting and affects the reader emotionally, but it also indicates the kinds of pleasure and understanding that your fiction will offer.

What beginnings should do

I've been thinking about beginnings here in terms of opening lines and paragraphs, but in a novel the beginning might extend for a hundred pages, a quarter of the total word length. It is the First Act of the story. The brief guidelines below may help to clarify what your beginning needs to do. Different stories might not tick every box, but if your beginning doesn't accord with any of these guidelines, you need to be very sure, both critically and creatively, why not.

1   Establish the nature of the story (the genre, the tone, the language).
2   Introduce a captivating character (usually the hero/ine) and place them in a compelling situation.
3   Anticipate and initiate the central conflict that will drive the story.
4   Make sure that the hero/ine reaches a point of no return.
5   Introduce the villain (either a person, a group, a force, an environment – whatever stands in the way of the hero/ine's success or happiness).
6   Begin to establish any sub-plots.
7   Introduce diverse and engaging supporting characters.

Questions to ask?

1   Will this opening scene intrigue the reader (does the first page make you want to read on)?
2   Does it provide the motivation for the story (rather than trying to tell the story)?
3   Is something significant at stake for the hero/ine?
4   Does the opening scene illustrate something about the hero/ine's personality?
5   Do the opening events change the lives of the characters or imply that they will be changed?
6   Why does the novel/story have to begin with this setting/event/character?
7   Does the story really begin in Chapter 3 (of the novel) or page 3 (of the short story)?

Middles

> *We are born and we die (beginning – end); the middle needs some significance.*
>
> Richard Kearney, *On Stories* (Routledge)

> *Surprise me with the believable.*
>
> E. M. Forster, *Aspects of the Novel* (Penguin)

The middle, as Richard Kearney implies, is the heart of fiction. The beginning provides the foundation for the story and the ending provides its resolution; but the middle *is* the story. Here is where we see the characters changing, the action intensifying, the stakes getting higher. This is why Joseph Campbell called the middle 'the road of trials', and Oakley Hall terms it 'complication'. For now the tensions established during the beginning take on new significance; they generate the conflict or, as I prefer to call it, struggle at the heart of fiction.[15]

I want to think about two ways in which writers keep their fiction focused upon struggle: scene choice and the use of suspense and surprise. The first point is very simple. The crucial difference between the story you imagine and the story you write is that the former is often a continuous narrative played out in your head, and the latter is distilled into scenes. In other words, the original story is broken into chunks, and to keep the middle of your fiction exciting, you need to decide which 'chunks' should be featured, which should be condensed, and which should be forgotten. If you like to plan, these decisions can be made during prewriting, if not, the triage method should help you to rewrite.[16]

Writing scenes

To stop the middle of your story 'sagging' you need to ask questions about every scene – I'm thinking of a 'scene' here as a continuous focus on one particular moment in the story (an argument, a car journey, a meal). A novel might have many scenes in one chapter, a short story can have anything between one and ten scenes, depending on its length. The first questions you should ask are:

Why do I need this scene?
Why will it interest the reader?
What does it add to the story?

Then consider your answers:

Does it move the story forward?
Does it move the story forward at the right pace?
If not, how could the pace be changed?
Does it reveal character?
Does it provide information?
Does this characterisation or information justify the scene?
Could it be placed somewhere else?

Then think about the reader's response to the scene:

How do you want the reader to feel at the end of this scene?
What should they know or think about your characters/plot?
What questions will be in their mind at the end of the scene?

If the reader has no questions or uncertainties after reading this scene (unless it is the final one), then ask yourself again:

Why do I need this scene?

Nancy Kress advises that writers use the fewest number of scenes to tell their story. She says: 'I've frequently been startled by how much a story can be sharpened by concentrating its events and emotions into the bare minimum of scenes.'[17] I think this a good rule of thumb for writing, whether you write short stories or novels, literary or pulp fiction. Scenes that do not move the story forward will make your middle sag.

Building suspense

Suspense is not just about curiosity, it's about anxiety. It is, as one critic observed, 'a curious mixture of pain and pleasure'.[18] But perhaps the most important feature of suspense is that it only exists in the reader's mind. The writer may work to construct suspense, but that curious mixture of pleasure and pain is a thrill *experienced* only by the reader.

The narratologist Mieke Bal has defined suspense in the following way: 'the reader or the character is made to ask questions which are only answered later ... If suspense is to develop, then the questions will, somehow, be recalled repeatedly.'[19] And she suggests three forms of suspense: firstly the riddle or search (like a detective story) where neither the character nor the reader knows what is to come; secondly the threat, where the reader knows something the character doesn't; and thirdly the secret, where the character knows something the reader doesn't. These different forms become clearer if we examine a clichéd moment of suspense: a young woman in an empty house hears a noise and goes to investigate. If we write this scene as a riddle or search, where neither reader nor character knows what caused the noise, we can create different levels of suspense.

Scenario 1: The girl hears a noise and runs out of the house to tell someone As readers, we feel some suspense because questions have been raised in our mind: What was the noise? Will the girl find someone? Where is she going? But the suspense will not be unbearable because it's been diluted by all the potential answers to these questions. We can anticipate all sorts of possibilities. To increase suspense the writer must raise questions in the reader's mind that have only a limited number of answers, answers that are predictable enough for the reader to anticipate (although of course the writer might ultimately do something entirely unpredictable with the story).

Scenario 2: The girl hears a noise and goes down to the cellar to investigate

Now the suspense is more extreme because the questions in the reader's mind are more focused: Is something/someone in the cellar? Will the girl be hurt? These questions have a limited number of predictable answers: either yes or no.

This is a very familiar example, but all suspense works in a similar way: by raising questions in the reader's mind that have only two or three possible answers. If, for example, a character we care about is dangerously ill, the reader knows that there are three possible outcomes. The character might die, the character might recover completely, or the character might be disfigured or disabled by the illness. Because the story has three predictable outcomes, the reader is caught between these possibilities, and if the writer withholds information about what happens (by moving to a sub-plot, or another character, or a memory) it creates suspense.

Scenario 3: A man carrying an axe crawls through the small cellar window. The girl hears a noise and goes down to the cellar to investigate.

Bal's second form of suspense, threat, occurs when the reader knows something the character doesn't. In this case, the reader is told that the noise was caused by a man with an axe crawling through the window. This time, the questions in our mind are even more focused and immediate: Will the girl see the axe-man in time? Will she escape? Will she be killed? Our anxiety increases. This is the suspense that directors like Alfred Hitchcock preferred. He argued that:

> It is possible to build up almost unbearable tension in a play or film in which the audience knows who the murderer is all the time, and from the very start they want to scream out to all the other characters in the plot, 'Watch out for So-and-So! He's a killer!' There you have real tenseness and an irresistible desire to know what happens ... I believe in giving the audience all the facts as early as possible.[20]

He illustrated this point with a famous example in which there is a bomb hidden in a school classroom. If the audience is unaware of the bomb, the explosion will be a terrible surprise, but if the audience sees it under the desk ticking away, the suspense will become unbearable. Then the director (or writer) can play on the audience's anxiety: first the teacher suggests the children play outside (relief), but then one child reminds her about their homework (anxiety) and so on.

Scenario 4: A man carrying an axe crawls through the cellar window. The girl hears a noise and goes down to the cellar to investigate. He finds the girl and kisses her.

Bal's third kind of suspense is the secret, where the characters know more that the reader. This form of suspense may initially arouse similar anxieties to the threat, and then resolve (or exacerbate) those anxieties by revealing the secret (in this scenario, the axe-man is the girl's secret lover). Most first-person narratives are based upon this kind of suspense (because the character-narrators have usually already lived through the events they now relate to the reader). Shirley Jackson's short story 'The Lottery' is a good example of a third-person form of this suspense. In the story the inhabitants of a New England town are preparing for a lottery and only at the end of the story do we realise the secret: the lottery determines who among the characters will be stoned to death. This kind of suspense works by foreshadowing, where the writer manipulates the reader's unease and sense of anticipation, and is close to narrative surprise.

When we use suspense in fiction, we need to balance the immediate thrills and instant gratification of the axe-murderer in the cellar with the extended suspense raised by questions that run throughout the entire narrative. For 'real suspense comes with moral dilemma and the courage to make and act upon choices. False suspense comes from the accidental and meaningless occurrence of one damned thing after another.'[21] To keep the suspense alive, to turn the screw in the reader's mind, we need to keep returning to the overall dilemma that underpins all the lesser incidents and excitements.

Creating surprise

Surprise differs from suspense in that, whereas we can imagine suspense like a fork in the road ahead of us (one way the girl is killed by the axe-man, the other way she escapes), surprise occurs when we thought the road was smooth and didn't see the fork coming (the axe-man is her lover). Michael Toolan makes this point when he argues that 'the essence of narrative surprise is that a reader experiences a new development as unforeseen but, upon reflection, foreseeable.'[22] In other words, the surprise isn't just arbitrary, like an accident, it was there as a possibility all the time, but as readers we overlooked the clues. In 'The Lottery', for instance, we see the children gathering stones at the beginning and misinterpret this as a childish game. To give another example, when in *Great Expectations* we discover that Pip's benefactor is not Miss Havisham, but the convict Magwitch, we are surprised, but we know that if we'd looked for it, we might have seen it coming. However, when, as a child, Pip was first grabbed by Magwitch in the lonely graveyard, this was a very different kind of surprise, and one that very few readers might have been expected to predict.

Narrative surprises give a 'little jolt of self-correction' to the reader, recasting the previous events in the story in light of the unexpected twist.[23] And this means that the surprise, although seeming to come out of the blue, needs to 'fit' with the rest of the story. The outcome of the lottery and Pip's comeuppance are fitting, but if the surprise had been outlandish, or insufficiently prepared, the reader might have felt cheated. Say the lottery had ended with an alien invasion, or Pip had discovered that Joe Gargery was his secret benefactor, as readers we may well have been astonished, but we would also have been unconvinced. When using surprise, remember E. M. Forster's advice, and surprise your readers with the believable.

What middles should do

1 Tell the story (the beginning introduces it, the ending resolves it)
2 Increase the momentum of the story
3 Complicate the hero/ine's path and the intensify the potential for failure
4 Build tension in the relationships between the characters
5 Reveal the hero/ine's emotional turmoil
6 Utilise suspense and surprise
7 Tantalise readers with a drip-drip of information
8 Vary the pace and rhythm of scenes
9 Develop the sub-plots in a novel (to avoid a one-dimensional story)
10 Introduce all remaining sub-plots and characters

Questions to ask

1 Have you used coincidence or contrivance to develop the plot?
2 Is the struggle weaker in the middle of the story than at the beginning?
3 Do you relieve the suspense too soon? Or too late (when the reader has begun to lose interest)?
4 Does every scene contribute to the forward momentum of the story?
5 If a scene does not move the story forward, why is it there?
6 Are the sub-plots interwoven with the main story?
7 Are surprises foreshadowed?

Endings

We cannot of course be denied an end; it is one of the great charms of books that they have to end. But unless we are extremely naïve ... we do not ask that they progress towards that end precisely as we have been given to believe.
    Frank Kermode, *The Sense of an Ending* (Oxford University Press)

An ending must seem inevitable without being predictable.
    Raymond Obstfeld, *Novelist's Essential Guide to Crafting Scenes*
                                                  (Writer's Digest Books)

As a writer, it's important to recognise that there is a difference between an ending, which all fiction will necessarily have, and closure. Closure is the moment when all questions are answered and all expectations fulfilled. In H. Porter Abbott's words: 'Closure brings satisfaction to desire, relief to suspense, and clarity to confusion.'[24] It is the moment the reader has been waiting for (and perhaps dreading): for as soon as there is closure the story is over. During the middle, and for most of the ending, writers will hold off such closure, keeping their readers oscillating between painful suspense and partial gratification. But during the final scenes the writer must provide those readers with some form of closure.

This does not mean to say, however, that everything must be neatly resolved, for, as literary theorists have pointed out, closure has two distinct levels: the level of expectations and the level of questions. I would suggest that to be a good writer we need to provide closure at the level of expectations. We need to think about what Nancy Kress has called 'the implicit promise' of the fiction, a promise that raised certain expectations about the way the story would end.[25] We made the promise in the beginning, then developed or re-stated it in the middle, and at the end we need to honour it. We need to fulfil the expectations it raised.

To give an example, if a novel opens with the murder of a politician, we might initially expect that the ending will reveal who murdered her and why. If the middle of the narrative continues to reinforce those expectations and then the novel ends without answering those questions, we would feel cheated. If, however, the middle of the novel revealed that the politician's murder was only a minor part of a much larger conspiracy, our expectations of the ending would change. We might still expect to find out something about the politician's murder (why she was killed, say, rather than precisely who killed her), but we probably wouldn't expect everyone involved in the conspiracy to be identified, convicted and imprisoned. If we did get such absolute closure we might even feel disappointed, because the twist in the middle has altered our expectations, and now such a 'happy ending' doesn't fit.

By saying that a good writer will provide closure at the level of expectations, I do not mean to imply that the ending cannot be a total surprise – in fact very often surprise is an expectation itself, as Frank Kermode implied – but the surprise should have its roots in the body of the story, rather than being an unforeseeable act of God tacked on in the final pages. Endings, then, should both fulfil and exceed the reader's expectations, 'seeming inevitable' without, as Raymond Obstfeld said, 'being predictable'. They should reach closure at the level of expectations, even if they do not reach such closure at the level of questions.

If we return to our political thriller, we can see that as a murder-mystery our initial questions (who killed the politician and why?) would carry us through the story. Along the way, there will be false or partial answers to these questions (red herrings, misleading evidence), but ultimately we expect the ending to provide closure: we expect the right answers. In the second version, the conspiracy, our questions will change. Now we want to know what connection the politician had to the larger conspiracy, and whether her death was significant. We expect these questions to be addressed at the end of the story, but recognise that as the situation becomes more complex, other questions will remain unanswered. This novel will end by providing partial closure.

In traditionally plotted short stories and novels, the ending will reach total resolution, with closure at the levels of expectations and questions. But many other stories refuse to give such comfortable resolution. Some fiction explores emotions or situations that cannot be resolved, and it's this ambiguity that fascinates both writer and reader. If we think back to Katherine Mansfield's story 'The Fly', which explores the unendurable nature of grief, we can see that the power of the story comes from its ultimate ambiguity. 'The Fly' fulfilled the implicit promise it made to the reader. It presented 'the question minus the answer' (to use French theorist Roland Barthes' description of literature), and the ending was appropriately indeterminate. The critic I. A. Richards called literature 'a machine to think with', a pleasant way of contemplating life's questions. A story that raises moral, philosophical or religious questions will not 'close' those questions at the end. Such a story may answer (or provide closure to) questions about the fate of its various characters and the consequences of their various actions (or it may not), but those more abstract questions will remain open. They will linger in the reader's mind.

What endings should do

1 Bring the struggle to its dramatic conclusion
2 Bring the main plot and sub-plots together (if they have not converged already)
3 Make the resolution of the hero/ine's struggle emotionally intense
4 Show how the character has grown (in a novel)
5 Include a short final scene/chapter after the climax (in a novel) to show the characters settling back into their life

Questions to ask

1 Have you left loose threads – characters abandoned or plot lines inappropriately unresolved?
2 Does the ending 'fit' the implicit promise and worldview of the story?
3 What kind of closure does the ending achieve?
4 If the ending is a surprise, has this ending been foreshadowed within the story or is it just a convenient accident?

9   S u b j e c t s

Literature is written by, for, and about people. . . . [But] the people with whom literature is concerned are not real people. They are fabricated creatures made up from fantasy, imitation, memory: paper people, without flesh and blood.

> Mieke Bal, *Narratology* (University of Toronto Press)

When writing a novel a writer should create living people; people not characters. A character is a caricature.

> Ernest Hemingway, *Death in the Afternoon* (Vintage)

A character is not a simulation of a living being. It is an imaginary being. An experimental self.

> Milan Kundera, *The Art of the Novel* (Faber & Faber)

Characters are the true subjects of fiction and whether we see our characters as 'living people' or 'paper people', 'fabricated creatures', 'imaginary beings', or 'experimental selves', their presence will fundamentally shape the stories we write. As novelists and short-story writers, we can question the construction of identity, the nature of humanity, or the enigmas of the psyche: we can manipulate characters as pawns within our plot or we can invest them with emotional and moral complexity. In this chapter, I consider three ways of presenting characters: as *autonomous subjects*, as *fragmented subjectivities*, or as empty vessels *subjected to* the vagaries of society or the author.

In *Orality and Literacy*, Walter Ong makes the point that 'rounded' characterisation in novels corresponded to the development in science of depth psychology, and he argues that: 'just as depth psychology looks for some obscure but highly significant deeper meaning hidden beneath the surface of ordinary life, so novelists from Austen to Thackeray to Flaubert invite the reader to sense some truer meaning beneath the flawed or fraudulent surface they portray.'[1] He suggests that novels and stories that are written down and read, rather than simply listened to, have changed the way people think about themselves and society, arguing that 'the feeling for human existence has been processed through writing and print.'[2]

In other words, written stories have developed an idea of character and characterisation that has then informed real human relationships in everyday life. Life has mimicked art. Fictional characters might be seen as people who 'happened never to exist', as Seymour Chatman puts it, but for Ong people who *do* exist become fictional characters through the 'novelisation' of life.[3] A similar point is made by the Russian critic Mikhail Bakhtin, for as Michael Holquist observes: 'the emergence of the novel is for him an event in not only the history of literature, but the history of *perception*: for those who have experienced novelness, the world will not look the same.'[4]

Fiction has always explored human relationships and individual identities, and by the end of the nineteenth century, the notion that characters were true *subjects* who had 'hidden depths' had become firmly established as the norm. But attitudes changed, and by the twentieth century writers began to challenge that idea of the stable, deep character in a number of ways. Writers like Virginia Woolf and Alain Robbe-Grillet focused on the inexpressibility of character, or the shifting, incoherent nature of the self. In novels like *Jacob's Room* or *The Erasers* they focused on the objects around the shadowy characters, rather than the characters themselves who remained fleeting and *fragmented subjectivites*. Other writers, like Franz Kafka, Samuel Beckett and Thomas Pynchon went further and hollowed out their characters, revealing their powerlessness within the world. Here characters were not so much subjects as *subject to* the faceless forces of society (as well as the whims of the author) and the idea of a stable self amidst the chaos was lost: characters were cogs in the wheels of a larger machine.

As contemporary writers in the twenty-first century we have many models of characterisation to inspire us when we populate our own fiction, but before I explore them in detail, I want to consider the role of simpler characterisations.

Creating characters

Characterization is not a virtue, it is a technique; you use it when it will enhance your story; and when it won't, you don't. . . . It's a mistake to think that deep, detailed characterization is an absolute virtue in storytelling.

Orson Scott Card, *Characters and Viewpoint* (Writer's Digest Books)

Orson Scott Card cuts across what he sees as 'the fashion of our time' and argues that complex or robust characterisation is not vital for all fiction. He goes back to E. M. Forster's influential distinction between flat and round characters in *Aspects of the Novel* and argues that the flat characters are just as important for fiction as the rounded ones: it all depends on the kind of story you want to write. Forster argued that 'really flat character can be expressed in one sentence,' and he gave several examples, from Dickens to Proust, of characters whose entire being could be summed up in this way: ' "I will never desert Mr Micawber". There is Mrs Micawber – she says she won't desert Mr Micawber; she doesn't, and there she is.'[5] In other words, flat characters are predictable and they are often used by writers to serve specific functions within the story.

By contrast rounded characters are unpredictable. Forster argues that 'the test of a round character is whether it is capable of surprising in a convincing way. If it never surprises it is flat. If it does not convince, it is flat pretending to be round.'[6] Seymour Chatman calls Forster's round characters 'open-ended', claiming that they are 'virtu-ally inexhaustible objects for contemplation'.[7] He focuses on the reader's response to the characters to decide whether they are flat or round, and in doing so, reminds us that characterisation is not simply 'done' by the author. It is a more complex process.

We can begin to unpick this process by considering Patrick O'Neill's suggestion that there are 'three interacting processes of characterisa-tion'. He argues that there is 'a process of construction by the author, a process of reconstruction by the reader, and, pre-shaping both of these, a process of *pre*-construction by contextual constraints and expectations, whether adhered to or rejected, such as that "heroes" should be tall, dark, and handsome, detectives should be clever, and the "boy" should meet the "girl" and live happily ever after.'[8] As writers creating characters we are already responding to the cultural expectations of our time, to the prevailing ideas about humanity and identity in life and art (even if we are doing so unconsciously). But if we develop a sense of critical-creativity we may be more aware of the ways in which we respond to these presumptions in our writing.

Our characters, then, are *born* from our particular reactions to the 'contextual constraints and expectations' around us, but our charac-ters *grow* in the mind of the reader. In characterisation, as in all else, the reader is our creative accomplice. The reader 'reads' the character, trying to decide upon their hidden traits and motivations, just as they try to figure out the people around them in daily life. We do not need to tell the reader every single detail from a character's biography, or create a photographic image of their appearance, to encourage them to 'picture' that character. We need to focus on particular details, the subtle nuances that make that character unique. From this, the reader will create an image of the character that is both rich with possibilities and intensely private.[9] William James makes the point very well: 'An unlearned carpenter of my acquaintance once said in my hearing "There is very little difference between one man and another; but what there is, is very important." This distinction seems to me to go to the root of the matter.'[10]

Characters as subjects

A character is interesting as it comes out, and by the process and duration of that emergence; just as a procession is effective by the way it unrolls, turning to a mere mob if all of it passes at once.
Henry James, Perface to Vol. 10 of the New York Edition,
www.henryjames.org.uk/prefaces/text10_inframe.htm

Another way to think about the differences between the 'flat' or 'round' character is through the work of Mikhail Bakhtin. Bakhtin was working in Russia, with no knowledge of Forster's book, but he came to very similar conclusions about character. In his view, a 'person' in literature was very different from a 'character'. He called characters 'monologic', meaning that they were somehow finished off, without the possibility of growth. A 'person' on the other hand was 'dialogic', a self that is still unfolding, like Henry James' procession, and thus unpredictable.[11] Bakhtin praised Dostoevsky as the master-creator of such people, populating his fiction not with 'voiceless slaves ... but free people, capable of standing alongside their creator, capable of not agreeing with him and even rebelling against him.'[12]

For Bakhtin the most successful character (or person) was one who would 'answer the author back', and he saw Dostoevsky's uniqueness as being able to 'visualize and portray personality as another, as someone else's personality, without making it lyrical or merging it with his own voice'.[13] He traced this ability back to Dostoevsky's perception of his characters as autonomous people who would hear him when he spoke about them, and argued that he wrote about his characters as if he were writing about 'someone actually present, someone who hears him (the author) and is capable of answering him'.[14]

Bakhtin's description of characters as autonomous subjects might help us avoid what John Gardner sees as the 'chief offence in bad fiction' which occurs when readers 'sense the characters are being manipulated, forced to do things they would not really do'.[15] If as writers we imagine our characters as people living in a different dimension, then it might make us more responsive to them. As writers working with a plot we will inevitably manipulate our characters into uncomfortable situations, but their reactions to those situations should be their own.

By 'visualising someone else's personality', as Bakhtin says, you allow your character to react to the situations you have created for them, rather than forcing them into certain behaviours, and this allows you to observe the way the character changes as a result of the experiences they have been through. This change is usually known as the character arc, and like the story arc it is a fundamental aspect of fiction. The character arc describes the central transformation of the main character, and there are many ways in which this transformation can be achieved. For instance, you could write about characters who change (for good or ill) when they break free from social or family constraints; or you could write about characters who desperately want to change but are pulled back again and again to their old self; or characters who change despite their best efforts to stay as they were.[16]

By thinking more carefully about how your characters would behave, you can explore the possibilities of their making wrong decisions. You can leave the reader wondering whether things would have been different if the character had made different choices; and whether they will realise their mistake as the story progresses. This sense of other possibilities, some not quite gone, will give the character more depth. And if it is through action that a character reveals who they really are, then their reactions to (the consequences of) previous (mistaken) actions will push such revelations further.

But what if, as a writer, you feel that your characters are less like Homo Fictus, as E. M. Forster called them, and more like Frankenstein's monster, when he needed to 'infuse a spark of being into the lifeless thing that lay at his feet'.[17] I have had characters like this; characters with traits, histories and motivations who despite all my efforts stare back at me like a collection of dead parts on the slab. We need lightning to strike. But in this case, the lightning is not the electric flash of inspiration so much as a long process of getting to know the character you are trying to create.

One way of doing this is to ask your character to write letters to you (or another character) about anything they think is important. If you ask characters 'to tell you about themselves' you often end up reciting the features and histories you already know. But by asking more indirect questions, such as 'What TV do you watch?' or 'Which politician would you vote for?', or by making them communicate with another character, you allow yourself to find out more about the character's own motivations. Short exercises like this can really help to understand and bring to life those characters you find difficult to write.

Fractured subjectivities

All novels, of every age, are concerned with the enigma of the self. As soon as you create an imaginary being, a character, you are automatically confronted by the question: What is the self? How can it be grasped? It is one of those fundamental questions on which the novel, as novel, is based.

Milan Kundera, *The Art of the Novel* (Faber & Faber)

One way to approach the 'enigma of the self' as a writer is to draw from Bakhtin's theories about character. We may accept that we can never represent the whole of a character in fiction. We may go further and argue that we can never truly understand the characters we invent, but only glimpse their identity through fragments of thought, appearance and action. Bakhtin suggests that the self cannot have an 'identity' in isolation, but exists only in relation to other selves; just as characters exist only in relation to other characters (even if those characters appear in memories or dreams). This is why he put so much emphasis on dialogue in fiction, because it is one way of working out the *relationship* between selves. The way a character is unique can only be understood in relation to other characters. We can think about this in more detail by focusing on the word 'I'.

We all use this word, and all our characters use it, but as a word it is totally empty. The linguist Roman Jacobson argued that the word 'I' is 'an empty no man's land' which each person fills with the meaning of themselves. And that is what we do. We fill the emptiness of 'I' with the (imaginary) essence of ourselves. 'I' becomes the position from which we look out onto the world, and because no one can stand where I am standing at precisely the same moment as me, this position gives my 'I' its uniqueness. The same is true of the characters we write. They fill their 'I' with the meaning of themselves because no one can stand where they stand. Their place in the world and their view of that world is unique.

For Bakhtin, the self (the perceiver) and the other (the perceived) exist not as separate entities, but as relations between two coordinates, each differentiating the other. In other words, a character's identity is only produced in relation to someone else: through reactions to, dialogues with, and thoughts about another. As one character in Iris Murdoch's *Nuns and Soldiers* says: 'Your life doesn't belong to you. . . . Who can tell where his life ends? Our being spreads out far beyond us and mingles with the being of others. We live in other people's thoughts, in their plans, in their dreams.'[18]

Many writers have explored this sense of subjectivity as relational, and some have taken it further, creating composite characters where one person's identity is divided between several different characters. Joanna Russ does this in her experimental novel *The Female Man*. The main character is Joanna (sharing the name of the author), who meets three other women of the same genotype living in different dimensions, Jeannine, Janet and Jael. Together these women, the four Js, constitute the alternative selves of one woman, different dimensions of one personality.

This is one way of suggesting the mutability of personality in fiction; one way of exploring how people are shaped and distorted by their environment. Other twentieth-century writers, from Iris Murdoch to Marguerite Duras, focused instead on characters that were fractured by their own memories, desires and neuroses. Influenced by Freudian psychoanalysis, these writers explored the vulnerability of personality, the alienation from society, and the symptoms of repression and denial that can be 'read' to reveal the true self underneath.

In Murdoch's *The Black Prince*, for instance, Bradley Pearson says: 'We are tissues and tissues of different personae and yet we are nothing at all. . . . Angels must wonder at these beings who fall so regularly out of awareness into a fantasm-infested dark. How our frail identities survive these chasms no philosopher has ever been able to explain.'[19] Writers such as Murdoch, who explore the *fractured subjectivities* of their characters, might be seen as tracing psychological symptoms to find a real self hidden beneath.

Drawing upon the work of psychoanalysts like Sigmund and Anna Freud enables writers to hint at 'symptoms' to suggest ways in which their characters are riven by anxiety and uncertainty. There is no space here to consider such theories in depth, but Anna Freud's work on what she calls 'defence mechanisms', ways in which we try to cope with a threatening world, offer useful insights for writers and are worth pausing over. An article in *The Journal of Psychotherapy Practice and Research* states that: 'In psychoanalytical theory, *character* is conceived of as the individual's attempt to bring the tasks presented by internal demands and by the external world into harmony, resulting in a typical constellation of traits by which we recognize the particular person.'[20] In other worlds, character is born out of struggle: the struggle to function when our own desires clash against the demands of the world around us.

Anna Freud's work detailed various ways in which we cope with this struggle, which we might more simply call anxiety, by using psychic defence mechanisms. These defences begin with simple denial, where a character will refuse to acknowledge a problem, or will imaginatively distort the real situation by creating a fiction that suits them better – denial in fantasy. Tobias Wolff's story, 'A Bullet to the Brain', offers a powerful version of such denial. When a jaded book-reviewer is caught up in a bank robbery he judges it loudly, with studied cynicism and contempt, as an appalling cliché. Only when the bullet is going through his brain does he shed this world-weary intellectualism, and savour the memory of lost pleasures. The bullet leaves 'the troubled skull . . . dragging its comet's tail of memory and hope and talent and love'.[21]

Another basic defence is repression, or as Anna Freud called it 'motivated forgetting', in which an experience, usually a traumatic experience, is completely forgotten, but emerges indirectly through such things as inexplicable phobias or unconscious gestures. In Sherwood Anderson's 'Hands', for example, the ageing schoolteacher, who has been (falsely) accused of sexually perverted behaviour, cannot prevent his hands from continuous movement.

The denial of desire can be a major motivation for characters, especially when this denial is unconscious. Asceticism is the form of defence in which people deny their desires, starving themselves either physically (as in Franz Kafka's 'The Hunger Artist') or emotionally (as Miss Havisham does in Dickens' *Great Expectations*) because they are afraid of their own desires, especially emerging sexual desires. Linked to this is isolation (or intellectualisation), in which a difficult or traumatic memory is stripped of emotion, so that, as George Boeree says: 'A person may, in a very cavalier manner, acknowledge that they had been abused as a child, or may show a purely intellectual curiosity in their newly discovered sexual orientation. Something that should be a big deal is treated as if it were not.'[22] Margaret Atwood's story 'Hairball', which explores a woman's intellectualisation of her abortions and childlessness, is a good example of such isolation. When the central character, Kat, has an operation to remove a dermoid cyst from her ovary she brings it home as her 'warped child' and calls it Hairball (dermoid cysts are made of hair, skin, bone and teeth). This confrontation with such horror and loss breaks down her psychic defence and she experiences emotional collapse.

Another defence mechanism that might particularise a character is displacement, where a desire or impulse is redirected from its real object onto something else, as in Raymond Carver's short story 'Little Things' where the fighting parents express their hatred for each other by pulling their baby apart. Displacement can involve the substitution of one emotion for another or of one object for another. For instance, a character who is angry with his parents may substitute his anger for a more acceptable emotion, becoming more affectionate with his mother and father (Anna Freud called this 'believing the opposite') only to vent his fury on others. This character may also displace his anger onto himself, causing depression or feelings of inferiority, or he may project it elsewhere, perhaps accusing other people of abusing their elderly parents. Finally, he may unconsciously take on the very characteristics he despises in his parents, treating others as they treat him (Annie Proulx has drawn upon this cycle of repeated abuse in her story 'Bedrock').

Many writers have explored such displacements in their fiction. Flannery O'Connor plays out the tragic consequences of displacement in her story 'The Lame Shall Enter First' when Sheppard displaces grief for his dead wife into affection for the wrong object: not his son Norton, but an impoverished teenage boy, Rufus, who manipulates him and precipitates Norton's suicide. R.V. Cassill also explores displacement in 'The Father'. After an accident, Cory Johnson was forced to amputate his son's hand, and although his son lives and does not blame him, the father's guilt is displaced onto a need for punishment that drives him to re-enact his crime.

Characters as empty vessels

If many early-twentieth-century writers presented their characters through 'symptoms' that could be deciphered by the reader, it can be argued that many late-twentieth-century writers lost faith in such a notion of the self, however neurotic or anxious that self may be. For these writers, a character's 'symptoms' did not reveal the troubled soul beneath, they simply reflected society back to itself. Character (indeed the self) becomes surface, a mirror which appears to show a person(ality), but which contains nothing. Character is a virtual image. A trick of the light. In the work of these writers characters are empty vessels, collections of words, fabricated beings without coherent identity.

In more experimental fictions, there has been a rebellion against what Michael Toolan terms the 'bourgeois self-determining subject'.[23] Novelists like Alain Robbe-Grillet and William Gass attacked what they saw as the cult of the individual, saying that 'novels that contain characters belong well and truly to the past'[24] and asserting that characters in fiction have no reality: '[s]tories and the people in them are made of words.'[25] Literary critics also rebuked those who saw characters as anything other than black marks on paper. In 1979, Joel Weinsheimer summed up this literalist approach when he claimed that 'Emma Woodhouse is not a woman nor need be described as if it were.'[26]

The sense that characters are not people, but simply a collection of words, denies the fact that the character lives not on the page but in the mind of the reader. However, many writers have played with this literalism, exploring the fact that their characters are 'paper people', born into words rather than bodies. Jeanette Winterson, for instance, creates characters like the Dog Woman in *Sexing the Cherry* or Villanelle in *The Passion* whose bodies defy physical possibility, and in *Written on the Body* she exposes the unreal, non-physical nature of her characters in two opposing ways. Firstly, the reader is told so little about the narrator-character's body that we are not even sure whether the protagonist is male or female, and secondly Winterson devotes chapter after chapter to a detailed anatomy of the lover's body, when 'flesh and blood' are precisely what fictional characters are missing.

Winterson's writing celebrates the uncertainty within her characters, and whereas previous writers might have responded to their characters' anxieties by tracing the symptoms back to their disturbed psyches, Winterson is part of a generation who, as philosopher Slavoj Žižek says, 'enjoy their symptom'. The symptom is no longer seen as evidence of the hidden self, but as evidence of the illusory self. For Žižek and other theorists, our identity is neither fixed nor stable. There is no core to our character, which can be expressed through actions and behaviour. Our identity is simply an image, a pretence that appeases other people's expectations and disguises our own emptiness. As writers, these ideas can be liberating (if life is a game of images, then our characters can push at the limits of possibility), but they can also be terrifying. If there is no 'self' or identity, if life is all image, surface with no depth, then how can we find meaning in our own existence?

This issue has been explored by very different writers, from Nick Hornby to Bret Easton Ellis. In *About a Boy*, Hornby introduces the character Will as a construction of his cultural moment:

> Sixty years ago, all the things Will relied on to get him through the day simply didn't exist: there was no daytime TV, there were no videos, there were no glossy magazines . . . Now though it was easy. There was almost too much to do. You didn't have to have a life of your own any more; you could just peek over the fence at other people's lives, as lived in newspapers and *Eastenders* and films and exquisitely sad jazz songs or tough rap songs. The twenty-year-old Will would have been surprised and perhaps disappointed to learn that he would reach the age of thirty-six without finding a life for himself, but the thirty-six-year-old Will wasn't particularly unhappy about it; there was less clutter that way.[27]

But if Will begins by proclaiming his shallowness, his sense of life as a pastiche of sound-bites and images, he ends by finding love. Friends and family are represented as the solution to Will's post-existential emptiness and the novel offers a humane response to such postmodern bleakness. But if Hornby's *About a Boy* could be accused of sentimentality, then Bret Easton Ellis's *American Psycho* could be seen as the nihilistic alternative. Ellis's character, Patrick Bateman, also exists 'in the banal hollow of popular culture'. As Alex E. Blazer argues: 'Bateman is an idea and an image, but empty and void of deep identity. . . . His character is a mask covering a void; his identity is an aberrational reaction to the abyss of being that founds his existence.'[28]

Whereas Hornby's Will escapes the meaninglessness of his existence through love, Bateman reacts to the loss of self and meaning in his world with violence: his own way, perhaps, of 'enjoying his symptom'. His society (and his narrative) is cluttered by material objects (designer clothes, beauty products, domestic technologies), and images (day-time TV shows, pornography, horror videos, MTV), but his sense of self is receding: 'there is an idea of a Patrick Bateman, some kind of abstraction, but there is no real me, only an entity, something illusory, and though I can hide my cold gaze and you can shake my hand and feel flesh gripping yours . . . : I simply am not there. It is hard for me to make sense on any given level. Myself is fabricated, an aberration. I am a noncontingent human being. My personality is sketchy and unformed.'[29]

Ellis is drawing attention to the fictionality of his character here (he does not exist beyond these pages), but he is also suggesting something about the dangerous fragility of identity within contemporary consumerist culture. As the novel progresses Bateman's narrative voice breaks down: the sentences stumble as the 'reality' presented becomes less and less credible. His voice betrays him as his subjectivity slips away. This approach to characterisation rejects the novelistic orthodoxy, whereby the reader comes to know and appreciate the subtleties of the characters. Instead, the more the reader attempts to understand a character like Patrick Bateman, the more he slips away, disintegrating into incoherent fragments.

As writers, the way we conceive our characters (as complex personalities; fractured, experimental beings-in-process, or inchoate deconstructions of the illusory self) will have a profound influence on the kind of fiction we write. Our perception of character will affect not only the subjects within our fiction but the style of our writing, and especially our use of voice and point of view. The next two chapters will explore these issues in more depth.

10 Voices

[A novel is] a diversity of individual voices, artistically organised.
Mikhail Bakhtin, *The Dialogic Imagination* (University of
Texas Press)

Fiction is made up of different voices: the narrator's, the characters'
and beneath them the disguised and whispered voice of the author.
Mikhail Bakhtin saw this cacophony of voices as the most exciting
thing about fiction and he called the novel 'polyphonic' because he
said it was a 'plurality of independent and unmerged voices and
consciousnesses'.[1] For Bakhtin, these voices gave fiction its distinct-
iveness, and if we think about the voices of our characters, the way
they use words (their ordering and rhythm, dialect and grammar,
loquaciousness or brevity) reveals much about their consciousness.
The same applies to the narrator's voice, whether or not the narrator
'appears' as a character in the story. The narrator's voice carries with
it a certain perspective, a point of view that frames their telling of the
events in the story.

I want to follow Bakhtin's argument that voice and point of view are
both expressions of the 'polyphonic' perspective of fiction. We cannot
fully understand voice (who speaks) unless we also understand point
of view (who sees), and so in this chapter I want to consider voice
and point of view together.

Point of view

The term 'point of view' is so familiar to writers that I think it's worth
keeping, even though most critical studies of narrative have rejected
it as confusing and vague. And the critics have a point. One of their
main objections to 'point of view' is that, as a term, it asks 'Who sees?'
without asking, or making clear, 'Who speaks?'. For these critics, the
term 'point of view' ignores the importance of voice in establishing
narrative perspective, and this is why Bakhtin's description of the
novel as 'polyphonic' is so useful.

To give an example of the difference between 'point of view' and 'voice' we can think of Henry James's *What Maisie Knew*. The main *point of view* character, the character who 'sees' the action, is Maisie, an innocent young girl who does not realise the sexual significance of the adult behaviour around her. But the *voice* of the narration is an adult voice, which uses words Maisie never would, allowing the adult reader to know more than Maisie 'sees', for example: 'Maisie received in petrification the full force of her mother's huge and painted eyes – they were like Japanese lanterns swung under festal arches.'[2] The overall perspective of the novella, then, is caught between the innocent eyes of Maisie and the knowing intelligence of the narrator.

Focalisation

The narratologist Shlomith Rimmon-Kenan also rejects the term 'point of view' and instead uses Gérard Genette's term 'focalisation' to suggest how the story is both seen and told.[3] She identifies several aspects of focalisation and I want to introduce three of them as potentially useful for writers: the perceptual, the psychological and the ideological. When we are thinking about point of view there are many questions we might ask about the position of our narrator: will he or she be a character or remain on the margins of the story?; will he use the first or third person?; will she tell the truth?, and so on. Rimmon-Kenan's analysis might help us to clarify the possibilities.

The *perceptual* aspect of point of view simply refers to how much a narrator sees. If the narrator is a character or a witness who stumbles upon the story, they may only see parts of the action, or piece together the whole story from other people's narratives (as Lockwood does in Emily Brontë's *Wuthering Heights*). If the narrator is a disembodied voice outside the story, they may see everything that happens, even when it happens in different places at the same time (as does the narrator in George Eliot's *Middlemarch*).

The *psychological* aspect of focalisation refers to the idiosyncrasies of the narrator, the personal hang-ups and quirks that make the narrator unique (such as Lemony Snicket's digressions in *A Series of Unfortunate Events*). If a character-narrator is emotionally involved in the action (as Lemony Snicket is), the narrative will be very different from one that is told by a distant, objective voice (even if, as readers, we are not made aware of their involvement until the end). The narrator will have their own slant on the events, positive or negative, that reflects their own self-interest. Agatha Christie's *The Murder of Roger Ackroyd* provides a twist on this technique: we ultimately discover that the narrator of the mystery is himself the murderer.

The third aspect of focalisation is the *ideological*, which represents the world-view of the narrator. For even invisible, third-person narrators frame the narrative (perhaps reflecting the unquestioned opinions of the author). We need to ask: how does the narrator judge the characters?; how does he or she interpret events?; how do his or her beliefs affect the narrative? Michael Holquist has argued that 'everything is perceived from a unique position in existence; its corollary is that the meaning of whatever is observed is shaped by the place from which it is perceived.'[4] In other words, the point of view within a story provides a frame of reference that can change not only the mood, but the meaning of the tale.

In the pages that follow I want to consider the way 'voice' and 'point of view' intertwine, firstly by thinking through the different ways of presenting perspective in a story, and secondly by considering how dialogue can work as a clash of competing, or dissimilar, points of view.

Viewpoint, voice and distance

> *Third person and first person are at least as different as major and minor keys.*
>
> Norman Mailer, *The Spooky Art* (Random House)

When thinking about voice and point of view, one of the fundamental decisions a writer makes is whether to write in the first, second or third person: to write using 'I', 'you' or 'he/she'. If, like Norman Mailer, we imagine this in terms of music, then first and third person are indeed as different as major and minor, but there are many other nuances in narrative approach that can change the feel of the story as much as changing from G major to G minor. I want to simplify these subtleties by thinking about point of view in terms of *viewpoint* (what the character/narrator sees, knows, believes and understands); *voice* (how the character/narrator tells the reader about what they see, know, believe and understand); and *distance* (the emotional distance created between the reader and the characters).

First-person narrative

First-person narration, where the protagonist addresses the reader directly (telling their own story using the 'I' pronoun), is where voice and viewpoint coincide in the character. The reader is drawn in as if they were a close friend, privy to the secret thoughts and feelings of the character, so that the emotional distance is minimal. As writers, though, we have to be aware of the restrictions as well as the possibilities of using the first person. We need to make sure that the voice and the viewpoint remain consistent throughout the narrative, and the reader only *sees* and *hears* the story from the narrator's perspective. This means that if the narrator sleeps or loses consciousness, there will be a gap in the narrative. And if the narrator is unlikely to know the difference between a beech tree and a birch, or recognise Gothic architecture when they see it, they cannot give this information to the reader, even if, as the author, you would like the reader to know.

But when used well, first-person narration is an effective way to tell a tale, and many writers have used it to intensify the relationship between reader and character. This doesn't mean that the reader entirely trusts the narrator, however. Many first-person narrators are unreliable, their version of the story being precisely that, a version, shaped by their perceptual, psychological and ideological focalisation. The reader may only gradually recognise the limitations of the narrator's perspective as they begin to read between the lines (which is, of course, part of the pleasure). In Kazuo Ishiguro's *The Remains of the Day*, the butler Stevens sees it as his duty to repress his emotions. The reader must then re-interpret the events he describes to understand the sad significance of his refusal to feel. Likewise in D. B. C. Pierre's *Vernon God Little* there is a secret within the narrative that is never told, and the reader must guess at Vernon's underlying motivation.

Sometimes, the limited or biased point of view of the first-person narrator is thrown into stark contrast when a different narrator takes over the tale. In John Fowles' first novel, *The Collector*, the reader is drawn into the warped perspective of the obsessive collector before experiencing a very different reality when the narrative is taken over by the girl he has abducted. The change in first-person narrators (other examples include William Faulkner's *The Sound and the Fury* and Sarah Waters' *Fingersmith*) can surprise the reader, forcing them to read the same events in a completely different way, but it can also confuse them, and so as writers, we need to think carefully about how and when we pluck readers out of the comfortable perspective our character has provided and make them see the world anew.

Second-person narrative

The second-person point of view is rarely used, and whereas both first and third have become familiar conventions and thus invisible to the reader, the second person declares itself as a technique. Jay McInerny's novel *Bright Lights, Big City* is an example of second-person narration and shows how it transforms the reader into a character in the story. It begins: 'You are not the kind of guy who would be at a place like this at this time of the morning. But here you are, and you cannot say that the terrain is entirely unfamiliar, although the details are fuzzy.'[5] If readers identify with the character, this can be a powerful technique, but if they don't they can be thrown out of the story. Thinking about this in terms of viewpoint, voice and distance, the reader is made to take on the voice and viewpoint of a character, collapsing any distance between themselves and the character as a distinct identity. It is a risky strategy that can provoke irritation and rejection, but, if it works, it can leave a powerful impression in the reader's mind.

There is another version of second person, which is really a hybridised version of first and second. This type of second person simply makes explicit the invisible 'you' in first-person narrative by acknowledging that the narrator is, after all, writing (or speaking) to someone, and that person is 'you', the reader. Some stories, such as *The.PowerBook* by Jeanette Winterson, play with combinations of first- and second-person narration so that the protagonist speaks to the reader, as if the reader were a particular character: 'Not knowing you, and knowing that small talk is not my best point, I started to tell you about George Mallory, the Everest mountaineer.'[6] Here the distance between the protagonist and the reader is maintained, but the reader is made to take on the voice and viewpoint, the identity, of a literary character. The effect is to blur the distinctions between the real and the fictional, to deprive the reader of a safe seat beyond the story, outside of the events. With second-person narration, the reader becomes an actor, forced to take on the role the writer has designated for them.

Third-person narration

Third-person narration is, in comparison, perhaps the most conventional way of telling a story. But within that general term there are so many variations of voice, viewpoint and distance, that many different effects can be created. A third-person narrative might stick closely to the voice and viewpoint of one particular character, so that the effect is almost as intimate as a first-person story, with only the use of 'he' or 'she' rather than 'I' creating emotional distance between the character and the reader; J. M. Coetzee's *Disgrace* is a good example of this technique, which is known as *third person limited*. Tim Winton's *Dirt Music* also shows how the single focus of the third-person-limited perspective can be loosened: the novel gives us both the voice and viewpoint of the main character Georgie Jutland, and a more objective impression of the other characters.

If your story has several viewpoint characters, like Armistead Maupin's *Tales of the City* series, limited third-person narrative can become the literary equivalent of serial monogamy. The reader enters the heads of each main character in turn, so that the renewed intimacy lessens the emotional wrench as the previous viewpoint character is left behind. Maupin, for instance, narrates each chapter from a different character's viewpoint, and these narrative breaks indicate the change to the reader. If you use several viewpoint characters you will need to flag up the voice and viewpoint changes, either with new chapters or with line breaks between scenes. When voice and viewpoint changes occur between lines or paragraphs, the reader can easily become disoriented, and unless this it the effect you wish to create, it's worth avoiding.

If you do not feel comfortable sticking rigidly to the voice and viewpoint of a particular character, or even a group of characters, third-person narrative allows you to treat voice, viewpoint and distance more flexibly. You might privilege the viewpoint of one particular character, and interweave the character's voice with the voice of an external narrator (as in *Dirt Music*); or you might keep the character's viewpoint, but tell the story in the narrator's voice (as in *What Maisie Knew*); or you might dip into the viewpoints of different characters, interweaving their voices with the narrator's own (as in Woolf's *Mrs Dalloway*).

With third-person narrative, as the viewpoint and voice are disconnected from the characters, so the emotional distance between the characters and the reader increases. At its extreme, when the viewpoint is taken from the characters completely, so that an external narrator simply reports the character's actions and speech, without understanding their motivations or world-view, then the emotional distance between the characters and the reader is at its greatest.

This narrative style is known as *third person objective* and is used frequently in mysteries, where motivations need to remain hidden. Ernest Hemingway used this objective narrative in his story 'Hills Like White Elephants' in which a man and a woman talk euphemistically about the woman having an abortion. We hear their words but need to guess at the emotions behind them.

In contrast to this objective style which reports from a distance, third-person narrative also allows the narrator to be all-knowing and all-seeing, like a god hovering over the world of the characters, able to dip in and out of their voices and viewpoints. This type of narration, known as *third person omniscient*, used to be seen as very much a nineteenth-century device but in recent years has made something of a literary comeback (in the work of A. S. Byatt among others). Omniscience though is not an easy option. It takes great skill to juggle different voices and perspectives within a single scene or paragraph, and as a writer you need to consider the rhythm and balance of these movements. The reader's confidence in the story world can be shattered by technical glitches in the narration. Rhythm is important for all styles of narrative, including the more limited third person, because if the reader is used to the viewpoint of the protagonist, and their narrative is interrupted by a paragraph from another character's perspective, it will read like a fly in the soup.

Voices

Distinctive voices make characters memorable. The reader may only have the sketchiest impression of what a character looks like, but an individual voice will bring that character to life. Bakhtin argued that 'the human being in a novel [or story] is first, foremost and always a speaking human being.'[7] We know characters through their voices and a character who does not speak or verbalise thoughts will simply be a blank space in the narrative, an empty shell.

For Bakhtin, however, the voices in fiction are never entirely what they seem. He coined the term 'double-voicedness' to describe what he saw as the dual nature of any character's speech, because he thought that the words a character speaks do two things at once: they express the intention and personality of the character who is speaking, whilst also suggesting 'the refracted intention of the author'. For Bakhtin this means there are 'two voices, two meanings and two expressions' in every character's voice, because behind their words sits the author, like a ventriloquist holding the dummy.[8]

We can work through this concept of 'double-voicedness' in several ways. An example that Bakhtin offers is skaz, the type of first person narrative that uses everyday street language, such as in J. D. Salinger's *Catcher in the Rye*. Holden Caulfield's words seem like real speech, but they are 'word[s] with a side-ways glance', as Bakhtin puts it, 'word[s] with a loop hole'.[9] Beneath the seeming spontaneity and naturalness of the character's voice is the author, shaping and crafting those words, giving them a subtle twist so that the reader can read between the lines.

The idea of ventriloquism is an interesting one in this context, for in many ways the fiction writer could be seen as a ventriloquist, imitating other voices, making it seem as if their own words have come from the mouths of strangers. And the notion of the writer as ventriloquist challenges the conventional idea that a writer has one true voice, because it's clear that the writer's voice can only be found through the voices of others. But here the analogy ends, because unlike the ventriloquist the writer is not trying to provide a voice-over for puppets. The writer, as Bakhtin says, should speak, 'not *about* the character, but *with* him', as if the character were a real person, with a real will and self-consciousness.[10]

Dialogue

Dialogue is not real speech, and characters do not have natural conversations because their words are manipulated by the author. Elizabeth Bowen offers some very useful advice for writing dialogue, which it would be helpful to think about in relation to Bakhtin's idea of 'double-voicedness'. Bowen suggests that:

1 dialogue should be brief
2 it should add to the reader's present knowledge
3 it should eliminate the routine exchanges of ordinary conversation
4 it should convey a sense of spontaneity but eliminate the repetitiveness of real talk
5 it should keep the story moving forward
6 it should be revelatory of the speaker's character, both directly and indirectly
7 it should show the relationships among people.[11]

Dialogue is serving many purposes here: it provides information to the reader, moves the plot forward and reveals the nature of the characters and their relationships. The seemingly natural conversation is stripped of all mumbling, hesitation and repetition to become pithy and engaging. But whilst dialogue is a useful way to 'add to the reader's present knowledge', all writers should beware of speaking over the characters' heads to give the reader information. Forcing characters to tell each other things they already know produces false and stilted dialogue, or long paragraphs of explanation simply framed by quotation marks.

Echoing Bowen's advice that dialogue should be brief, Oakley Hall suggests this rule of thumb: 'one thought at a time, and keep the lines short.'[12] Whilst agreeing with his emphasis on economy, I think such rules tend to typecast fiction. If you put information into the mouths of characters, the most important thing to remember is not simply brevity. It is that the information needs to be communicated in the character's voice and from their point of view, with the number of thoughts and length of line appropriate to that character.

Dialogue can keep the story moving, creating tension or kindling the reader's curiosity, and often dialogue increases the pace of the story simply because it is quick to read, with lots of white space on the page. But again, we need to think about the rhythm of our writing: pages of uninterrupted dialogue without thought, action, reaction, emotion or description can become monotonous.

When I was first writing, I got it into my head that what made dialogue monotonous was the over-use of the word 'said' and so I tried to avoid it at all costs; not by replacing 'said' with 'argued', 'shouted', 'exclaimed' and so on, which would have been bad enough, but by trying to avoid speech tags altogether. And since I was writing a comic novel with more characters than you could shake a stick at, this became increasingly difficult. In the end, my characters were constantly fidgeting, drinking, smoking and smiling, just so I could show where the mystery voice was coming from. Consider this scene when my character Cass tries to persuade the radical workers at the Cosmic Café to accept middle-aged, middle-class Pearl onto the soon-to-be bankrupt collective:

[Buzz] fixed Pearl with his good eye. 'I don't want her.'
There was an edgy silence. Cass looked at Pearl, then back to Buzz.
'What?'
'She's not right for the café.'
'What do you mean, not right for the café? This is our chance to save the bloody café.'
He sneered at her. 'You mean this is our chance to join the oppressors.'

Cass appealed to him. 'Oh come on, Buzz, Pearl's hardly an agent of
the state.'
He stood up. 'She's buying you! And you all jump at the chance to
sell out.'
Dee shook her head. 'Nobody's buying anyone, you stupid Trotsky.
She's joining as a member of the collective, an equal member.'
'Yeah!' Buzz spoke directly to Pearl. 'And some members are more
equal than others, isn't that right?'
Pearl flushed. She wasn't used to being the focus of ideological debate.
And her idea of unequal members was more Jackie Collins than
George Orwell.[13]

I now realise that the word 'said' is fairly invisible to the reader's eye,
and a few 'saids' might have eased the flow of the writing, enabling
me to avoid some of the more awkward constructions. It is possible to
overdo the word 'said' so that it clangs like a gong at the end of every
exchange, but generally speaking words like 'exclaimed' or 'argued'
are far more obvious. (I now use 'said' for most direct speech.)

Bowen's final points about dialogue concern relationships and
characterisation. Voice is an important tool for characterisation, and
by differentiating your characters' speech patterns, you will crystallise their individual identities. Sol Stein suggests that one of the
best ways to bring out the individuality of different voices is to
use speech markers. He says: 'Vocabulary is an important marker.
Throwaway phrases are markers. Tight or loose wording is a marker.
Run-on sentences are markers. Sarcasm is a marker. Cynicism is
a marker. Poor grammar is a marker. Omitted words are markers.
Inappropriate modifiers are markers. Consider all these a mine for
the jewels of dialogue.'[14] Such markers are important features of
characters' speech, but, like all other aspects of characterisation,
they need to grow from the character rather than being imposed
upon them.

Although dialogue is a simulation of speech, rather than a re-
creation of the way people actually talk, I think it's also worth remembering Ford Madox Ford's point about real conversation. He said that
in real life hardly anyone ever listens to anyone else because they are
too busy thinking about what they will say next, and so he advised
writers not to make speakers actually answer each other directly, but
to answer to their own agenda, promoting their own point of view
and only responding indirectly or belatedly to the other speaker's
demands.[15] James Frey makes a similar point, arguing that 'good

dialogue should be in conflict, indirect, clever, and colourful.'[16] The effect of such contrivance is that dialogue appears to be sparkling with spontaneity and yet, in reality, it's driven by the needs and conventions of the story. This is what Bakhtin calls double-voiced discourse, where the words serve two masters: the character and the author.

Double-voiced speech

Bakhtin also argued that characters themselves do not use words in a straightforward way, but he approached this question slightly differently. He suggested that when reading or writing dialogue, 'what matters is not the direct meaning the word gives to objects and emotions – that is the false front of the word; what matters is rather the actual and always self-interested *use* to which this meaning is put and the way it is expressed by the speaker.'[17] In other words, we should pay attention not only to the direct meaning of the characters' words, but also think about how a character will use words to skew a situation to their own advantage.

If we allow our character to simply say what they mean, then our dialogue will be flat and transparent. We can give depth, both to the dialogue and the character, if we remember that everyone, however amiable they appear, uses words to manipulate and control situations. Characters sometimes present 'false fronts', words which say one thing and imply another, words which contain meanings that other characters, and the reader, may partially detect, even if the character him or herself remains unaware. As Sol Stein says, 'what counts is not what's said but the effect of what is meant.'[18]

This double-voicedness, where words are not all they seem, can also be true of the narrator's voice, especially where the narrator is a character or a witness to the action. But where the narrator's voice interacts with the character's voice there are other ways in which the double-voicedness of fiction can be seen. If we think about the narrator in more detail, the narrative can be told by a fully developed character or a disembodied voice. And yet even an unseen narrator who exists 'beyond' the action of the story can still be characterised as hesitant and self-questioning, uncertain about what's coming – or authoritative, with a tale to tell (and anything in between). Patrick O'Neill argues that narrators exist somewhere in the spectrum between 'personality or abstraction, participation or non-participation, knowledge or ignorance, reliability or unreliability, independence or relativization'.[19] But however we characterise our narrator, their voice will set the tone of the tale.

O'Neill outlines three basic ways of presenting a character's speech. Firstly there is *direct speech*, where we hear the character's voice speaking the words ('Just leave me, Greg,' said Fran. 'You still don't get it, do you? I'm sick of you.'). This is the most immediate way of presenting dialogue, where the reader feels that they can hear the words coming out of the character's mouth. At the other extreme, *indirect speech* means that the character's actual words are lost, but the sense of the exchange is reported by the narrator. The only voice the reader 'hears' is the narrator's own. (Fran told Greg to leave her alone, spitting the words at him, screaming into his pallid face.) The third possibility is *free indirect speech* or what O'Neill calls *compound speech*, where the voices of the character and narrator become entwined (Fran spat her words into Greg's pallid face. Did he still not get it? She was sick of him.) The character's words are, as O'Neill says, 'filtered' by the narrator so that some of their flavour enters the narrator's own speech, reminding us that there are two distinct voices within these sentences.

The thing to remember about terms like direct, indirect and free indirect speech is that although they come from literary criticism they only exist to label techniques that writers had already developed. As writers we don't necessarily need to remember the terms, but the possibilities they describe are useful. Becoming aware of the ways in which voices can be amplified, muted or woven into the narration allows us to identify rhythms and patterns that contribute to a writer's style, and this is something I will consider in more detail in the next chapter.

11   Styles

Style and Structure are the essence of a book; great ideas are hogwash.
Vladimir Nabokov, *Writers at Work* (Viking)

In this chapter I want to consider one of the most important aspects of style, the rhythm of the narrative. By rhythm I don't simply mean the balance or cadence of sentences, although that of course is important. But rhythm is about more that syllables and sentences. It's about the balance of the whole story: the pace, the fractured chronologies, the difference between the story and its telling. If the same story were told by two different writers, it would not only be word choice or point of view that made their fictions unique, it would be the more subtle rhythms of time and technique. Great ideas may count for more than 'hogwash', but, like Nabokov, I would argue that structure and style are the essence of fiction.

The work of Gérard Genette

The French theorist Gérard Genette investigatcd the rhythms of fiction in order to understand the hidden structure of narrative.[1] He was interested in the way a story creased time in its telling: condensing certain moments and lingering over others, using or avoiding repetition. So when he analysed a novel he didn't worry about character motivation or conflict, he was interested in the way story events were rearranged in the telling. This may seem a rather uninspiring way to read stories, but this kind of structuralist criticism reveals the deep rhythms of style, rhythms we might well miss if we focused purely on individual pages or paragraphs by our favourite writers.

Genette described the stylistic structure of fiction using three categories: *order* (the sequence in which story events are narrated), *duration* (how long the story events are narrated for) and *frequency* (how often the story events are narrated).

The most important aspects of *order* for writers are analepsis (flashback) and prolepsis (flashforward). I'm using Genette's terms here – 'analepsis' and 'prolepsis' – rather than the more familiar film language – 'flashback' and 'flashforward' – because the film terms aren't quite right for fiction; they miss the subtleties. In film everything has to be shown, and although most writers want their fiction to be highly visual we can still reveal a character's mind in a way film can't. We can reach backwards and forwards in the narrative without having to show an entire scene. For instance, analepsis can weave memory into the present as well as 'flashing back' to previous action. And prolepsis can include foreshadowing, omens, anticipation, projection as well as the more literal 'flashforward' to future events.

Genette's second category, *duration*, is important for writers because it reveals how, at a fundamental level, a writer's style must balance pace against atmosphere. The term duration indicates the difference between the time an event took to happen in story time and the time it takes to read about it; but when we break this down, it touches upon some of the vital decisions writers make about how to tell their story. We have several options: fictional time can be faster than the 'actual' story time, as in summary ('He slept for fifteen hours'); or the same as story time, as in dramatic scene ('Go to hell!' she said); or slower than story time, as in description ('The gnawed end of my pencil reveals naked wood beneath its painted shell').

The third category, *frequency*, concentrates on the stylistic use or avoidance of repetition. For instance, an event that happens in the story only once may be narrated five times, and conversely, an event that happens in the story five times may be narrated only once. These choices have a major effect on the stylistic 'feel' of our fiction and so I will now consider each of Genette's categories in more detail.

Order

As writers we can manipulate time. We do not have to follow the chronological order of a story, instead we can turn the hourglass back and forth, moving the reader from present to past, or present to future, as we wish. Genette used the term 'anachrony' to talk about these moments in fiction, where time is twisted out of shape. Anachronies can be fundamental structuring devices for fiction (such as in mystery novels, where Chapter 1 shows the dead body, and Chapter 20 reveals how that person was murdered) or they can be minor creases in the unfolding story (such as in sentences that reverse chronology: 'Jane ran through the deserted streets. She had left the children behind, still trapped in the car.'). In this section I want to consider two of the most significant ways in which writers manipulate time to see what we can learn from Genette's analysis.

Analepsis (flashback)

Many writing-teachers warn writers not to use 'flashbacks' in their prose for the simple reason that flashbacks stop the story. They give information and background about the character, but they pause the forward motion of the action. As a writer you have to make decisions about your story that are also decisions about your style. In story terms, you have to decide whether the extra information in the analepsis increases the momentum of the story (by giving more depth to the character or the situation). In stylistic terms, you have to decide whether the rhythm of the story demands forward or backward movement, chronological telling or sweeping reversals. When writing, we often make these decisions unconsciously and only become aware of them when we rewrite the manuscript. During rewriting we have to consider where the analepsis 'fits' in terms of style and story, and how we will include it.

The least intrusive analepsis comes from the character's own memory (rather than being explained by an outside narrator) and is prompted by events that mirror or connect to earlier experiences. Michael Toolan argues that 'grief and trauma are powerful triggers of character-based analepsis', but memory need not always be so dramatic.[2] Suppressed memories of the past may well erupt into the character's present because a situation, sight, smell, has recalled their pain; but memories might also drift in and out of the character's present in less traumatic ways. Either way, using memory can prevent the analepsis seeming like an abrupt stop in the story. Unless you want to create a fractured narrative, analepsis should also be brief, giving the reader only enough detail to hint at greater depth of character or suggest the true resonance of the present scene.

If the analepsis is several pages long, this will inevitably disrupt the forward momentum of the story, and may well disorientate the reader. The decision to include a scene from the past should be considered in terms of story and style. Has the story enough momentum to sustain the interruption (especially at the beginning)? Would an analepsis disrupt the rhythm of the fiction (as a whole and of this scene in particular)? Is this analepsis part of the fictional style or simply an easy way to give the reader information? If you answer this last question honestly, it might help you to see whether the analeptic scene is one that should be dropped, re-worked, or even repeated. I say repeated, because the repetition of analepsis can be a powerful stylistic technique. In *Beloved*, Toni Morrison's story of slavery, guilt and ghosts, moments of trauma (such as Sethe's murder of her daughter and the hanging of the Sweet Home men) are told and re-told so that they come to haunt the story (and thus the reader) as much as the characters.

Prolepsis (flashforward)

Prolepsis works differently from analepsis. Instead of asking the reader to understand the present story in terms of the past, prolepsis teases the reader by offering fragments of what is to come. It is often used in first-person narratives, where the character has already lived through events they are narrating, and provides the reader with glimpses of the future. Phrases like: 'If only I had listened to her', or 'That was the last time I saw her alive', tease the reader, playing on their anticipation of what is going to happen, and tempting them to read on.

Prolepsis can also be used in third-person narratives where there is an omniscient narrator. In *The Prime of Miss Jean Brodie* (which tells the story of a manipulative teacher who is betrayed by one of the girls she has taught) Muriel Spark uses prolepsis in two major ways. Firstly, she uses prolepsis to characterise the girls by telling the reader about their adult lives: 'Mary Macgregor, although she lived into her twenty-fourth year, never quite realized that Jean Brodie's confidences were not shared with the rest of the staff . . . she died while on leave in Cumberland in a fire in the hotel. . . . But at the beginning of the nineteen-thirties, when Mary Magregor was ten, there she was sitting blankly among Miss Brodie's pupils.'[3] And secondly, she uses prolepsis to outline the fictional crisis and therefore stimulate the reader's curiosity: 'It was twenty-eight years after Eunice did the splits in Miss Brodie's flat that she, who had become a nurse and married a doctor, said to her husband one evening . . . "She was betrayed by one of her own girls, we were called the Brodie set. I never found out which one betrayed her." '[4]

By telling the reader about the fire that killed Mary, an event that occurs several years after the story finishes, Spark provides a frame for that character. The reader knows that she will die young and alone after a failed romance, and the weight of that knowledge makes us judge this ten-year-old, and Miss Brodie's behaviour towards her, very differently than we otherwise would. But the prolepsis also distances the reader from this character. The frame around Mary MacGregor constructs her as an object for our gaze, more like a creature under the microscope than an empathetic human being. In this way, the style of the novel mirrors the way Miss Brodie herself treats her girls – as specimens to be moulded rather than as individuals to be respected or understood. The omniscient third-person narrator, who tweaks our curiosity, heightening the suspense by hinting at what is to come, ultimately keeps us emotionally distanced from the fate of these characters, and so what is gained (suspense, characterisation) comes at a price (emotional distance). In other words, prolepsis works best, as here, where its stylistic effect echoes and reinforces the mood and tone of the story, which in *The Prime of Miss Jean Brodie* is driven by the decorous tyranny of Miss Brodie herself.

Duration

The concept of duration refers to the time it takes the narrative to relate a story event, whether it dwells over details or condenses years into a sentence. Duration is a way of alerting us to the pace of our narratives. For Genette there are four distinct modes of narration (ellipses, summary, scene, and pause) and these modes determine the pace and atmosphere of our storytelling.

Ellipses

Ellipses need not appear as a series of dots (. . .). Ellipses are simply gaps in the narrative that reveal that something has been left out. Very often ellipses occurred in nineteenth- and early-twentieth-century fiction when two characters clutched in embrace. Rather than describing a sexual encounter, however briefly, these novels and stories left it to the reader's imagination. The chapter ended and the invisible ellipses obscured those aspects of human behaviour that remained culturally taboo.

In the twenty-first-century Western world, however, writers continue to expose and explore any remaining taboos, and ellipses often have a more mundane function. We might read about a character making a lunch-date, and, with the ellipsis signalled by a break in the paragraphs, begin the next sentence with her sitting in the restaurant. As readers we simply do not need to see her driving across town, parking the car, doing a bit of shopping and so on. This is not to say that ellipses can't be used more thematically and experimentally to obscure story events, but generally their main function is one that we often take completely for granted.

Thinking about ellipses reminds us that when we write our story, we don't write it as one long narrative. We write it in scenes. We make decisions about the events we will dramatise and the events we will leave out. As writers, we might well need to know how our characters get from A to B, but do our readers? We ask ourselves (consciously or unconsciously) what such a journey would add to the scene. If it allows us to reveal the character's emotional turmoil about the date, or heighten suspense by showing how she almost didn't make it in time, then we might keep it. But it has to do something beyond revealing the mechanics of her movement. If it doesn't, we consign it to ellipses, assured that our readers will know the codes (a break in the paragraphs, a gap between chapters) and realise that irrelevant action has been missed out.

Henry Fielding proclaimed himself one of the first writers to use ellipses in this way when he skipped twelve years of Tom Jones's life because 'nothing worthy of a Place in this History occurred within that Period'. And he attacked dull writers who 'fill up as much Paper with the Detail of Months and Years in which nothing remarkable happened'. He compared their books to a stage-coach 'which performs constantly the same Course, empty as well as full'.[5] As writers we need to avoid those empty journeys. But it is up to us how we signal these missing sections of the story.

Genette categorises ellipses in three ways: explicit (when the narrative tells us that a certain time has passed), implicit (where we know something is missing from the narrative but are not sure how much time has passed) and hypothetical (where the temporal coherence of the narrative is stretched to its limits and we only realise that something is missing by its inclusion later in the story as an analepsis). The way we use ellipses depends upon the kind of fictional experience we wish to evoke for the reader. We might leave a scene out because 'nothing remarkable happened', or because we are creating suspense, or because we are experimenting with chronology. If you use ellipses to experiment with the reader's experience of time, however, you need to be very clear about how this stylistic experimentation will continue to intrigue your reader once the 'continuous dream' of the story world is shattered. What kinds of pleasure and understanding does the narrative offer? For those story events that are not to be consigned to ellipses, Genette offers three other modes of writing.

Summary

Henry James's famous advice, to show not tell, has often been interpreted as meaning that everything must be shown in full scene. But this is not true. Narrative summary, Genette's second mode of telling, is a vital aspect of storytelling. He calls it 'the connective tissue par excellence of novelistic narrative' because the 'fundamental rhythm [of fiction] is defined by the alternation of summary and scene' (p. 97). Summary enables us to indicate situations and events quickly, accelerating the pace. If I write: 'For several weeks after the accident Lucy refused to leave the house,' this narrative summary condenses action that took place over a long period into one sentence.

The problem with such summary is that it distances the reader, who is not shown and therefore does not experience the character's situation, in this case Lucy's suffering. But as a writer we need to make choices about pace and atmosphere, the speed of the scene against the emotional reality of the story. Summary is a tool particular to fiction, and one that we should not under-value: other media, like cinema, find it very difficult to condense scenes in this way. What we need to remember though, is that we live in a very visual culture, where readers are brought up on TV and film, and direct scene is the dominant mode of storytelling. Within film, everything must be shown rather than summarised, so that exposition (background information about a character or situation) can only be presented through dialogue or flashback. In prose fiction, writers are more tempted to simply tell the reader what we need them to know.

Traditionally novels often started with just such expository narrative summary, where the voice of the narrator loomed large, as in the opening line of Jane Austen's *Emma*: 'Emma Woodhouse, handsome, clever, and rich, with a comfortable home and happy disposition, seemed to unite some of the best blessings of existence; and had lived nearly twenty-one years in the world with very little to distress or vex her.'[6] But since the early twentieth century, and the development of cinema, such chunks of narrative summary have been discouraged. Ford Madox Ford, a novelist and critic himself, argued that 'lumped summary' should be avoided. Instead he encouraged writers to: 'get in the character first with a strong impression, and then work backwards and forwards over his past'.[7]

But there are other ways to summarise a story. 'Lumped summary' which tells the reader about events that occur off-stage, events that the reader cannot 'see', can be replaced by dramatic summary, which allows the reader to experience the illusion of an on-stage scene. In dramatic summary we have the advantage of pace (the summary time is faster that the story time) but we do not lose the immediacy of a scene. Consider this passage from Yann Martel's *Life of Pi*, which, incidentally, uses almost uninterrupted narrative summary for the first four chapters: 'I repeated the stunt with every teacher ... Between one commonly named boy and the next I rushed forward and emblazoned, sometimes with a terrible screech, the details of my rebirth. It got to be that after a few times the boys sang along with me, a crescendo that climaxed ... with such a rousing rendition of my name that it would have been the delight of any choirmaster. A few boys followed up with a whispered, urgent "Three! Point! One! Four!" as I wrote as fast as I could ....'[8]

Here we have a summary of repeated events that are compressed into one telling. As readers we are aware that this one glimpse is a summary and stands in for other, unseen, occurrences ('sometimes' the chalk screeched) but we 'see' enough of the scene to make it feel immediate (Pi rushing forward, the chalk screeching, the boys singing) and the addition of one line of speech ('Three! Point! One! Four!') makes the event seem more immediate. But this one line is the only moment when story time (how long an event took) is accurately represented in the fiction. The other sentences condense repeated actions into summary form with the dramatic details balancing the pace of the summary against the immediacy of a direct scene.

Scene

Genette's third mode of telling is one where the story time equals the reading time: the scene. The word 'scene' comes from the theatre and this captures the sense of action unfolding before the eyes of the reader as if it were on a stage. The scene is the 'as it happens' mode of writing, and is the basis for most contemporary fiction. It is the most immediate form because the writer is there with the characters experiencing events as they unfold. Consider this passage from 'Sonny's Blues' by James Baldwin:

> He sort of shuffled over to me, and he said. 'I see you got the papers. So you already know about it.'
> 'You mean about Sonny? Yes, I already know about it. How come they didn't get you?'
> He grinned. It made him repulsive and it also brought to mind what he'd looked like as a kid. 'I wasn't there. I stay away from them people.'

> 'Good for you.' I offered him a cigarette and I watched him through
> the smoke. 'You come all the way down here just to tell me about
> Sonny?'
> 'That's right.' He was sort of shaking his head and his eyes looked
> strange, as though they were about to cross.[9]

The writing corresponds to the action. We see what the character
sees, hear what he hears and says. Although even in direct scene of
course, writers do not present things exactly as they happen. We miss
out anything that would detract from the intensity of the scene. Even
writers trying to represent 'real life' in all its detail, like Marguerite
Duras, are forced, as Mieke Bal points out, to 'abridge' real life 'on
pain of unreadability'.[10]

Genette suggests that the stylistic rhythm of fiction in the nineteenth
century was an alternation of 'nondramatic summaries, functioning
as waiting room and liaison, with dramatic scenes whose role in the
action [was] decisive' (p. 110). After Marcel Proust's *À la Recherche
du Temps Perdu*, however, twentieth-century fiction abandoned the
traditional rhythm of summary / scene / summary / scene, and priv-
ileged scenes over all else. Writing gurus like Sol Stein echo this
point, arguing that nowadays there is no need to connect different
scenes with summary: 'Today's reader', he says, 'is used to jump
cutting'.[11] For contemporary (non-experimental) writers who want to
be published there is no place for 'waiting rooms' in their fiction.
Waiting rooms are by their nature boring. So it's best to avoid using
summary to anticipate future action (go straight to the action) or to
debrief after the action (if debriefing is needed, write it as a scene).

Pause

Descriptions necessarily slow or stop the forward movement of the
story because we step out of the action to contemplate the situation,
characters or setting in more detail. But there is a difference between
the narrator's descriptions and the character's own perceptions. For
instance, in the passage from 'Sonny's Blues' the dialogue is inter-
spersed with short passages of description:

> He was sort of shaking his head and his eyes looked strange, as
> though they were about to cross. The bright sun deadened his damp
> dark brown skin and it made his eyes look yellow and showed up
> the dirt in his kinked hair. He smelled funky. (p. 3)

The description slows the narrative by presenting what the character observed in the blink of an eye. As readers, we are still with the character, still within the scene, but the moment has been stretched as we read what he sees.

Descriptions by a third-person narrator, not mediated through a character's thoughts, can be equally vivid, but they inevitably speak over the heads of the characters, and so distance the reader. Toni Morrison begins *Beloved* with a description that reinforces the reader's sense of being an outsider: '124 was spiteful. Full of baby's venom.'[12] This brief description raises question upon question: what is 124? (it's a house); how can a house be spiteful?; how can babies have venom? The description confuses categories, making the inanimate animate and the innocent wicked. It makes clear that the narrative will not be conventional or easy (it's neither), and that to know these people and their story, the reader will have to work.

Sixty years earlier, Virginia Woolf had also used description to create unusual stylistic effects. She isolated the reader from her characters, denying the reader the dramatic scenes (of death in war and child-birth) that a novel would usually provide and focused instead upon elaborate description. In *To the Lighthouse*, a story about the difficult relationships within the Ramsay family, Woolf dedicated the middle section, 'Time Passes', to a description of their empty holiday house, confining the characters to parenthesis, their lives bracketed off in summary:

> What people had shed and left – a pair of shoes, a shooting cap, some faded skirts and coats in wardrobes – those alone kept the human shape and in the emptiness indicated how once they were filled and animated; how once hands were busy with hooks and buttons; how once the looking-glass had held a face; had held a world hollowed out in which a figure turned, a hand flashed, the door opened, in came children, rushing and tumbling; and went out again. . . . [A shell exploded. Twenty or thirty young men were blown up in France, among them Andrew Ramsay, whose death, mercifully, was instantaneous].[13]

The prolonged description of the decaying house (over sixteen pages) devalues the human world of action and interaction (the fundamental ingredients of fiction) and concentrates instead on the rhythms of nature and time. Woolf effectively stops the story and forces the reader to recognise cosmic time as a non-human force, indifferent to the trivial and fleeting concerns of humanity. She uses description as a stylistic device to reinforce the theme of her novel.

Frequency

Genette's third category of stylistic structure is frequency – how often an action appears in a novel or short story compared to how often it took place in the story world. He puts it like this: 'a narrative, whatever it is, may tell once what happened once, n times what happened n times, n times what happened once, once what happened n times' (p. 114). All these ways of telling have different effects on the style of the story. To tell something once when it happened once (as in a scene) or once when it happened n times (as in a summary) are the stock methods of fiction, and are so conventional that as readers we don't notice them as stylistic devices. The other ways of telling though, n times when it happened n times, or n times when it happened once, are less conventional and as such stand out as stylistically experimental.

To take Toni Morrison's *Beloved* as our example, we can see how these different frequencies might work. When Beloved seduces Paul D in the shed, it is narrated only once: 'Beloved dropped her skirts as he spoke and looked at him with empty eyes' (p. 116). Most of the book is constructed in this way, telling once what happened once. Morrison's use of the other convention, telling once what happened n times, is much less frequent, and its absence is one of the stylistic features of this book that gives it such immediacy. A rare example occurs near the end of the novel when Denver persuades the town to help feed her starving family, and the different gifts are summarised: 'Every now and then, and all through the spring, names appeared near or in gifts of food' (p. 249).

But what defines *Beloved*'s particular style is Morrison's use of repetition, telling n times what happened once. And these repetitions are usually episodes of trauma (the loss of Sethe's mother, Halle's humiliation, the hanging of the Sweet Home men, School-teacher's arrival and Sethe's murder of her baby) which erupt again and again into the narrative. When Sethe kills her baby girl, fragments of this event reappear in the narrative in various ways: 'the baby blood that soaked her fingers like oil' (p. 5); 'From the pure clear stream of spit that the little girl dribbled onto her face to her oily blood was twenty-eight days' (p. 95); 'a nigger woman holding a blood-soaked child to her chest' (p. 149); 'She just flew. Collected every bit of life she had made, all the parts of her that were precious and fine and beautiful, and carried, pushed, dragged them through the veil' (p. 163), and so on.

Genette's final example, telling *n* times what happened *n* times, is more unusual and doesn't really appear in *Beloved*, but the sense of repetition it carries (Genette's example is 'Monday I went to bed early, Tuesday I went to bed early, Wednesday I went to bed early') can be seen in the four successive chapters narrated by Sethe, Denver and Beloved that begin: 'Beloved, she my daughter. She mine' (p. 200); 'Beloved is my sister' (p. 205), and 'I am Beloved and she is mine' (p. 210 and p. 214). Here, three separate 'actions' of possession are narrated four times, and the sense of repetition draws attention to itself, exposing the way the narrative is constructed.

Morrison uses repetition to show how the three major characters (Sethe, Denver and Beloved) are beginning to lose their distinct identities, but this unconventional way of storytelling also draws attention to the words themselves. They become visible to the reader at a new level. This strategy has its risks as well as its benefits. It breaks the 'vivid continuous dream' that Gardner argues for, by snapping the reader's attention back to the words, but it also allows the reader to appreciate the complexity of the novel, both in terms of its stylistic construction, and in terms of the way meaning can only be understood through the interplay of story and style.

The three categories of stylistic structure that Genette identified, Order, Duration and Frequency, might well be aspects of style that we take for granted when we initially write our fictions. But they are worth pausing over when we prewrite and rewrite, for they help us to ask questions about the way we use scene and summary, analepsis and prolepsis, reiteration and repetition. They help us to consider how style and story interweave, and whether the rhythm of our fiction is right for the tale we want to tell.

12 Speculations in Fiction

To write what is worth publishing, to find honest people to publish it, and get sensible people to read it, are the three great difficulties in being an author.

Charles Caleb Colton, *Lacon, Or Many Things in Few Words*
(Melrose Books)

In this final chapter I want to think about the 'great difficulties in being an author' by exploring the different ways new writers 'speculate' upon their writing. There are many different meanings within the word 'speculate' and the *Oxford English Dictionary* gives several. From the sixteenth century onwards 'to speculate' has meant 'to consider or reflect upon with close attention; to contemplate; to theorise upon'. Then there are more contemporary meanings: 'to undertake ... a business enterprise or transaction of a risky nature in the expectation of considerable gain'. These different meanings of 'speculate' are both relevant for writers; for we are often required to reflect upon our own work, and if we want to publish, we are forced to gamble on the market.

In this chapter I want to consider two examples of our 'speculations' to consider how we can make them work for us. The first is reflective, the second is commercial.

Speculating on the process: writing reflective commentaries

I never know what I think about something until I read what I've written on it.

Attributed to William Faulkner

Universities cannot teach their students to write, but they can provide one of the best atmospheres for students to learn about fiction writing and to develop their own critical and creative abilities. This learning is a self-reflexive experience: a process of working out how you write, of exploring new ideas and techniques, of discovering how to edit your material. At undergraduate and (post)graduate levels, this self-reflexive experience is part of the degree itself, and creative writing students are often asked to write about their own processes of composition in the form of commentaries, perhaps, like Faulkner, working out what they think by writing about it. But even if you are not writing within a university structure, being able to think and talk intelligently about your own work and the work of others is a necessary skill. Agents, editors, interviewers will all expect a writer to be able to communicate the uniqueness and energy of their own work, and so it is important for writers to develop their critical-creative skills in this way.

For degree students, however, there are particular issues about assessment and grading within the university system that affect the form of the reflective commentary. Commentaries should not be seen as diaries, progress reports, political essays or literary criticism; although they might borrow from each of these forms. The commentary is a piece of writing that enables a student to develop and understand their own critical-creative approach to writing fiction, and as such, it can take many forms. For instance, imagine that a student-writer has submitted a short story about a homeless teenager rejecting the patronising charity of a passer-by. The commentary for this piece might:

1 contemplate a real-life incident that prompted this story and discuss the way the writer reworked his or her observations and feelings in the fiction
2 discuss the political context for homelessness and the personal anger that inspired this story
3 analyse other fictions about homelessness that moved or infuriated the writer and provoked him or her to develop this particular story
4 discuss theories of narrative, and the ways they helped the writer to focus the story
5 reflect upon any theories (ethical, historical, philosophical, political, sociological) that inspired the ideas in the fiction
6 consider the planning, drafting and rewriting of the story, explaining what creative decisions were made and why

7 unravel any experimental writing in the story and discuss the effects the writer wanted to achieve by writing in this way
8 describe and explain the motivations of the characters
9 explore the role of the reader in interpreting the story, and explain how the writer anticipated the reader's role when rewriting
10 discuss why the writer thought the story submitted didn't work as he or she had envisaged and suggest why
11 explore what the student has learned as a writer through the experience of writing the story

These suggestions are not exclusive (many could work well together), but they convey something of the flexibility of the commentary and show how it can be used to help students explore and develop their own writing. Tutors want to see a student's commitment to their own work. If you are writing creatively for a degree, your tutors want you to show how your writing has developed in response to your own learning: whether that be through a new knowledge of craft; or through reading a particular writer, or through engaging with philosophical, literary, cultural or social debates. You need to demonstrate the three Rs: research, reading and reflection.

Research could include travelling, walking the streets, observing people's speech and behaviour, visiting museums or archives, interviewing people, shadowing workers or volunteering. *Reading* can include fiction, poetry, screenplays, magazines and newspapers, but also non-fictional material, such as theory, philosophy, politics, sociology. *Reflection* will respond to the research, reading and writing you have done. It will consider how the research has informed, and perhaps even transformed, the writing process; how the writing process was itself a form of research (through which you discovered and refined the form, structure, rhythm, vision, perspective, subject and story of your piece), and how the reading has inspired and influenced the different stages of the process (prewriting, writing and rewriting).

It is not enough to simply show that you have read widely, using the university as a site of knowledge (although that is important). You also need to show how this learning has influenced (and continues to influence) your development as a writer. That does not mean that you must claim to thoroughly understand your writing process, or the deeper meanings of everything you write. It simply means that you are exploring ideas about the world, exploring your perspective upon the world, and exploring the techniques you use to represent that vision. You are developing a critical-creative approach to fiction writing.

Below are some questions to consider that might help you plan and shape a commentary. The order of the questions moves from close focus on your own writing to a broader consideration of writing and research, but when writing your commentary, it's best to integrate these different perspectives. Remember, when considering these questions, to reflect upon the reading and prewriting that you have done, thinking about how that work has been transformed in the writing and rewriting stages of composition.

1   What is this novel or story about?
2   What is/are the theme(s) of the story (or chapter)?
3   (For novels): How does this chapter contribute to the novel?
4   What problems did you encounter in the writing process? (point of view, voice, form, structure, dialogue, characterisation and so on)
5   How did you identify and address these problems?
6   How do you evaluate the changes you made?
7   How has the feedback received (in class and elsewhere) contributed to the process of writing and rewriting?
8   How do you position your short story / novel in relation to other short stories / novels that you've read? Does it challenge or develop other fictions?
9   How have these other fictions influenced you – technically or thematically?
10 What ideas (ethical, historical, philosophical, political, spiritual) about the world/humanity have influenced you?
11 How did you question or appropriate these ideas?
12 How did theories of writing help you to clarify your own ideas (about this piece of work in particular and writing/creativity more generally)?
13 How did you identify precisely what research you needed to do?
14 What was the importance of this research for the fiction?
15 What have you learned from this writing experience?

When writing your commentary you will be directed primarily by your own experience of prewriting, writing and rewriting, but I hope that these questions might offer useful ways for thinking about your own writing process and help you to understand and express your interests and ambitions as a writer.

Speculating on the market: submission to publishers and agents

> *More people fail at becoming successful businessmen than fail at becoming artists.*
>
>   John Gardner, *On Becoming a Novelist* (W. W. Norton)

> *If and when [your manuscript] comes back, you must turn it around and send it out to someone else. If and when it comes back that time, you must have the persistence to send it out again . . . You must persist. Until the manuscript has been rejected six to eight times, it hasn't even been tried yet!*
>
>   Jack M. Bickham, *The 38 Most Common Fiction Writing Mistakes*
>   (Writer's Digest Books)

Dorothea Brande argued in *Becoming a Writer* that the writer is a dual personality, and she recommended that writers should try to separate the critical and the creative aspects of themselves by putting a 'transparent barrier' between the two. Throughout this book I have repeatedly argued against this, suggesting that the writer needs a fluid and dynamic relationship between creativity and criticality. But even I would agree that there is one moment in a writer's life when that 'transparent barrier' would be very useful: the moment when you have to cope with rejection. Brande says: 'by all means see to it that it is your prosaic [critical] self which reads rejection slips!'.[1]

Now if you can do that, if you can be worldly and prosaic when you read rejection letters, and shield the vulnerable, needy part of your writer self from the disappointment, then I would wholeheartedly support the separation; it will save you much pain and despondency. But I have never been able to separate the critical and the creative. When I receive rejection letters or negative criticism it always hurts; and the wide-eyed creative part of myself is always there, reading the rejection along with the sceptical critic.

Rejection is not personal, neither is it always fair, and rarely is it explained. You must not allow it to crush you. If you are like me, and cannot coldly read rejection letters in terms of the 'law of averages' or any such comforting intellectualism, then there are still ways of coping that can make rejection a spur to better work. You can take heart by remembering, as John Gardner says, that more people fail in business than as writers. You can adopt Jack Bickham's pragmatism and think that until you've gathered eight rejection letters you've not even started. I've learnt to deal with rejection by putting my critical-creative energies into an active response rather than a passive despondency. This works in several ways (and might also be adapted for painful feedback from tutors or workshops).

If I receive several form rejection letters, I will return to the story or sample chapters and re-read them, first thinking about what I would enjoy (if I were a reader), and on a second reading thinking about why I would reject the story (if I were an editor). If you read as an editor the first time around, it's too easy to indulge in a form of writerly sado-masochism and pull your fiction (and your ego) to bits. I make notes after both readings, and read them through together afterwards. If I still believe that the work is as good as it can be, or as good as I can make it, then I send it out again. But if I have doubts, I hold back. I muse over it for a week or so and then come back and read the story and my notes again. It's tempting to be lazy at this point and send it out anyway, hoping someone will like it as it is. But if my instincts tell me it's not quite there, I try to work out why that is and rewrite.

We can think of the form letter as stage one of the rejection process, the lowest rung on the ladder we are trying to climb. Stage two is a letter that addresses the story you have written. If an editor or agent has offered me any crumb of feedback, I mull over it for a while. If, on reflection, I think it would improve my story (and only then) I use it as the basis for rewriting. You need to draw on both your critical and creative sensibilities here to avoid being buffeted by different, possibly contradictory, feedback. Only if you have a clear sense of your own story, and your ownership of that story, can you resist being swept along by the casual comments of editors or agents who might have only glanced at your work. But, if someone has bothered to *respond* to your work in any way, then take heart. You may have a rejection letter now, but someone has recognised that you may be a potential talent.

The third stage of rejection is a letter that rejects the story you sent in, but asks if you would send in other material. This is confirmation that you have the potential to be a writer. Perhaps the story you sent wasn't quite right for that agent or editor (and this could be for a number of reasons: an editor might have commissioned something too similar, an agent might know that the story falls out of market categories), but that person has seen something in the writing that they liked.

The fourth stage in this process goes beyond rejection. It is the letter that says yes. It is the stage we are all reaching for. We won't all get a blockbuster novel, but we might all get the satisfaction of seeing our writing published somewhere. It is not rejection that stops a writer writing. No one else has that power. Only the writer can throw in the towel. And this means that how you cope with rejection will shape your career as a writer: if you let rejection undermine you, then you will not be a writer – but if you learn from each setback, always aspiring to be better, then who knows? So don't give in. Learn. Make your own luck by writingrewritingsubmitting / writingrewritingsubmitting / writingrewritingsubmitting. The rest of this chapter offers some advice about how best to go for the letter that says 'yes'.

Submitting to the market

If you send your work to an agent or editor you normally include a covering letter, a synopsis and three chapters, roughly fifty pages (for a novel); or a covering letter and the story itself for a short story. I'm focusing my discussion here on novels, but the advice about the letter and the presentation of creative work applies equally to short stories.

Perhaps the most challenging part of the submission for novelists is the synopsis. Different editors and agents have different ideas about the synopsis, some read it before the chapters, some after, and some not at all: I've heard one publisher say that 'the synopsis is to the book what the zombie is to the body.' The advice about how long the synopsis should be also varies widely, as does advice about whether to include character biographies. As writers we are squeezed between two seemingly incompatible demands. On the one hand, the synopsis needs to be as short as humanly possible (I'd say a maximum of four sides of double-spaced A4, although many publishers I've spoken to have baulked at more than one); on the other hand, it needs to tell the basic story whilst keeping the flavour and tone of the novel itself. Needless to say, this is incredibly difficult. It's not that hard to write a bare-bones summary in a couple of sides – what's really tricky is bringing the zombie to life.

In the face of such contradictory advice, writers need to find a model that works for them, and the suggestion by Carole Blake in *From Pitch to Publication* is one that is both concise and yet gives the writer a little room to show off their talents. She suggests that an ideal submission should include:

- a brief blurb
- biographies of the main characters
- a synopsis

- the first two or three chapters
- an author biography[2]

This expands the more traditional submission of letter, synopsis, chapters and moves closer to the model used by screenwriters when they present film treatments, which in some way resolves the problem of trying to cram everything into a one-page synopsis. In this section I want to work through Blake's model, beginning with the first thing the agent or publisher reads: the letter.

The letter

The covering letter is perhaps one of the most important things that you will write, and you should spend at least as much time on it as you would on a page of your fiction. The agent or editor will judge you by your letter: the letter sets the tone, it shows the reader how you use words, it influences the way they read the rest of the package, or the short story itself. Remember that the person you're writing to wants to advance or consolidate their career by finding the next big thing (the prize-winning novel, the bestseller, the anthologised story, the new talent) and the letter is the first stage in the process of convincing them that your fiction is what they're looking for.

The letter will include a brief 'blurb' about the novel or story (although for a novel you may want to write a separate blurb as part of your submission), but you should avoid telling the reader what they should think or how they should respond to your story. If you are submitting a short story, don't tell the reader what the story's *really about*, it suggests that you don't believe that the story can speak for itself. As C. Michael Curtis says: 'the more sophisticated and successful writers resist the impulse to encapsulate stories that, to borrow from Archibald MacLeish, "must not mean, but be".'[3] Trust the reader to read intelligently.

In the letter you should tell the agent/publisher something about yourself, especially any previous publications. You want to show them that you are professional, so if you have graduated with honours from a Creative Writing degree course, say so; if you have a professional career, say so. You only need to include a separate author biography if there is too much information. In the letter brevity, courtesy and self-belief are key, so it should not go over one page of A4 if single-spaced. Here are my dos and don'ts for the ideal letter:

DO

1 Be confident in yourself and show your passion and commitment to your story.
2 Say why you are writing to this particular publisher / agent / publication (reference authors they represent / books they've edited / stories they have published that you enjoy).
3 Give key details about the book / story (title, length, genre, themes) and show that you know your readership.
4 Show the voice and tone of the novel / story. Give a smattering of detail about characters or plot to draw the editor / agent in.
5 Say who you are, give previous publications and any positive reviews. Tell them anything interesting about you that they can 'sell' or that gives your work authority.

DON'T

6 Don't be wacky.
7 Don't be buddy chummy.
8 Don't be sloppy.
9 Don't try to grab grab grab.
10 Don't go on and on.
11 Don't over-state or over-sell yourself or your work.
12 Don't say move over J. K. Rowling / Dan Brown, here I come.

The blurb

If you include a separate blurb for your novel, this should be no more than two paragraphs and should not repeat anything from the letter. The purpose of the blurb is to whet the appetite of the reader, piquing their curiosity and encouraging them to turn the page. Read back-covers in bookshops to think about the way in which they sell rather than tell the story, but don't mimic the over-blown style unless it's appropriate for your own novel. Instead, focus on the main character, a key moment in the story, and the overall feel of the drama.

Character biographies

The character biographies allow you to offer thumbnail sketches of your main characters, and if a reader has your characters in their mind's eye before they read the synopsis, then the story line takes on a new significance (make sure you include a biography for each character mentioned in the synopsis). The biographies, though, need to be impressionistic as too much detail can be confusing. Aim to write a paragraph for each of your main characters (perhaps two for your main or viewpoint character) outlining their age, appearance, and motivation. Focus on the aspects of their appearance or personality that distinguish them from others, the key features that reveal their attitude to life.

The synopsis

The synopsis is both selling the story and telling the story. The synopsis is the storyline, and as such it's important to cover all the main plot lines, including the ending; but the storyline stripped of voice, tone, and emotion is 'to the novel as the zombie is to the body'. To give the synopsis life you need to show the emotional impact of the plot events on the characters, to show how they struggle. You also need to use the voice and tone of the book itself to show the style and viewpoint as well as literally telling what happens next. Conventionally, the synopsis is written in the present tense and the third person (even if the novel is in the first person and the past tense), so you might be offering the reader a 'taste' of the character's voice, rather than replicating it in full.

Inevitably, you won't be able to include the entire story: what you need are the critical moments that move the story forward (if you don't need to mention minor characters, don't. You want to avoid clutter). Don't worry about including every detail and limit yourself to a maximum of four pages of double-spaced A4. Whoever is reading your synopsis will be a professional who is very aware that these pages do not contain the richness of the finished novel; but the more involving you make them, the better.

The chapters / short story

The three chapters (roughly fifty pages) or the short story now need to live up to the claims you made in the letter and the rest of the package. Hopefully the reader is feeling curious and excited as they turn to these pages. You do not want to disappoint them. The chapters you submit should usually be the first three. If you submit later chapters because you know the first chapters are boring, then you will need to work on them before you send in the entire manuscript. If you do choose later chapters they need to be consecutive (otherwise they will seem confusing) and you will need to explain where they fit in the story (otherwise the reader won't understand what's happening). For these reasons, I'd stick with the first three chapters. All the work you submit should be professionally presented, and the following guidelines apply to novels and short stories (where magazines state their preferred format for story submissions you should follow them):

1 The title page should have the title and your name halfway down (not too big and no strange fonts). Name, address, email, phone/fax number in the bottom left-hand corner.
2 Double space the chapters/story.
3 Use Times Roman or Courier (Courier has less words to the page so the text moves faster). Font size 12.
4 No drawings or wacky fonts.
5 Always paginate.
6 Keep all margins 3cm minimum.
7 Justify the left margin only.
8 Indent paragraphs – only leave an extra line to signal a shift in time, place, viewpoint and so on.
9 Use standard white A4 paper.
10 Use one side of the paper only.
11 You can use a footer with name and title if you wish.
12 Keep a copy!

The author biography

There is no need to include this unless there is impressive detail that could not be included in the letter. Generally you want to present yourself as a professional person who plans a career as a writer. Beyond that, saleable personal experience is useful, such as hardship (J. K. Rowling writing *Harry Potter* in an Edinburgh café); youth (Zadie Smith writing *White Teeth* in her early twenties); or unusual jobs (Bruce Coville being a gravedigger and a toymaker before becoming a children's writer). You might even want to say something about why you write. But remember not to become self-indulgent. You are trying to sell yourself to a professional reader, not applying to a dating agency.

Advice about 'selling yourself' is perhaps not the way you expected this book to end. You might have thought that a critical-creative approach to writing would not conclude by 'submitting to the market' with everything that entails. But unless you are a writer who writes simply for your own pleasure or for the pleasure of those around you, you will have to face this hard fact of writing life. The critical-creative approach is not about denying the commercial world of publishing in favour of the creative freedom of the universities. Instead it offers writers a way of thinking about their own writing process. It suggests a way of learning from the universities as well as the best-seller charts so that writers can develop their own potential. A critical-creative approach to writing enables writers to engage with the worlds they live in as well as imagining better ones. And by developing our criticality as well as our creativity we might just become better writers. I wish you every success.

Speculations: Exercises

Practice, practice, practice writing. Writing is a craft that requires both talent and acquired skills. You learn by doing, by making mistakes and then seeing where you went wrong.

Jeffrey A. Carver, www.starrigger.net/advice.htm

These exercises are designed to complement and develop the ideas in Part II of this book. They focus more directly upon the practicalities of writing than the exercises in Foundations, and encourage you to apply the ideas in this book to your own writing-in-progress: to 'learn by doing'.

Chapter 7: Exploring Possibilities

1   Think back to a family celebration when you were a child (a birthday, perhaps, or a holiday or festival). Try to visualise the room, the people, yourself as a child. Pay attention to the smells (food, perfume, bodies), the noises (laughter, music, chatting), the physical sensations (the feel of your clothes, of being embraced), and the tastes (food, drink) and so on. Note the way your body reacts to this memory, then:

   (a)   Write for five minutes about your 'felt sense' of the memory.
   (b)   Choose five details that crystallise the atmosphere and significance of this memory. Write a short paragraph exploring each one.
   (c)   Using these details, write this scene for your 'memoirs'.
   (d)   Devise and write a fictional scene or short story that uses this memory.

2   Write thirty-five ideas for the title of the novel or story you are working on / plan to write. Do not allow yourself to stop until

you have written down exactly thirty-five potential titles. Then put them away and look over them the next day. Often when you force yourself to keep going you come up with something that surprises you.

3   Keep a scrapbook for one month. Use it to collect quotes and ideas as well as cuttings from newspapers, magazines, adverts and so on.

Chapter 8: Forms and Structures

4   Devise a simple story which features six or more key events (for instance: a man argues with his wife, leaves home in temper, drives chaotically, knocks down a pedestrian, drives away then returns to the scene, phones for medical aid, waits at the hospital to see if the person survives, speaks to the police, phones his wife). Write each event as a self-contained paragraph on a different sheet of paper. Shuffle the papers and consider the effect of changing the chronology.

5   Use the situations below as the beginnings of three stories. For each situation write two beginnings: one that opens just before the moment of crisis, one that opens with the moment of crisis. Consider the impact of the different beginnings:

   (a)   a suicidal businessman jumps off a bridge
   (b)   a woman walks out on her husband
   (c)   a pedestrian is knocked down in a hit-and-run accident

6   Plan the way you would write the following scenes to build and sustain suspense:

   (a)   a mother tries to find her child in a shopping mall
   (b)   a lion escapes from the zoo
   (c)   a group of teenagers drive a stolen truck too fast

7   Using an anthology of short stories, read stories that you do not know – but do not read the last page. Devise the ending that would match your expectations and write it in the style of the story. Then compare your ending to the original. Consider the advantages and disadvantages of the two endings.

Chapter 9: Subjects

8   If you have a character you find difficult to write (or one you would like to know more about) answer the following questions (one each day for a week) in the voice of the character:

    (a)   If you had three wishes what would they be?

    (b)   What is the most important issue in the world today (or in your time)? Why?

    (c)   Is there anyone you would die for? Who? How does that make you feel?

    (d)   Where would you like to be in twenty years' time? Why?

    (e)   If you were able to erase one memory, which would it be, and why?

    (f)   What is the meaning of life? What is the meaning of your life?

    (g)   What is your biggest fear? Why?

9   Write a questionnaire and fill it out for each character in your story. On the questionnaire ask both obvious and less obvious questions. Obvious questions might be about hobbies, political beliefs, religious beliefs, personal morality, hopes, fears, pets, family, habits, mannerisms, obsessions, love-life, work, education, favourite food/sport/colour/music/book/film, and so on. Less obvious questions might ask about embarrassing or traumatic memories, middle-of-the-night anxieties, sexual fantasies/experiences, deepest regrets, personal hygiene, body image, dreams, and so on.

10   'Even those beliefs he's sure of, the artist puts under pressure to see if they will stand.' (John Gardner) Write a short story in which the characters or narrator have radically different beliefs from your own (beliefs you might even find offensive). Make their voices and beliefs convincing. Come back to the story after a week and consider its effectiveness.

11   Create a sense of character by:

    (a)   writing about the environment in which the character lives; the objects they own; the movements they make

    (b)   revealing their stream-of-consciousness responses to the environment in which they live; or the objects they own; or the movements they make

Do this for a number of characters, but do not describe them phys-ically in any way. Give these sketches to different readers to see how they picture these faceless characters.

Chapter 10: Voices

12   Write three versions of the same short scene. In the first version use first-person narrative; in the second use second-person narrative, and in the third version use the third person. Consider the emotional distance created between the characters and the reader:

(a)   a child trying to get money from a parent
(b)   an activist trying to persuade a crowd
(c)   a new immigrant trying to find somewhere to stay

13   Plan a scene in which there is an argument between a man and a woman, witnessed by another person. Develop the characters and setting. Now write the scene in these different ways, considering the effect of changes in voice and viewpoint:

(a)   as a first-person narrative from the woman's point of view
(b)   as a limited-third-person narrative from the man's perspective
(c)   as a second-person narrative using the voice and viewpoint of the witness
(d)   as a third-person narrative using the voice and viewpoint of an invisible third-person narrator
(e)   as a third-person narrative that slides between the voice and viewpoint of the man, the woman, the witness and an objective narrator

14   Write a scene of dialogue in which the two speakers have very different points of view and neither will reveal their ulterior motives or weaknesses. The following situations might be useful as prompts:

(a)   The dating couple. The woman wants a romantic holiday. The man has pretended to be wealthy, but doesn't have enough money for the trip. The woman wants the man to

show his commitment and suspects that he is losing interest
in her. The man fears he'll lose the woman if she knows he's
broke.

(b)   The pensioner and the salesperson. The pensioner is lonely
and simply wants to talk. The salesperson has targets
to meet.

Chapter 11: Styles

15   Write a scene incorporating analepsis, for one (or more) of the
following situations:

(a)   a person stealing a child (their own baby died two months
before)

(b)   a person hosting an extravagant dinner-party (they often
went hungry as a child)

(c)   a person building a house (their old house was bombed)

16   Write a scene for one (or more) of the following situations using
all four of Genette's modes of telling: ellipses, summary, scene,
and pause:

(a)   four people trapped in a house-fire

(b)   a person floating out to sea on a lilo

(c)   a cyclist racing through rush-hour traffic

17   Write two short short stories (up to 1,000 words). One tells once
what happened once, and n times what happened n times; the
other tells n times what happened once and once what happened
n times. Choose from the following situations and develop setting
and characterisation:

(a)   a child staying for a week with grandparents who is praised
every evening for good behaviour, and beaten once for bad
behaviour

(b)   an insomniac walks the empty streets every night for a week
and one night sees a strange sight

(c)   a temporary worker who is spurned by everyone s/he works
with is surprised by an act of kindness

Chapter 12: Speculations in Fiction

18   Write character biographies for:

    (a)   people you know
    (b)   characters in a novel or short story you have read
    (c)   characters in a fiction you are writing

19   Write a synopsis for a novel you have read. Try to bring the storyline to life by using the voice, tone and style of the original and including the emotional impact of the action upon the characters.

20   Write a short commentary about a creative piece that you have written recently or are currently writing. Consider the influences on your writing and the decisions you made during the prewriting, writing and rewriting stages.

Notes

Introduction: A Critical-Creative Approach to Fiction

1 P. Elbow, *Writing with Power* (Oxford and New York: Oxford University Press, 1998), p. 9.
2 Quoted in M. Schorer, 'Technique as Discovery' in *The Theory of the Novel*, ed. by P. Stevick (New York: Free Press, 1967), p. 73.
3 Quoted in Schorer, p. 73.
4 R. Queneau quoted in I. Calvino, *Six Memos for the Next Millennium* (1988) (London: Vintage, 1996), p. 123.
5 J. Gardner, *On Becoming a Novelist* (1983) (New York and London: Norton, 1999), p. 15.
6 F. Weldon, 'Harnessed to the Harpy' in *The Agony and the Ego*, ed. by C. Boylan (Harmondsworth: Penguin, 1993), p. 38.
7 G. LaFemina, 'Lab Work: Creative Writing, Critical Writing, Creative Obsessions and the Critical Essay' in *TEXT* 8:1, www.griffith.edu. au/school/art/text/april04/lafemina.htm
8 E. Hemingway, *Ernest Hemingway on Writing* (1984), ed. by L. W. Phillips (New York and London: Scribner, 2004), p. 91.
9 V. Woolf, *A Room of One's Own* (1929), *A Room of One's Own / Three Guineas* (Oxford: Oxford University Press, 1998), p. 96.

1 Establishing Practice

1 F. Smith, *Writing and the Writer* (Oxford: Heinemann, 1982).
2 Smith, p. 105.
3 Smith, p. 104.
4 Smith, p. 104.
5 Smith, p. 125.
6 W. B. Yeats, 'The Circus Animals' Desertion', *Collected Poems* (London: Macmillan (now Palgrave Macmillan), 1982), p. 392.
7 N. Goldberg, *Writing Down the Bones: Freeing the Writer Within* (London and Boston: Shambhala, 1986), p. 14.
8 W. James, *The Principles of Psychology* (1890), vol. 1 (New York: Dover, 1957), p. 462.
9 W. Whitman, *Prose Works* (Philadelphia: David McKay, 1892), Bartleby.com, 2000, www.bartleby.com/229/
10 I'm grateful to Richard Gwyn for bringing Geertz's phrase to my attention.

11 J. Gardner, *On Becoming A Novelist* (New York and London: W. W. Norton, 1983), p. 71.

12 D. Brande, *Becoming a Writer* (1934) (London: Macmillan (now Palgrave Macmillan), 1996), p. 120.

13 V. Shklovsky, 'Art as Technique', in *Modern Literary Theory: A Reader*, 2nd edition, ed. by P. Rice and P. Waugh (London: Edward Arnold, 1992), pp. 18–19.

14 H. James, *The Art of Fiction*, in *Longman's Magazine*, 4 (September 1884), http://guweb2.gonzaga.edu/faculty/campbell/engl462/artfiction.html

15 P. Lubbock, *The Craft of Fiction* (1921) (London: Jonathan Cape, 1954), p. 24.

16 Longinus, 'On the Sublime', in *Aristotle/Horace/Longinus: Classical Literary Criticism*, trans. by T. S. Dorsch (Harmondsworth: Penguin, 1965), p. 119.

17 K. Brophy, *Explorations in Creative Writing* (Melbourne: Melbourne University Press, 2003), p. 3.

18 The phrase 'creative conspirators' is taken from S. Chatman's *Story and Discourse: Narrative Structure in Fiction and Film* (Ithaca and London: Cornell University Press, 1978).

19 H. Porter Abbott, *The Cambridge Introduction to Narrative* (Cambridge: Cambridge University Press, 2002), pp. 93–104.

20 P. Auster, *The Invention of Solitude* (New York: Penguin, 1988), p. 146.

21 See W. K. Wimsatt and M. Beardsley, 'The intentional fallacy', in *The Verbal Icon: Studies in the Meaning of Poetry* (Lexington: University of Kentucky Press, 1954), pp 3–18.

22 F. Kermode, *The Genesis of Secrecy: On the Interpretation of Narrative* (Cambridge, MA: Harvard University Press 1979), p. 113.

23 Longinus, p. 120.

24 H. Bloom, *The Anxiety of Influence* (Oxford: Oxford University Press, 1997).

25 John Gardener makes a similar point about characterisation in *On Becoming a Novelist*. He says: 'What one needs is not the facts but the "feel" of the person not oneself' (p. 31).

26 E. M. Forster, *Aspects of the Novel* (1927) (Harmondsworth: Penguin, 1976), p. 99.

27 R. Kearney, *On Stories* (London and New York: Routledge, 2002), p. 132.

28 P. Ricoeur, *Time and Narrative*, vol. 1, trans. by K. McLaughlin and D. Pellauer (Chicago and London: University of Chicago Press, 1984), p. 59; and G. LaFemina, 'Lab Work: Creative Writing, Critical Writing, Creative Obsessions and the Critical Essay', *TEXT*, 8:1, April 2004, www.griffith.edu.au/school/art/text/april04/lafemina.htm

29 R. B. Tobias, *20 Master Plots and How to Build Them* (Cincinnati: Writer's Digest Books, 1993), p. 34.

30 J. L. Borges, 'A Universal History of Infamy' (1935), in *Collected Fictions*, trans. by A. Hurley (New York and London: Penguin, 1998), p. 325.

2   Form and Structure

1   R. Tarnas, *The Passion of the Western Mind* (London: Pimlico, 1991), p. 17.
2   H. Arendt, *The Human Condition* (Chicago: Chicago University Press, 1958), p. 72.
3   Aristotle, 'On the Art of Poetry', in *Aristotle/Horace/Longinus: Classical Literary Criticism*, trans. by T. S. Dorsch (New York and Harmondsworth: Penguin, 1965), p. 39. All further quotations have page numbers after the text.
4   H. James, 'The Art of Fiction', *Longman's Magazine*, 4 (September 1884).
5   M. Kundera, *The Art of the Novel* (London: Faber and Faber, 1988), p. 23.
6   Quoted in J. Gardner, *The Art of Fiction* (1983) (London: Vintage, 1991), p. 37.
7   See P. O'Neill, *Fictions of Discourse: Reading Narrative Theory* (Toronto: University of Toronto Press, 1994), p. 20.
8   E. M. Forster, *Aspects of the Novel* (1927) (London and New York: Penguin, 2000), p. 42.
9   Forster, p. 87.
10 S. Chatman, *Story and Discourse: Narrative Structure in Fiction and Film* (Ithaca and London: Cornell University Press, 1978), pp. 45–6.
11 R. McKee, *Story: Substance, Structure, Style, and the Principles of Screenwriting* (New York: Regan Books, 1998; London: Methuen, 1999), p. 33.
12 McKee, p. 34.
13 P. Pullman in interview with A. Yentob, *Imagine: Unsuitable for Children*, BBC1, Wednesday 30 June 2004.
14 J. Gardner, p. 188; and www.glasswings.com.au/Storytronics/Tronics/plot/single8.htm
15 Forster, p. 95.
16 L. Sterne, *The Life and Opinions of Tristram Shandy* (1759–67) (London and New York: Penguin, 1967), p. 453.

3   Subject

1   V. Propp, *Morphology of the Folktale* (1928), 2nd edition, trans. by L. A. Wagner (Austin: University of Texas Press, 1968).
2   M. Toolan, *Narrative: A Critical Linguistic Introduction*, 2nd edition. (London and New York: Routledge, 2001), p. 19.
3   F. Schlegel, *Dialogue on Poetry and Literary Aphorisms* (1798), trans. by E. Behler and R. Struc (University Park: pennsylvania University Press, 1968), p. 67.
4   J. Campbell, *The Hero with a Thousand Faces* (1949) (London: Fontana, 1993), p. 12. All further page references will be given after the quotations.
5   J. Gardner, *On Becoming a Novelist* (1983) (New York and London: W. W. Norton, 1999), p. 5.

6   T. Davis, Lecture on Jung, University of Birmingham, UK, 2005.
    www.bham.ac.uk/english/bibliography/CurrentCourses/Freud/jung/
    junglecture.html
7   Quoted in D. Brande, *Becoming a Writer* (1934) (London: Macmillan
    (now Palgrave Macmillan), 1996), p. 117.

4 Voice

1   D. Brande, *Becoming a Writer* (1934) (London: Macmillan (now
    Palgrave Macmillan), 1996), p. 112.
2   T. Pateman, 'The Empty Word and the Full Word: the Emer-
    gence of Truth in Writing', in *The Self on the Page: Theory
    and Practice of Creative Writing in Personal Development*, ed. by
    C. Hunt and F. Sampson (London: Jessica Kingsley, 1998), p. 159,
    www.selectedworks.co.uk/creativewritingemptywordfullword.html
3   L. Althusser, 'Ideology and the State', in *Modern Literary Theory*, 2nd
    edition, ed. by P. Rice and P. Waugh (London: Edward Arnold, 1992),
    pp. 54–62.
4   T. Pateman, 'The   Subject   and   the   Speaking   Subject',
    www.selectedworks.co.uk/speakingsubject.html
5   Brande, p. 146.
6   M. Bradbury, 'Foreword', in Brande, *Becoming a Writer*, p. 15.
7   I. Calvino, *Six Memos for the Next Millennium* (1988), trans. by
    P. Creagh (London: Vintage, 1996), p. 124.
8   M. Bakhtin, *The Problems of Speech Genres and Other Late Essays*
    (Austin: University of Texas Press, 1996), p. 69.
9   M. Bakhtin, 'Discourse in the Novel', in *The Dialogic Imagination*,
    trans. by C. Emerson and M. Holquist (Austin: University of Texas
    Press, 1991), p. 280. Further page numbers will be given after the
    quotations.
10 See S. Vice, *Introducing Bakhtin* (Manchester: Manchester University
    Press, 1997) for a discussion of the three types of dialogism.
11 See M. Toolan, *Narrative: A Critical Linguistic Introduction*, 2nd
    edition (London and New York: Routledge, 2001).
12 W. Iser, *The Act of Reading: A Theory of Aesthetic Response* (Baltimore:
    Johns Hopkins University Press, 1978), p. 108.
13 J. P. Sartre, *What is Literature?* (London and New York: Routledge,
    2001), p. 35 and p. 27.
14 P. Ricoeur, 'Life in Quest of Narrative', in *On Paul Ricoeur: Narrative
    and Interpretation*, ed. by D. Wood (London and New York: Routledge,
    1991), p. 27.
15 Longinus, 'On the Sublime', in *Aristotle/Horace/Longinus: Classical
    Literary Criticism*, trans. by T. S. Dorsch (Harmondsworth: Penguin,
    1965), p. 135.
16 Toolan, p. 68.
17 W. J. Ong, *Orality and Literacy: the Technologizing of the Word* (London
    and New York: Methuen, 1982), p. 102.
18 S. Chatman, *Story and Discourse: Narrative Structure in Fiction and
    Film* (Ithaca and London: Cornell University Press, 1978), p. 151.

19 L. Sterne, *The Life and Opinions of Tristram Shandy* (1759–67) (Harmondsworth: Penguin, 1967), p. 82.
20 See W. Booth, *The Rhetoric of Fiction* (Chicago: Chicago University Press, 1961).
21 R. Silverberg, 'Who is Tiptree, What is He?', in J. Tiptree Jr, *Warm Worlds and Otherwise* (New York: Ballantine, 1975), p. xii; and A. Sheldon in M. Siegel, *James Tiptree Jr*, Starmont Reader's Guide 22 (Mercer Island: Starmont, 1985), p. 7.
22 A. Sheldon quoted in C. Platt, 'Profile: James Tiptree, Jr', *Isaac Asimov's Science Fiction Magazine*, April 1983, p. 42.
23 Ong, p. 177.

5 Style

1   É. Zola, *Le Roman Expérimental* (1880), quoted in D. Grant, *Realism* (London: Methuen, 1970), p. 21.
2   See I. Watt, *The Rise of the Novel: Studies in Defoe, Richardson and Fielding* (1957), (London: Pimlico, 2000).
3   H. Fielding, 'Preface', in *Joseph Andrews* (1742) (London: Penguin, 1999).
4   J. Gardner, *The Art of Fiction* (1983) (New York: Vintage, 1991), p. 49.
5   T. Pateman, 'Space for the Imagination', in *Journal of Aesthetic Education*, Vol. 31, No 1, Spring 1997, pp. 1–8, www.selectedworks.co.uk /imagination.html
6   T. S. Eliot, 'Tradition and the Individual Talent', in *The Sacred Wood: Essays on Poetry and Criticism* (London: Methuen, 1922), www.bartleby.com/200/sw4.html
7   Eliot, www.bartleby.com/200/sw4.html
8   P. Ricoeur, 'Life in Quest of Narrative', in *On Paul Ricoeur: Narrative and Interpretation*, ed. by David Wood (London and New York: Routledge, 1991), p. 25.
9   Zola, quoted in Grant, *Realism*, p. 30.
10 See www.metmuseum.org/toah/hd/rlsm/hd_rlsm.htm
11 G. Courbet quoted in Grant, *Realism*, p. 26.
12 Champfleury quoted in Grant, *Realism*, p. 23.
13 G. Flaubert quoted in P. Nicholls, *Modernisms: A Literary Guide* (London: Macmillan (now Palgrave Macmillan), 1995), p. 13.
14 Letter to A. N. Maykov, 11 December 1868, in *The Brothers Karamazov* (New York: W. W. Norton, 2005).
15 S. Beckett, *Proust* (New York: Grove, 1994), p. 59.
16 H. Read, *A Concise History of Modern Painting* (London: Thames and Hudson, 1975), p. 8.
17 V. Woolf, 'Modern Fiction' (1919). http://etext.library.adelaide. edu.au /w/woolf/virginia/w91c/chapter13.html
18 Ibid.
19 G. Orwell, 'Inside the Whale' (1940), in *Essays* (London and New York: Penguin, 2000), p. 115.
20 J. Barth, 'The Literature of Exhaustion', in *The Novel Today: Contemporary Writers on Modern Fiction*, ed. by M. Bradbury (London: Fontana, 1977), p. 70.

21 J. Barth, 'Lost in the Funhouse' and 'Life-Story', in *Lost in the Funhouse* (New York: Bantam, 1988), p. 72 and p. 125.

22 A. Robbe-Grillet, www1.chapman.edu/comm/english/events/robbe-grillet

23 Longinus, 'On the Sublime', in *Aristotle/Horace/Longinus: Classical Literary Criticism*, trans. by T. S. Dorsch (Harmondsworth: Penguin, 1965), p. 103.

24 G. Flaubert quoted in O. Hall, *How Fiction Works* (Cincinatti: Writer's Digest Press, 2001), p. 27.

25 E. Pound in P. Jones, *Imagist Poetry* (London: Penguin, 1972), p. 131.

26 I. Calvino, *Six Memos for the Next Millennium* (1988), trans. by P. Creagh (London: Vintage, 1996), p. 56.

27 G. Orwell, 'Politics and the English Language' (1946), in *Essays*, p. 350.

28 T. LeClair, 'William Gass and John Gardner: A Debate on Fiction', in *Conversations with John Gardner*, ed. by A. Chavkin (Jackson and London: University Press of Mississippi, 1990), p. 174.

29 J. Gardner, in ibid., p. 177.

6 Foundations of Fiction

1 J. Gardner, *The Art of Fiction* (1983) (New York: Vintage, 1991), p. 39.

2 P. Ricoeur, *Time and Narrative Vol. 1*, trans. by K. McLaughlin and D. Pellauer (Chicago and London: University of Chicago Press, 1983). All further page references to this volume are given after the quotations

3 P. Ricoeur, 'Life in Quest of Narrative', in *On Paul Ricoeur: Narrative and Interpretation*, ed. by D. Wood (London and New York: Routledge, 1991), p. 27.

4 Ricoeur, 'Life in Quest of Narrative', p. 33.

5 Ricoeur, 'Life in Quest of Narrative', p. 32.

6 H. White, *The Content of the Form: Narrative Discourse and Historical Representation* (Baltimore: Johns Hopkins University Press, 1987), p. 181.

7 P. Ricoeur, 'Initiative', in *From Text to Action: Essays in Hermeneutics Vol. 2*, trans. by K. Blamey (Evanston: Northwestern University Press, 1991), p. 214.

8 A. Golden, 'Author Q+A', www.randomhouse.com/vintage/catalog/display.pperl?isbn=9780679781585&view=qa

9 É. Zola, *Le Roman Expérimental* (1880), quoted in D. Grant, *Realism* (London: Methuen, 1970), p. 23.

10 W. J. Ong, *Orality and Literacy: the Technologizing of the Word* (New York and London: Methuen, 1982), p. 155.

11 T. Pratchett, 'Terry Pratchett: Discworld and Beyond', *Locus*, December 1999, www.locusmag.com/1999/Issues/12/Pratchett.html

12 P. Ricoeur, 'The Function of Fiction in Shaping Reality', *Man and World* Vol. 12, No. 2 (1979), 123–41, at 139, emphasis in original.

13 Ricoeur, 'Life in Quest of Narrative', p. 28.

14 Ricoeur, 'Life in Quest of Narrative', p. 20.

15 K. J. Vanhoozer, 'Philosophical Antecedents to Ricoeur's *Time and Narrative*', in *On Paul Ricoeur: Narrative and Interpretation*, ed. by D. Wood (London and New York: Routledge, 1991), p. 48.

16   U. Eco, *Six Walks in the Fictional Woods* (Cambridge, MA: Harvard University Press, 1994), p. 85.
17   Eco, pp. 85–6.
18   Eco, p. 86.

7   Exploring Possibilities

1   F. Smith, *Writing and the Writer* (Oxford: Heinemann, 1982), p. 124, p. 104 and p. 127.
2   Smith, p. 104.
3   E. Hemingway, *Ernest Hemingway on Writing* (1984), ed. by L. W. Phillips (New York and London: Scribner, 2004), p. 38.
4   See P. Elbow who develops this idea in *Writing with Power* (Oxford and New York: Oxford University Press, 1998).
5   E. Gendlin, *Focusing* (London and New York: Bantam, 1982), p. 32.
6   See S. Perl, *Felt Sense: Writing with the Body* (Portsmouth, NH: Boyton/Cook, 2004).
7   C. Tucker-Ladd, *Psychological Self-Help*, http://mentalhelp.net/psyhelp/chap15/chap15q.htm
8   J. Gardner, *On Becoming a Novelist* (New York and London: W.W. Norton, 1999), p. 19.
9   E. Hemingway, *Death in the Afternoon* (London: Arrow, 1994), p. 192.
10   J. Webb Young, *A Technique for Producing Ideas* (London and New York: McGraw-Hill, 2003), p. 15. All further page numbers will be given after quotations.
11   A. Koestler, *The Act of Creation* (London and New York: Macmillan, 1975), p. 120.
12   J. Foster, *How to Get Ideas* (San Francisco: Berret-Koehler, 1996), p. 32.
13   D. Knight, *Creating Short Fiction* (New York: St Martin's Griffin, 1997), p. 156.
14   S. Beckett, http://samuel-beckett.net/
15   S. Stein, *Stein on Writing* (New York: St Martin's Press, 1995), p. 281.
16   C. S. Lewis quoted in Knight, *Creating Short Fiction*, p. 86.

8   Forms and Structures

1   M. Saporta, *Composition No. 1*, trans. by R. Howard (New York: Simon & Schuster, 1963). Quoted at www.madinkbeard.com/archives/saportacompo.html
2   P. Ricoeur, 'Life in Quest of Narrative', in *On Paul Ricoeur: Narrative and Interpretation*, ed. by D. Wood (London and New York: Routledge, 1991), p. 27.
3   O. Hall, *How Fiction Works* (Cincinnati: Writer's Digest Books, 2004), p. 156.
4   I. Calvino, *If on a Winter's Night a Traveller* (London and Sydney: Vintage, 1998), p. 4 and p. 10.
5   J. Gardner, *The Art of Fiction* (London: Vintage, 1991). p. 56.

6   J. Frey, *How to Write a Damn Good Novel* (New York: St Martin's, 1987), p. 72.
7   J. M. Bickham, *The 38 Most Common Fiction Writing Mistakes* (Cincinnati: Writer's Digest Books, 1997), p. 10 and p. 12.
8   J. Campbell, *The Hero with a Thousand Faces* (1949) (London: Fontana, 1993), p. 49.
9   Horace, 'Ars Poetica', in *Aristotle/Horace/Longinus: Classical Literary Criticism*, trans. by T. S. Dorsch (New York and Harmondsworth: Penguin, 1965), p. 84.
10 S. Stein, *Stein on Writing* (New York: St Martin's, 1995), p. 16.
11 E. M. Forster, *Aspects of the Novel* (1927) (London and New York: Penguin, 2000), p. 87.
12 T. Morrison, *Beloved* (London: Picador, 1988), p. 3.
13 A. Boulter, *Around the Houses* (London: Serpent's Tail, 2002), p. 1.
14 A. Boulter, *Back Around the Houses* (London: Serpent's Tail, 2003), p. 1.
15 'Conflict' has become the generic term for the energy and movement in fiction, but I prefer to use the word 'struggle' as it suggests greater flexibility and dynamism.
16 See N. Kress, *Beginnings, Middles and Ends* (Cincinnati: Writer's Digest Books, 1999), pp. 67–70 for a fuller discussion of scenes.
17 Kress, p. 70.
18 Quoted in S. Chatman, *Story and Discourse: Narrative Structure in Fiction and Film* (Ithaca and London: Cornell University Press, 1978), p. 59.
19 M. Bal, *Narratology: Introduction to the Theory of Narrative*, 2nd edition (Toronto and London: University of Toronto Press, 1999), p. 160.
20 Quoted in Chatman, p. 60.
21 J. Gardner, *On Becoming a Novelist* (London and New York: W.W. Norton, 1999), p. 49.
22 M. Toolan, *Narrative: A Critical Linguistic Introduction*, 2nd edition (London and New York: Routledge, 2001), pp. 100–1.
23 Toolan, p. 102.
24 H. Porter Abbot, *The Cambridge Introduction to Narrative* (Cambridge: Cambridge University Press, 2002), p. 60.
25 Kress, p. 7.

9   Subjects

1   W. J. Ong, *Orality and Literacy: the Technologizing of the Word* (New York and London: Methuen, 1982), p. 154.
2   Ong, p. 155.
3   S. Chatman, *Story and Discourse: Narrative Structure in Fiction and Film* (Ithaca and London: Cornell University Press, 1978), p. 137.
4   M. Holquist, *Dialogism: Bakhtin and his World* (London and New York: Routledge, 1990), p. 163.
5   E. M. Forster, *Aspects of the Novel* (1927) (London and New York: Penguin, 2000), p. 73.

6 Forster, p. 81.
7 Chatman, pp. 132–3
8 P. O'Neill, *Fictions of Discourse: Reading Narrative Theory* (Toronto: University of Toronto Press, 1994), p. 49.
9 W. Iser, *The Act of Reading* (Baltimore: Johns Hopkins University Press, 1978). (see p. 193)
10 William James, 'The Importance of Individuals' in *The Will to Believe and Other Essays in Popular Philosophy* (1897) (Mineola, NY: Dover, 1956), p. 107.
11 M. Bakhtin, *Problems in Dostoevsky's Poetics*, trans. by C. Emerson (Minneapolis: University of Minnesota Press, 1984), p. 297.
12 Bakhtin, p. 6.
13 Bakhtin, p. 26 and p. 12.
14 Bakhtin, p. 63, emphasis in original.
15 J. Gardner, *On Becoming a Novelist* (New York and London: W. W. Norton, 1999), p. 20.
16 O. Scott Card, *Characters and Viewpoint* (Cincinnati: Writer's Digest Books, 1988), pp. 120–2.
17 M. Shelley, *Frankenstein: or the Modern Prometheus* (New York and Boston: Bedford Books, 1992), p. 57.
18 I. Murdoch, *Nuns and Soldiers* (London: Vintage, 2001), p. 467.
19 I. Murdoch, *The Black Prince* (London and New York: Penguin, 1973), p. 200.
20 http://jppr.psychiatryonline.org/cgi/content/full/7/1/23
21 T. Wolff, 'Bullet in the Brain', in *The Night in Question* (New York: Knopf, 1996).
22 G. Boeree, *Personality Theories*, www.ship.edu/%7Ecgboeree/freud.html
23 M. Toolan, *Narrative: A Critical Linguistic Introduction*, 2nd edition (London and New York: Routledge, 2001), p. 80.
24 A. Robbe-Grillet in R. Kearney, *On Stories* (London and New York: Routledge, 2002), p. 127.
25 W. Gass in T. Leitch, *What Stories Are: Narrative Theory and Interpretation* (University Park: Penn State University Press, 1986), p. 154.
26 J. Weinsheimer in Toolan, p. 80.
27 N. Hornby, *About a Boy* (London: Indigo, 1998), pp. 14–15.
28 A. E. Blazer, 'Chasms of Reality, Aberrations of Identity: Defining the Postmodern through Brett Easton Ellis's American Psycho', Americana: The Journal of American Popular Culture (1900–present), 1:2 (2002), www.americanpopularculture.com/journal/articles/fall_2002/blazer.htm
29 B. Easton Ellis, *American Psycho* (London: Picador, 1993), p. 376.

10 Voices

1 M. Bakhtin, *Problems of Dostoevsky's Poetics*, trans. by C. Emerson (Minneapolis: University of Minnesota Press, 1984), p. 6.
2 H. James, *What Maisie Knew* (1897) (London and New York: Penguin, 1985), p. 124.

3   S. Rimmon-Kenan, *Narrative Fiction: Contemporary Poetics* (London and New York: Routledge, 1990).

4   M. Holquist, *Dialogism: Bakhtin and his World* (London and New York: Routledge, 1990), p. 164.

5   J. McInerney, *Bright Lights, Big City* (London: Bloomsbury, 1992), p. 3.

6   J. Winterson, *The.PowerBook* (London: Vintage, 2001), p. 57.

7   M. Bakhtin, 'Discourse in the Novel', in *The Dialogic Imagination*, trans. by C. Emerson and M. Holquist (Austin: University of Texas Press, 1981), p. 332.

8   Bakhtin, 'Discourse in the Novel', p. 324.

9   Bakhtin, *Problems of Dostoevsky's Poetics*, p. 196 and p. 232.

10 Ibid., p. 63.

11 Quoted in O. Hall, *How Fiction Works* (Cincinnati: Writer's Digest Books, 2004), p. 57.

12 Hall, p. 59.

13 A. Boulter, *Around the Houses* (London: Serpent's Tail, 2002), pp. 153–4.

14 S. Stein, *Stein on Writing* (New York: St. Martin's, 1995) p. 116.

15 Quoted in Hall, p. 63.

16 J. Frey, *How to Write a Damn Good Novel* (New York: St Martin's, 1987), p. 138.

17 Bakhtin, 'Discourse in the Novel', p. 401.

18 Stein, p. 114.

19 P. O'Neill, *Fictions of Discourse: Reading Narrative Theory* (Toronto: University of Toronto Press, 1994), p. 60.

11   Styles

1   G. Genette, *Narrative Discourse: An Essay in Method*, trans. by J. E. Lewin (Ithaca: Cornell University Press, 1980). All further page references are given after quotations.

2   M. Toolan, *Narrative: A Critical Linguistic Introduction*, 2nd edition (London and New York: Routledge, 2001), p. 45.

3   M. Spark, *The Prime of Miss Jean Brodie* (London: Penguin, 1965), p. 15.

4   Spark, pp. 26–7.

5   H. Fielding, *Tom Jones* (Oxford: Oxford University Press, 1998), p. 107.

6   J. Austen, *Emma* (1816) (Harmondsworth and New York: Penguin, 1966), p. 37.

7   Quoted in S. Chatman, *Story and Discourse: Narrative Structure in Fiction and Film* (Ithaca and London: Cornell University Press, 1978), p. 67.

8   Y. Martel, *Life of Pi* (Edinburgh: Canongate, 2003), p. 23.

9   J. Baldwin, 'Sonny's Blues' (1957), in *American Short Story Masterpieces*, ed. by R. Carver and T. Jenks (New York: Bantam, 1989), p. 3.

10 M. Bal, *Narratology: Introduction to the Theory of Narrative*, 2nd edition (Toronto and London: University of Toronto Press, 1999), p. 106.

11 S. Stein, *Stein on Writing* (New York: St Martin's, 1995), p. 102.

12 T. Morrison, *Beloved* (London: Picador, 1988), p. 3. All futher page references are given after quotations.
13 V. Woolf, *To the Lighthouse* (1927) (London and New York: Granada, 1979), p. 120 and p. 124.

12   Speculations in Fiction

1 D. Brande, *Becoming a Writer* (1934) (London: Macmillan (now Palgrave Macmillan), 1996), p. 49.
2 C. Blake, *From Pitch to Publication* (London: Macmillan (now Palgrave Macmillan), 1999), p. 31.
3 C. M. Curtis, 'How to Read Rejection', *Poets and Writers Magazine*, 1999, vol. 27, no 5, www.pw.org/mag/curtis.htm

Selected Further Reading

Creative writing

D. Brande, *Becoming a Writer* (1934) (London: Macmillan (new Palgrave Macmillan), 1996).

K. Brophy, *Explorations in Creative Writing* (Melbourne: Melbourne University Press, 2003).

P. Elbow, *Writing with Power* (Oxford and New York: Oxford University Press, 1998).

E. M. Forster, *Aspects of the Novel* (1927) (London and New York: Penguin, 2000).

J. Frey, *How to Write a Damn Good Novel* (New York: St Martin's, 1987).

J. Gardner, *On Becoming a Novelist* (New York and London: W. W. Norton, 1999).

J. Gardner, *The Art of Fiction* (London: Vintage, 1991).

N. Goldberg, *Writing Down the Bones: Freeing the Writer Within* (London and Boston: Shambhala, 1986).

E. Hemingway, *Ernest Hemingway on Writing* (1984) ed. by L. W. Phillips (New York and London: Scribner, 2004).

N. Kress, *Beginnings, Middles and Ends* (Cincinnati: Writer's Digest Books, 1999).

P. Lubbock, *The Craft of Fiction* (1921) (London: Jonathan Cape, 1954).

R. McKee, *Story: Substance, Structure, Style, and the Principles of Screenwriting* (New York: Regan Books, 1998; London: Methuen, 1999).

O. Scott Card, *Characters and Viewpoint* (Cincinnati: Writer's Digest Books, 1988).

S. Stein, *Stein on Writing* (New York: St Martin's, 1995).

Writing/philosophy/creativity

L. Althusser, 'Ideology and the State', in *Modern Literary Theory*, 2nd edition, ed. by P. Rice and P. Waugh (London: Edward Arnold, 1992).

I. Calvino, *Six Memos for the Next Millennium* (1988), trans. by P. Creagh (London: Vintage, 1996).

J. Campbell, *The Hero with a Thousand Faces* (1949) (London: Fontana, 1993).

J. Foster, *How to Get Ideas* (San Francisco: Berret-Koehler, 1996).

A. Koestler, *The Act of Creation* (London and New York: Macmillan (new Palgrave Macmillan), 1975).

M. Kundera, *The Art of the Novel* (London: Faber and Faber, 1988).

W. J. Ong, *Orality and Literacy: the Technologizing of the Word* (New York and London: Methuen, 1982).

G. Orwell, *Essays* (London and New York: Penguin, 2000).

P. Ricoeur, 'Life in Quest of Narrative', in *On Paul Ricoeur: Narrative and Interpretation*, ed. by D. Wood (London and New York: Routledge, 1991).

P. Ricoeur, *Time and Narrative Vol. 1*, trans. by K. McLaughlin and D. Pellauer (Chicago and London: University of Chicago Press, 1983).

J.-P. Sartre, *What is Literature?* (London and New York: Routledge, 2001).

F. Smith, *Writing and the Writer* (Oxford: Heinemann, 1982).

J. Webb Young, *A Technique for Producing Ideas* (London and New York: McGraw-Hill, 2003).

V. Woolf, *A Room of One's Own* (1929), *A Room of One's Own / Three Guineas* (Oxford: Oxford University Press, 1998).

Literary theory

Aristotle/Horace/Longinus: Classical Literary Criticism, trans. by T. S. Dorsch (New York and Harmondsworth: Penguin, 1965).

M. Bal, *Narratology: Introduction to the Theory of Narrative*, 2nd edition (Toronto and London: University of Toronto Press, 1999).

M. Bakhtin, 'Discourse in the Novel', in *The Dialogic Imagination*, trans. by C. Emerson and M. Holquist (Austin: University of Texas Press, 1981).

M. Bakhtin, *Problems of Dostoevsky's Poetics*, trans. by C. Emerson (Minneapolis: University of Minnesota Press, 1984).

S. Chatman, *Story and Discourse: Narrative Structure in Fiction and Film* (Ithaca and London: Cornell University Press, 1978).

T. S. Eliot, 'Tradition and the Individual Talent', in *The Sacred Wood: Essays on Poetry and Criticism* (London: Methuen, 1922).

G. Genette, *Narrative Discourse: An Essay in Method*, trans. by J. E. Lewin (Ithaca: Cornell University Press, 1980).

W. Iser, *The Act of Reading: a Theory of Aesthetic Response* (Baltimore: Johns Hopkins University Press, 1978).

R. Kearney, *On Stories* (London and New York: Routledge, 2002).

P. O'Neill, *Fictions of Discourse: Reading Narrative Theory* (Toronto: University of Toronto Press, 1994).

H. Porter Abbot, *The Cambridge Introduction to Narrative* (Cambridge: Cambridge University Press, 2002).

V. Propp, *Morphology of the Folktale* (1928), 2nd edition, trans. by L. A. Wagner (Austin: University of Texas Press, 1968).

S. Rimmon-Kenan, *Narrative Fiction: Contemporary Poetics* (London and New York: Routledge, 1990).

V. Shklovsky, 'Art as Technique', in *Modern Literary Theory: a Reader*, 2nd edition, ed. by P. Rice and P. Waugh (London: Edward Arnold, 1992).

M. Toolan, *Narrative: a Critical Linguistic Introduction*, 2nd edition (London and New York: Routledge, 2001).

Index of Names